KARL MAIER was born in Kentucky in 1957 and studied at Columbia University, New York. In the early 1980s he worked as a journalist in Central America and in 1986 moved to Africa; he has reported from Angola, Somalia, Mozambique, Liberia, South Africa and Zimbabwe for *The Independent*, *Washington Post*, *The Economist* and *Africa Confidential*. Author of *This House Has Fallen: Nigeria in Crisis* and *Into the House of the Ancestors: Inside the New Africa*, he currently works as a journalist in Khartoum.

How many dead in this war? How many homes abandoned, how many refugees in neighbouring countries, how many separated families? For what? When I think of all the suffering, the individual hopes destroyed, futures torn apart, the blood, I feel anger, impotent anger, but against what? It is not even against the enemy. He carried out his role as coloniser. The colonialist is colonialist, finished. There is nothing to expect from him. But from us? The people expected everything from us, we promised a paradise on earth, freedom, the tranquil life of tomorrow. We always spoke of tomorrow. Yesterday was the dark night of colonialism, today is the suffering of war, but tomorrow will be paradise. The tomorrow that never comes, an eternal today. So eternal that the people forget the past and say that yesterday was better than today.

Pepetela, Angolan novelist, *A Geração da Utopia (The Utopia Generation)*

Angola: Promises and Lies

Karl Maier

Serif
London

This edition first published 2007 by
Serif
47 Strahan Road
London E3 5DA

1 3 5 7 9 8 6 4 2

First published, in slightly different form, 1996

British Library Cataloguing-in-Publication Data.
A catalogue record for this book
is available from the British Library.

Library of Congress Cataloging in Publication Data.
A catalog record for this book is available
from the Library of Congress

ISBN 13: 978 1 897959 52 7
ISBN 10: 1 897959 52 4

Printed and bound in Malaysia by Forum

Contents

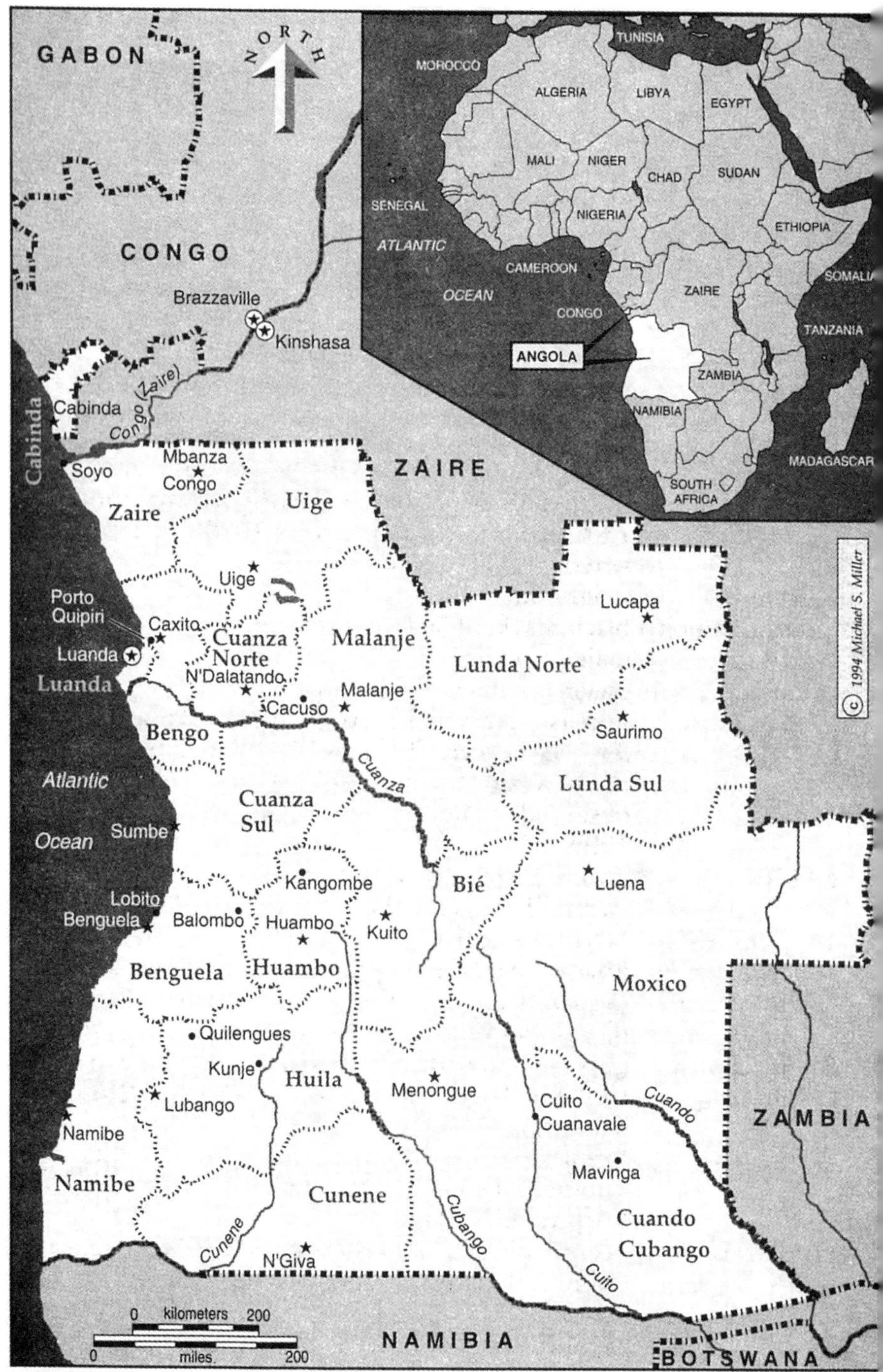
GABON
NORTH
CONGO
Brazzaville
Kinshasa
Congo (Zaire)
Cabinda
Cabinda
Soyo
Mbanza Congo
ZAIRE
Zaire
Uige
Uige
Porto Quipiri
Caxito
Luanda
Luanda
Cuanza Norte
N'Dalatando
Malanje
Malanje
Cacuso
Lunda Norte
Lucapa
Saurimo
Lunda Sul
Bengo
Cuanza
Atlantic Ocean
Cuanza Sul
Sumbe
Lobito
Benguela
Balombo
Kangombe
Huambo
Kuito
Bié
Luena
Benguela
Huambo
Moxico
Quilengues
Kunje
Huila
Lubango
Menongue
Namibe
Cuito Cuanavale
Cuando
Mavinga
ZAMBIA
Namibe
Cunene
Cubango
Cuando Cubango
Cunene
N'Giva
Cuito
0 kilometers 200
0 miles 200
NAMIBIA
BOTSWANA
TUNISIA
MOROCCO
ALGERIA
LIBYA
EGYPT
MALI
NIGER
CHAD
SUDAN
SENEGAL
NIGERIA
ETHIOPIA
ATLANTIC
CAMEROON
OCEAN
ZAIRE
SOMALIA
CONGO
TANZANIA
ANGOLA
ZAMBIA
NAMIBIA
MADAGASCAR
SOUTH AFRICA
© 1994 Michael S. Miller

Angola

Foreword to the 2007 Edition

All wars end eventually, wiser heads repeatedly told me, even in Angola. At the time I wrote the pages that follow, it was difficult to imagine that the flames of the country's civil war might ever die down, or how its people, most of whom knew nothing but armed conflict, could start living their lives free of gunmen and the land mines that littered their farms. It is true that in Mozambique, the erstwhile Portuguese colony on the other side of the African continent, a peace agreement had been signed in 1992 and was still holding. Even the champions of apartheid had finally given up their dream of endless white minority rule in South Africa. But Angola was the scene of the ultimate clash between the immovable object, President José Eduardo dos Santos's ruling Popular Movement for the Liberation of Angola, or MPLA, and the irresistible force of Jonas Malheiro Savimbi, the rebel leader with an unquenchable thirst for power. It was hard to believe that it could ever be different.

They had been fighting since before Angola gained independence from Portugal in 1975 and there was no sign that they were going to stop. During the 1990s two peace agreements came and went, both of them followed by the eruption of full-blown war on a scale rarely seen in Africa. The United Nations and countries such as the United States, Russia and Portugal slowly transformed themselves from meddlers to mediators, wringing their collective hands in anger and despair, passing resolutions and imposing sanctions on both Savimbi's UNITA and the government, but war remained the central feature of Angola's day-to-day reality.

By 1998, the Lusaka Protocol signed four years earlier was collapsing. Savimbi refused to honour commitments to hand over UNITA-controlled territory to the government, the disarmament and demobilisation programmes were a sham and both sides geared up for another round of fighting. The agreement had been suspect from the outset; it was simply a delaying tactic. Savimbi had refused to attend the signing ceremony, and instead sent Eugenio Manuvakola, UNITA's former secretary general, who was later arrested on Savimbi's orders and held for two years until he fled with his family to Luanda. The government didn't believe in the peace deal because it knew Savimbi wouldn't respect it. Ceasefire violations by both sides occurred in 1996 and increased in number during 1997, with the government capturing significant areas of UNITA-held territory in the diamond-rich north-east. In April 1997, a government of national unity was formed with representatives from both the MPLA and UNITA, but, with Savimbi still on the outside, the root cause of the war had not gone away.

Both sides used the false peace to re-arm, UNITA paying for weapons with illicitly traded diamonds and the government with bank loans and 'signature bonuses' from companies desperate to grab a slice of Angola's burgeoning oil industry. Young men, many of them little more than children, were forcibly conscripted as fighters. Both sides sowed new land mines, reinforcing Angola's unenviable status as the most heavily mined country in the world, with nearly 1 million explosives and as many as 80,000 men, women and children living out their lives as amputees. As Angola teetered on the brink of renewed war, the UN Special Representative Blondin Beye died when his chartered plane crashed near Abidjan, capital of the Ivory Coast. He had been trying to persuade UNITA-supporting governments in West Africa, such as those in Togo and Ivory Coast, to pressure Savimbi to meet his peace commitments.

When the final stage of the conflict exploded into a full-blown war in December 1998, the United Nations estimated that another 1 million people, almost a tenth of Angola's population, had fled their homes, joining the quarter of the nation's inhabitants who had already done so. The warring rivals were guilty of torture, summary executions and the forced displacement of civilians. UNITA shelled government-held cities such as Malanje, Kuito and Huambo indiscriminately, killing hundreds of civilians and sparking food shortages, while the government bombed rebel-controlled towns such as Bailundo, Mungo and Andulo in the central highlands. If the war were fought today, there would almost certainly be voices describing the slaughter as 'genocide'.

And then, quite unexpectedly on 22 February 2002, the war ended in a brief hail of bullets. Government troops shot Savimbi and two dozen of his bodyguards dead on the banks of the River Luvuei in the eastern province of Moxico, where his drive to take power had started nearly a quarter of a century earlier. He was buried under a tree in a graveyard outside the city of Luena.

A darling of the right in the United States, Savimbi was sometimes portrayed as an anti-Communist Che Guevara. For the left, he was a lackey of apartheid South Africa and the CIA. In truth, he was neither. His cause – personal power – was morally flawed, but Savimbi had a domestic constituency among the central highlands people traditionally regarded as Angola's second-class citizens and others elsewhere in the country disgusted by the MPLA's often brutal misrule. Just as surely as South Africa and the United States used Savimbi in their battle against the ogre of Marxism, he manipulated them to acquire money, weapons and respectability. Savimbi accepted help from anyone who offered it. His army received military training from the Chinese, troops, intelligence and equipment from the South Africans and covert aid from the CIA. At different times, and for different audiences, he espoused socialism, capitalism, Chinese-style communism, democracy and Negritude. Savimbi's ability to be all things to all people was his true genius. That, fused with an iron will, brought him almost within reach of his goal of becoming king of Angola.

However welcome his demise, Savimbi's departure and the formal end of the conflict have robbed President dos Santos and his government of their primary excuse for failing to care for their citizens' welfare. Four years to the month after he died, Angola returned to the familiar rhythm of a preventable slaughter, although this one wasn't directly caused by the armed violence that over the decades claimed hundreds of thousands of lives and made Angola a symbol of Africa's killing fields. On this occasion, the immediate cause was the worst outbreak of cholera in the country's history. Erupting in February, the epidemic killed 1,400 people in just three months and infected as many 600 people a day. It spread like fire through the slums of Luanda, where 70 per cent of the capital's 4 million inhabitants live, mainly in shacks.

Sitting in Khartoum, Sudan, and watching the television interviews with residents of Luanda's impoverished *bairros* explaining how they live without access to clean water and their children play in refuse heaps, I found it easy to forget that – on paper – Angola has become one of Africa's richest countries. Multinational oil companies such as Chevron, Exxon Mobil, BP and Total are scrambling to reinforce their hold on Africa's second biggest oil industry, which by 2010 should double its current production of more than a million barrels a day. The International Monetary Fund estimates that in 2006 the economy could grow by as much as 26 per cent, one of the highest rates in the world, but the provision of healthy drinking water for the residents of their capital appears to be beyond Angola's rulers.

Angola is no exception to the rule that holds true in Africa and beyond that an influx of petro-dollars and rising gross domestic product do not necessarily mean improved well-being for the majority of an oil-producing nation's citizens. This is why Juan Pablo Pérez Alfonso of Venezuela, a founder of the Organisation of Petroleum Exporting Countries, once described oil as 'devil's excrement'. In fact, Angola is making the transition from a war economy to the petro-capitalism typical of African oil producers and characterised by an urban elite living a luxurious European lifestyle surrounded by massive shantytowns deprived of even the most basic necessities. Luanda, with its ever-expanding traffic jams, looks more and more like a mini-Lagos. Nigeria, Africa's biggest oil producer, has earned $300 billion in oil export revenues since the 1960s and today two-thirds of the population still live on less than $1 a day. In Sudan, which in 2005 saw its 21-year civil war come to an end, while another in the western region of Darfur rages on, a growing economy and expanding oil production haven't helped more than 6 million of the country's citizens who still depend on international food aid.

Despite the oil bonanza, almost three-quarters of Angola's people live on less than $1 a day. About 45 per cent of its children are malnourished and, according to the UN World

Food Programme, in the central highlands, where Savimbi grew up, some 52 per cent of those under five are stunted. In 2005 the UN Development Programme ranked Angola 160th out of 177 countries in its human development index.

The key to the problem is how the rulers use the oil riches. According to the IMF, Angola's government was unable to account for $4.22 *billion* in revenues between 1997 and 2002. Many suspect that the money disappeared into what is often called the Bermuda Triangle – the opaque financial world linking the Presidency, the Banco Nacional de Angola and Sonangol, the state oil company. This is almost the same amount as that spent on health, education and the humanitarian needs of the population by the United Nations, the government and public and private groups over the same period. In 2005 Transparency International, the Berlin-based corruption watchdog, ranked Angola as one of the ten most corrupt countries in the world.

Today, the principal suppliers of the revenues that help to keep the dos Santos government in power are, ironically, two countries that at different times backed Savimbi. China and the United States are now the biggest consumers of Angolan oil. US and other Western oil companies still dominate the oil industry, but the world's most populous nation, ever hungry for resources, is gaining ground rapidly.

China, where Savimbi and his top brass once received military training, is today providing Angola with $3 billion in loans, which will help the authorities avoid uncomfortable questions about transparency from the IMF and Western creditors. It has also become a leading player in Angola's construction industry, with its companies involved in rebuilding the Benguela railway, developing a new airport at Viana outside Luanda and constructing a major oil refinery in Lobito, the port city where UNITA once enjoyed strong political support. Meanwhile, President dos Santos appears to be delaying until 2007 the first elections since the 1992 polls, whose results Savimbi rejected with the homicidal consequences described later, in the hope that his government's programme to rebuild roads and bridges may bolster its popularity.

When Savimbi's death was announced, there were spontaneous celebrations in Luanda, mournful tributes to his charisma and supposed status as a statesman in Portugal and expressions of good riddance in a variety of Africa countries. The celebratory mood has died down since then as the vast majority of Angolans confront new battles, such as the deadly cholera epidemic, in another, more modern conflict – a war of neglect by their rulers. As the then Namibian foreign minister, Theo-Ben Gurirab, commented at the time, 'The devil himself is dead, but his footprints will still be there.'

Khartoum
June 2006

Glossary

Bacongo	One of Angola's three major ethnic groups, based in the north of the country and southern Zaire. Base of support for the FNLA, but in the September 1992 elections voted largely for the MPLA.
Bairro	neighbourhood
Candonga/ueiro	black market/black-market trader
Degredado	exiled convict
Dono	owner, politician (figuratively)
FAA	Forças Armadas Angolanas, Angolan Armed Forces, the new Angolan government army formed on eve of the UN-observed general election in September 1992.
FALA	Forças Armadas de Libertação de Angola, Armed Forces for the Liberation of Angola, UNITA's army
FAPLA	Forças Armadas Populares para a Libertação de Angola, Popular Armed Forces for the Liberation of Angola, the MPLA government's former army
Fitinha	vigilante (figuratively, from the word for bandanna or ribbon)
FLEC	Frente para a Libertação do Enclave de Cabinda, Front for the Liberation of the Enclave of Cabinda
FLEC-FAC	Frente para a Libertação do Enclave de Cabinda-Forças Armadas de Cabinda, Front for the Liberation of the Enclave of Cabinda-Armed Forces of Cabinda

FNLA	Frente Nacional de Libertação de Angola, National Front for the Liberation of Angola, one of three nationalist groups which fought for independence; leader, Holden Roberto.
ICRC	International Committee of the Red Cross
Galinha	chicken
Lavra	farm
Limpeza	cleaning/cleansing
Mestiço	mixed race
MPLA	Movimento Popular de Libertação de Angols, Popular Movement for the Liberation of Angola, the governing party; leader, José Eduardo dos Santos
Musseque	shanty-town
Mutilado	amputee
Nacas	winter-planting season
Planalto	the central highlands
Poder popular	people's power
Povo	people
Praça	market
Soba	traditional chief
SWAPO	South West Africa People's Organisation, the main Namibian independence movement and since 1990 the ruling party; leader, Sam Nujoma.
Umbundu	Commonly referred to by its plural form Ovimbundu, this ethnic group is based in the central highlands and is considered to have felt the colonial penetration least of the three main ethnic groups. Traditional base of support for UNITA.
UNAVEM	United Nations Angola Verification Mission
UNITA	União Nacional para a Indepencia Total de Angola, National Union for the Total Independence of Angola, the armed opposition movement; leader, Jonas Malheiro Savimbi.
WFP	United Nations World Food Programme

Preface

As I sit down to write this book in a flat in central Luanda there is an explosion nearby. From the veranda I see a crowd gather quickly on the Rua da Missão several streets away. An old man, a tramp, sits calmly on the pavement surrounded by several hundred people. Blood is splattered all over him. His right leg and left arm have been blown off.

I am standing close to him, inhabiting almost the same space, yet our worlds, our realities, have nothing in common. We exist in different dimensions. As I make coffee before beginning work, he is rummaging through a pile of rubbish, looking for something to eat, or perhaps, if he is lucky, a discarded item to sell. As I sit down in front of my computer he steps unwittingly on an old explosive someone has left lying around. As the sound of the boom reaches my startled ears, parts of his body are being ripped away.

Moments later I reach the scene. A couple of teenage boys selling cigarettes look on and walk away saying, 'He'll live.' Seconds later a police van pulls up, a minor miracle in its own right, and hauls the old man away. The crowd begins to disperse, as if nothing ever happened. Maybe if everyone agrees to forget, it never did.

Acknowledgements

I am deeply grateful to Sarah Longford and Chris Simpson for their strong encouragement to write this book.

I am indebted to many others for their support and company: Katia Airola, Alex Vines, Jeremy Harding, Richard Fritz, Moises, Fernando Pacheco, Maria Conceição Neto, Brennon Jones, Amy Janello, Eduardo Minvu, Vita, Toby Lanzer, Peter Hawkins and John Liebenberg, none of whom, however, bear any responsibility for the book's contents.

Many thanks also to the World Food Programme, Save the Children UK, the International Committee of the Red Cross and Concern for hospitality and transport.

This book is dedicated to all those who gave their time to speak with me and put up with endless questions.

1 In the Time of *Guerra*

Sílvia Neyala Zinga looks like a little black doll in a pink dress when she answers the door, nonchalantly relieves herself on the floor and withdraws into the interior of the flat. Perhaps it is her natural reaction to a white face, or perhaps it is just time to go. Sílvia is two years old. She is quite practised at opening the front door, although her greeting might be improved upon. Her mother, Deofina Chinima, has not been able to walk very quickly ever since a mortar shell blew away half of her left foot. Her father, Fernando Denis, died two months before she was born. Her eldest brother, Alberto, is missing, and her other brother, Inácio, just returned after a two-year disappearance, spends most of his time on the street. Sílvia is growing up in the time of *guerra*, war.

With fluffy white clouds drifting across a deep blue sky atop the rolling green hills of Angola's central highlands, the view from the veranda of their sixth-floor flat in the city of Huambo is picture-perfect. Inside the panorama is rather more sombre. The dark brown wooden floors are clean but bare. There is one little table in the centre of the living room, three peg-leg stools for visitors and mats for beds. Deofina's wardrobe consists of a couple of shirts and skirts. Everything else, the furniture, clothes and cooking utensils, has been sold over the past two years to buy food. The kitchen is empty too, except for a small plastic bag of maize meal which Deofina has received from the International Committee of the Red Cross. That and tremendous will-power are the only things keeping the family alive.

Almost all of Huambo's 300,000 people depend on hand-outs of food and medicine sent by the United Nations and international aid agencies. Angola's vast reserves of oil and diamonds should make it one of Africa's richest countries, but the politicians – Deofina calls them the *donos*, or owners – spend everything either on the war or themselves.

Inácio, Deofina's twelve-year-old son, was missing for two years before returning home earlier in the month. Deofina does not care that Inácio is another mouth to feed, too young to contribute to the family's groceries but old enough to eat like an adult. He has grown into a young man since he has been away, Deofina says admiringly, but she has no trouble in making him feel at home. 'It is never difficult for a mother,' she mutters below a shy smile. Deofina only wishes that Alberto, aged sixteen, would come back too. He ran away to live as a street kid in the capital, Luanda. 'I don't know how he is living, but I really want that boy back.'

Things started falling apart for Deofina's family in October 1992 when Angola's *donos* decided that the civil war, already Africa's oldest conflict, had not run its course. Jonas Savimbi, the leader of the UNITA rebel movement, claimed that President José Eduardo dos Santos's MPLA government had cheated him in the country's first general elections. No matter that the United Nations and the entire world said the polls had been relatively free and fair, that they were a remarkable demonstration by yet another oppressed people of the universal desire to have a say in their own lives. What mattered was that one side lost, and the only recourse was to take power, or to hold onto it, by armed force.

When the initial battle erupted in Huambo, a soldier named Fernando Denis, Deofina's husband, was one of the first casualties. The United Nations negotiated a temporary ceasefire, but three months later UNITA told the world to go to hell and launched its final drive to capture Huambo, which Savimbi hoped would become the capital of his 'new Angola'.

The siege began on 8 January 1993, just after Sílvia's birth. She and her mother were in the stairwell on the back of their high-rise block when a mortar shell slammed into the wall and sent shards of burning metal ripping through Deofina's foot. Alberto and Inácio went scampering down the stairwell. 'I told them "Run, boys, run and hide",' says Deofina. 'I knew it was too dangerous to stay in the building. But I couldn't follow them. I crawled back into the apartment with Sílvia and stayed here for four days until some neighbours found us.'

The boys disappeared. After the siege ended 55 days and 10,000 lives later, friends helped Deofina to reach the Bomba Alta complex of the International Committee of the Red Cross, and from there she was sent to a hospital in Bailundo, a small town 40 miles to the north, where she spent the next six months. She emerged from the treatment as an amputee, a *mutilada*, one of tens of thousands of people who have been maimed in the fighting, either by shrapnel or landmines.

Deofina's neighbours told her that the boys would never return, that they were dead, just as her husband was. But she would not listen. When other families held traditional symbolic funerals for their missing loved ones, Deofina refused. 'I just could not do it. I kept making excuses to wait longer.'

Alberto and Inácio had fled Huambo during the siege to escape the constant firefights and mortar bombardments. They joined one of the massive human columns of government soldiers and civilians who walked 100, sometimes 150 miles, through the bush, through the rain, over mined roads and fields, to garrison towns near the Atlantic Ocean. For most, it took about two weeks to reach their destination. They swam across rivers, trudged through mud and climbed hills. Some women even gave birth along the way.

Inácio remembers that the most difficult part of the journey came when they reached the River Catumbela. To cross the swift current swollen by the summer rains, the soldiers removed the straps from their AK-47 assault rifles, tied them together to make a long chord and tried to drag everyone across. 'Many people died there, especially the older ones,' says Inácio. 'They were too weak to hold on and were swept away in the water.'

After government forces recaptured Huambo from Savimbi's UNITA in early November 1994, a cousin told Deofina that the International Committee of the Red Cross was helping to bring separated families back together. Then came word that the boys were alive. They were at an orphanage in Lobito, a port city about 150 miles west of Huambo. Alberto had written a letter to the British charity, Save the Children, saying his mother lived in the Benfica neighbourhood of the city and requesting help in finding her.

For three weeks Save the Children asked around the

neighbourhood until they located Deofina. In the meantime Alberto stowed away on a boat and, like thousands of other homeless children his age, gravitated to the bright lights of Luanda where he could hustle money in the company of petty criminals and guarding or, if he was lucky, washing rich people's cars.

It is February 1995 and there should be a feeling of new hope in Huambo. The war is supposed to be over, again. The MPLA and UNITA signed another ceasefire three months ago and the United Nations is sending in observers and 7,000 troops to ensure that this time the peace will hold. Many Angolans fear, however, that the new deal will work no better than its predecessors. There are ample signs that the two sides are simply using the lull in the fighting to re-arm and re-equip their forces to have another go at a war neither can ever win.

UNITA and the MPLA have been fighting back and forth over the two decades since independence, switching international alliances and ideologies as needed, rounding up young men when their ranks are thin, buying millions of dollars' worth of arms when they are short of firepower, even hiring foreign mercenaries, but the result is always the same: a grinding military stalemate that has left thousands more civilians dead or homeless and hungry, more schools and health posts gutted, an entire generation shell-shocked.

The first chance for peace collapsed on the eve of independence from Portugal in November 1975, when the MPLA, supported by the Soviet Union and Cuba, drove Savimbi's UNITA and a third, now effectively defunct, faction, Holden Roberto's FNLA, both backed by the United States and South Africa, out of Luanda. The second opportunity fell apart after the 1992 elections. The United Nations and the most powerful nations on earth were unable to stop the return to war. Since then some observers estimate that 500,000 people have died in the fighting and the famine and disease it has provoked.

Only God can intervene, Deofina believes, to save a people condemned to damnation by their leaders. She is a deeply religious woman, a member of the Seventh Day Adventist Church, and she is hoping God will do away with the politicians and self-appointed messiahs – the *donos* – who have dragged the country, her family, to ruin. 'The problem is that the *donos* never die.'

Welcome to Angola, home of the worst war in the world, a massive international relief effort, white mercenaries, black megalomaniacs, diamond smuggling, arms dealing and record numbers of amputees, like Deofina, so many *mutilados* that it seems the country has spawned a new species of limbless human beings. It is also a land of natural treasures and a people of humbling determination. Doctors and teachers who earn the equivalent of a six-pack of beer a month, if they are paid, truck drivers who risk their lives on every run, street-market women who must constantly evade police-turned-robbers just to make a sale. Angola is the new world order in its purest form, a nasty stain left over by the Cold War which has proved almost impossible to remove.

The first time I heard of Angola I never imagined it, or any place, could be like this. Now I seem to see Angola everywhere, most obviously in other decaying African nations such as Somalia, Nigeria and, until its recent peace settlement, Mozambique, and in the television images from the countries of the former Soviet Union and Yugoslavia. Even in the streets of American cities, where crack gangs and corrupt politicians vie for power, or among the homeless families in the cities of Western Europe, there is a little whiff of Angola.

My first contact occurred just before Angola's independence twenty years ago while I was visiting Lisbon. I was seventeen years old and on my first trip outside the United States, indeed on one of only a handful of forays beyond my home state of Kentucky. After I graduated from high school a friend invited me to visit her mother in Holland for the summer. My friend's mother was a Marxist and her idea of a holiday was to travel to Spain to witness the death throes of Generalissimo Francisco Franco's dictatorship. It turned out to be a very good idea.

We also visited Portugal, which was still in turmoil a year after the Revolution of Carnations had thrown out the fascist dictatorship and set free Lisbon's colonies. The excitement of the new order in Lisbon was like springtime compared to the gloom of Madrid. Monuments, walls, buildings and banks, literally everything was painted in red by a kaleidoscope of Marxist mini-parties calling for workers' revolution.

One day I was walking in the central area of Lisbon near the

Bairro Alto district when I came upon a demonstration by thousands of Portuguese demanding bread and jobs from the new government. Portugal had sent its poor, illiterate, unemployed and its exiled convicts, the *degredados*, out to colonies such as Angola and Mozambique, and with the collapse of the colonial administrations they were returning home *en masse* to claim a good turn from their country. I walked up to one elderly man and asked where he had come from. The place he named sounded magical. 'Angola,' he said.

I did not realise it at the time, but Angola had become a flash point in the Cold War rivalry. Smarting from its recent defeat in Vietnam, Washington had latched onto another anti-communist crusade. The US Central Intelligence Agency, the Soviets, the South Africans, the Cubans and dozens of European and American mercenaries were attempting to outdo each other in supporting the various factions in a game of one-upmanship in the African bush. All sides pumped hundreds of millions of dollars' worth of arms into the country, weapons Angola's politicians were only too happy to hand out to young troops who were largely press-ganged to fight it out.

With the support of the United States, the South Africans invaded to bolster UNITA and to defend the region against the communist onslaught that existed more in their minds and their need to justify their warped system of apartheid. A South African armoured column roared across the border with Namibia, the south-west African colony illegally occupied by Pretoria, and was within 100 miles of Luanda before it was routed by thousands of Cuban troops dispatched by Fidel Castro to defend the MPLA. Angola's independence was born in blood. Its democracy would maintain the tradition.

Angola possessed great wealth in oil and diamonds and had been the world's fourth biggest coffee producer. It was just another dubious beneficiary of Portugal's civilising mission in Africa: up to four million of its fittest youth had been shipped to the Americas in the slave trade, and at independence the illiteracy rate was over 90 per cent and the number of doctors could be counted on two hands.

None of this mattered to Henry Kissinger and his strategic planners in Washington. So strong was their taste for war that when Jonas Savimbi attempted to initiate peace discussions with the MPLA in September 1975, the United States objected. No one supported by the CIA had any business being soft on communism. In the ensuing years the war dragged the country down and helped to lift up the arms dealers' bottom line. Thousands of Cuban troops and oil revenues kept the MPLA government afloat, while repeated South African invasions and millions of dollars in American aid to UNITA ensured military stalemate.

Eleven years later, in 1986, I quit my job in New York City and travelled to southern Africa to become a freelance journalist. Angola was my first assignment. It nearly ended in disaster.

The flight from Harare touched down on a dull grey Sunday afternoon. Only one other person, a Swedish diplomat, disembarked, and the rest of the passengers who were continuing to Lisbon looked at me as if I was insane. Why would anyone want to stop in Luanda? Only after I reached the arrival lounge did I understand their astounded expressions. The airport was abandoned except for a couple of teenage soldiers manning the immigration desk. Pools of water emerged from under the lavatory doors. The stench was overpowering.

My visa was a typed letter signed by a deputy trade minister whom I had met in New York. The soldiers holding down the temporary immigration jobs, their AK-47 assault rifles at the ready, could not understand why the visa was not stamped in the passport itself. Frankly, neither did I. The real problem, though, was that they could not read the paper. They asked me to decipher its words. Since I did not speak Portuguese at the time, they were treated to a distinctly Spanish version of my entry permit. It worked up to a point.

We reached a compromise whereby they would keep the letter to show their superiors while I was free to go. There was, of course, a complication. They had placed the entry stamp not in my passport but on the visa paper, so if I was stopped by the police on the street I had no proof that I had entered the country legally. Paranoia about South African and American spies was running high. President Ronald Reagan had just resumed official American aid to Savimbi's 'freedom fighters'. The likelihood of being questioned by the police was a virtual certainty in those days, and without the visa stamp the chances were good that I would spend a night or two in the local jail.

I caught a lift into town and luckily reached the house of a Uruguayan aid worker who was a friend of a friend. He handed me the keys to an empty flat on the Rua dos Massacres and bid me welcome to Angola. No food, no water, and Luanda was in the midst of one of its regular cholera epidemics. The state radio, Rádio Nacional de Angola, kept broadcasting warnings to boil tap water before using it. At 6 o'clock the next morning I queued at a communal tap outside with a group of women who thought I presented a humorous spectacle.

The Aníbal de Melo press centre was about one mile away, and when I walked in to introduce myself to the director he said that since he had no prior knowledge of my visit I must leave the country immediately. The ticket to Luanda had cost me about one-fifth of my entire savings and I could see my cherished journalistic career vanishing before me. Then Katia Airola, a 60-year-old Finnish woman who worked at the press centre, took pity on me. She convinced the director to relent and began organising a tour of the country for me.

A few days later I casually mentioned my visa problem to Katia. She rushed out to the airport with me in tow and retrieved my visa after rifling through a three-foot-high stack of papers on the floor of the immigration office. Then, for good measure, Katia proceeded to lecture a group of flabbergasted officials about the folly of their actions. How could you take this man's visa? What would happen if he were arrested? she demanded. My luck was beginning to change. Being on hand when Katia, a naturalised Angolan, was dressing down the agents of the country's stifling bureaucracy became one of life's great pleasures. Her age was one of the reasons she always got away with it. In Africa elderly people still command respect.

I was back in Angola in 1988 hoping to reach a little town called Cuito Cuanavale, the site of the biggest battle in Africa since the Second World War. The clash held out the promise of changing the course of history not only in Angola but in the rest of southern Africa as well. The drama was unfolding in the remote south-eastern bushlands of Cuando Cubango province, which because of their harshness, their complete despair, the Portuguese used to call *as terras do fim do mundo*, the lands at the end of the world.

2 Hitching to Africa's Stalingrad

> Angola's UNITA rebels, reportedly backed up by 6,000 South African troops, are locked in a fierce battle with Angolan government forces for control of the strategic town of Cuito Cuanavale in the south-east of the country. The battle, said to have begun ... with heavy artillery bombardments and airstrikes, marks the climax to one of the bloodiest phases yet in the twelve-year Angolan civil war.
>
> *Daily Telegraph*,
> 16 January 1988

> Mr Chester Crocker, the US Assistant Secretary of State for African Affairs, resumes talks with the Angolan government in Luanda today as a fierce battle continues for control of the strategic garrison town of Cuito Cuanavale in the south-east of the country.
>
> *The Times*,
> 28 January 1988

A pungent bouquet of jet fuel fumes with a dash of sea salt in the moist earthy air of the west coast of Africa announces my arrival at Luanda's 4 de Fevereiro airport. Something special is up this evening. Half a dozen black Mercedes Benzes appear in front of the VIP lounge. Who are they for? I do not recall seeing any government ministers on board when the Portuguese plane took off from Harare three hours before, though someone may have slipped into first class at the last minute. Waiting at the foot of the stairs is Katia, the press centre official who is like a surrogate mother to foreign correspondents visiting Angola. Her smile is always reassuring. Suddenly it dawns on me and the other journalists on the plane that the red carpet reception is for us.

We are ushered into the VIP lounge, known as *protocol*, where officials quickly process our passports and make us feel downright giddy for not having to endure the lengthy queues at the normal arrival lounge just 100 yards away. Within minutes we are whisked away in a high-speed race through central Luanda, with our driver, a certain Fernando who seems to speak only French, keeping beat with his foot, the one which is supposed to be on the accelerator, to Zairean music pulsating from the car's tape deck.

The special treatment has been arranged for a group of reporters I have joined in a quest to reach the ever elusive front line of the Angolan civil war, a small town called Cuito Cuanavale in the distant south-eastern province of Cuando Cubango.

It is late February 1988. The Angolan army, together with thousands of Cuban troops and dozens of Soviet military advisers, are engaged against the South African Defence Force (SADF) and its UNITA allies in the biggest set-piece battle in Africa in recent memory. We are counting on a government promise to take us there, to become the first reporters to witness the clash. It is an opportunity I do not want to miss, a rare chance to see the bully boy of southern Africa, the apartheid government in Pretoria, finally receive a richly deserved bloody nose.

Scepticism and a certain amount of dread abound among us, however, since what Angolan officials promise and what they deliver are usually two very different things. 'I cannot guarantee anything,' Katia responds in her clipped Finnish accent to our persistent enquiries about whether the trip is a serious proposition. 'Let us wait and see.'

Our dread increases the next morning when we board a plane, though unfortunately one heading not to Cuito Cuanavale but to the south-western city of Lubango, about 400 miles west of our intended destination. It is *inconveniente* to go to Cuito Cuanavale just now. So the military has decided to fill the time with a visit to the southern air base at Chamutete, where, it is said, Angolan anti-aircraft gunners recently brought down a South African Mirage jet. At least we are moving, though, and the first rule in covering the war in Angola, or any civil war for that matter, is to take what you can get.

We sit at the airport. Our Antonov-26 cargo aircraft

remains dormant on the tarmac. It seems for a while that even this trip too might be *inconveniente*. Several military officers accompanying us explain that we are waiting for the air space over Lubango to re-open. They cannot, or will not, say why it was closed. An hour later we take off.

The delay in Luanda means that we do not touch down in Lubango until the early afternoon, too late to continue the journey to Chamutete until the following morning. So we hang around Lubango airport, admiring a dozen Russian-built MiG-23 jets, the most sophisticated planes in southern Africa, which are tucked away neatly in their bunkers alongside the airstrip, and waiting for our Angolan minders to ride into the city and arrange transport for the rest of us.

Having minders along can be one of life's more unpleasant experiences. In Angola, government minders are routinely young lads trained in East Germany or the Soviet Union whose sole mission is to ensure that reporters do not get into any trouble and that they stay well clear of sensitive subjects. They are part censors, part chaperons and part captors. On rare occasions minders can smooth the way onto over-crowded planes or into fully-booked hotels, sometimes even arrange an important interview.

In the mid-1980s, when the MPLA was still clinging to its status as a Marxist vanguard party, press minders underwent special training by the intelligence services. One minder in Luanda told me that things were so bad in 1985 that when he had to accompany a journalist or visiting dignitary, he was usually followed by an intelligence operative, who, in turn, was followed by another. Inevitably, the vehicle carrying a foreign journalist, perhaps even a minister, was followed around town by a trail of others. It was a good thing that Angola was Africa's second biggest oil producer.

Our minders have been gone for about 30 minutes when we start getting bored with our surroundings at Lubango airport. So we take the only sensible option available: hitch-hike into town. Fortunately, just as we walk out of the airport entrance an ageing lorry passes by, tilting badly to the left under the weight of a modest mountain of potatoes. It is going our way so we climb aboard for the fifteen-minute ride to the Grande Hotel de Huila in central Lubango.

Sitting in the hotel lounge the minders are surprised by our arrival, as if we should have waited for them indefinitely at the airport. Don't leave the hotel, they say. We leave anyway. They will not say why, but they are very nervous. The team leader hardly inspires confidence. He is the director of the Aníbal de Melo press centre in Luanda, Miguel de Carvalho, 'Wadigimbi', a particularly sinister character, said to be a former officer in the secret police and given to beginning a healthy daily intake of scotch whisky at 10 in the morning. Wadigimbi has told me on several occasions that journalists are a waste of time, which is certainly an arguable position but surely not one that the director of the foreign press centre should hold. On one occasion he banned me from leaving Luanda for no particular reason and I retaliated by visiting and writing a story about the city's biggest black market, Roque Santeiro, named after a Brazilian soap opera and strictly out of bounds to the press at the time because the government did not want the world to know that while its mismanaged socialist policies had helped the war to wreck the economy, traditional markets were booming.

The reason for our minders' strange behaviour is revealed when we tune in to the 7 p.m. news bulletin of Rádio Nacional de Angola. The lead item is about the early morning air strikes by South African jets on camps of Namibian refugees and fighters for the South West Africa People's Organisation (SWAPO), the Namibian independence movement, just outside Lubango. Our frustration reaches breaking point. Communications with Luanda are so bad that there is no way for us to file the story to our newspapers and agencies. The provincial government refuses to comment on the affair or to permit us to visit the bomb sites. Besides, our minders say we can not deviate from the *programa* set up for us, and SWAPO camps are not part of it. My sense of dread deepens as a sense of deja vu begins to settle in.

The first time I came to Lubango was in 1986. The governor of Huila province then was Lopo do Nascimento, one of the most open-minded people in the government who, despite his leadership role in the avowedly Marxist MPLA. was an avid reader of magazines such as *Institutional Investor*. He had given me permission to photograph the annual celebration of Armed Forces Day which was being held in Lubango that year. The government army, known as the Popular Armed Forces for the Liberation of Angola (FAPLA), was to stage a procession of its heavy weaponry, including Soviet T-54 tanks and SAM-8 anti-aircraft missile systems, and I, a hungry young freelance reporter, was positively salivating at the prospect of capturing it all on film. Lopo had instructed the minders accompanying me and an American colleague to wait for special credentials before leaving the hotel to take the photographs. All would be in order, he said.

By 9 a.m. when the parade started, the MPLA official designated to deliver our papers had not arrived. He did not come an hour later and by 11 o'clock, when the heavy weaponry was passing by the hotel on its way out of town, there was still no sign of him. He had taken our credentials and our vehicle to spend the day with his mistress. It was, after all, a public holiday. I was able neither to take pictures nor even to attend the celebration.

Our main concern was to reach the airport for the trip back to Luanda. We were very low on money. The plane we were due to catch had already arrived, but the two youthful security agents were sticking to the governor's order that we could not leave the hotel until our credentials had arrived. They were unmoved by the argument that the credentials were for a parade which had already ended. Orders were orders, they said. Flexibility was not among their strong points. A few days before the same pair had arranged interviews with people displaced by the war, but answered all the questions themselves before the refugees could speak.

In a state of near panic, we turned to Katia, who luckily had accompanied us from Luanda. Would it help, we asked, if we told the minders that unless we were allowed to make the flight to Luanda, we would report in our newspapers that we had been detained? 'A very good idea,' she said. Katia was positively glowing as she marched up to our guardians and formally relayed the message. It caught their attention. They made a few frantic telephone calls, all unsuccessful since their superiors were enjoying an Armed Forces Day lunch. Katia stood there poker-faced, respectfully awaiting their decision. After a moment they commandeered a vehicle passing on the street outside and drove us straight to the airport, running over a dog on the way.

The crowd at the departure gate was massive and

preparing to dash to the airplane. Flying with the national airline was, for Angolans, one of the world's great bargains. Because fares were pegged to the official, incredibly low exchange rate to the dollar, Angolans could pay in local currency to fly to Rio de Janeiro or Lisbon for the equivalent of a couple of bags of tomatoes sold on the black market. Internal flights, to say the least, were packed and grabbing a seat on them was like fighting one's way through a riot. This was one of those occasions when minders could come in very handy. Sensing the problem, they led us through a small opening on the luggage conveyor belt to avoid the throng and onto the ageing Boeing-737 for the flight back to Luanda.

So our current dilemma in Lubango is a mere twist on an old theme. No visits to the sites of today's attacks by South African jets, it is not on the *programa*, and no, there is no way of calling Luanda to report the story.

The next morning we are duly flown out to the Chamutete air base, complete with a stomach-wrenching spiral down to the airstrip to avoid government and UNITA anti-aircraft missiles. Army officials produce a fairly modest piece of unidentifiable metal which they describe as a remnant of a South African jet they shot down a week before. It is far from convincing.

How was it, we ask the local military commander, Captain Brancão Armindo Fraternidade, that South African jets so easily avoided the sophisticated Soviet-built air defence systems, which cost tens of millions of dollars, and attacked Lubango yesterday? Embarrassed glances pass between the assembled army officers. At first Captain Fraternidade casts blame on 'the carelessness of our rearguard troops. They always think they will be warned by the forces at the front line.' Then, he says, UNITA spies must have told the South African pilots they could fly at the precise moment the radar and anti-aircraft batteries were not properly manned. Saving the best excuse for last, Captain Fraternidade admits that sometimes the Angolans have to 'rest the system for maintenance'. His explanations do little to inspire confidence when, three days later, we finally embark on the historic visit to Cuito Cuanavale. What if the defence systems there suddenly needed to relax?

Cuito Cuanavale had been in the news since November 1987, a month after crack South African troops smashed an offensive by the FAPLA army outside the UNITA-held town of Mavinga at the River Lomba. FAPLA had mounted a huge force and spent over $1 billion on Soviet weaponry to capture Mavinga, from where it hoped to be able to strike at Savimbi's headquarters in Jamba, just 150 miles to the south-east. Since UNITA captured Mavinga in 1980 it had become a vital arrival point for supplies from South Africa.

The Angolan military strategy was designed by Soviet advisers, who had ignored warnings from their Cuban allies that such an attempt was inviting disaster, that they would be once again over-stretched and bogged down in Cuando Cubango. Cuban officials around southern Africa had been briefing reporters for months on the idiocy of such an offensive, assuring anyone who would listen that Fidel Castro wanted no part of it. But the idea of wiping out UNITA had been an obsession ever since the MPLA took control of Luanda at independence in November 1975, and the mirage of total victory had clouded the leaders' vision once again.

In the event, the Cubans were right. The Angolan government forces were routed, at the cost of thousands of casualties and the loss of hundreds of millions of dollars' worth of equipment, and had to retreat 120 miles with the South Africans in very hot pursuit. Until then the South African government had refrained from admitting its army's role in the battle and, as always, Jonas Savimbi claimed that UNITA troops were fighting alone.

This time Savimbi's bluster reached the absurd. On 13 November 1987 he flew a group of South Africa-based reporters into Jamba to hear his announcement to the world that the heroic UNITA fighters had destroyed a Cuban/FAPLA offensive on their own. 'We have had aid from South Africa but not men fighting at our side. That is categorical,' he declared. Unfortunately for Savimbi, on the same day that he was making this claim South African Defence Minister Magnus Malan admitted for the first time that the South Africans had intervened in Angola to halt Russian expansion and to save UNITA from annihilation. In fact, the battle at the River Lomba had been a strictly Angolan-South African affair. The Cubans were not directly involved at all and UNITA's own role was minimal.

By mid-November, the Angolans were in full retreat and Cuito Cuanavale looked set to fall to the South Africans, although they would later say that they had never been interested in taking the town. Several Angolan commanders likened Cuito Cuanavale to the heroic Soviet defence of Stalingrad against Hitler's Wehrmacht. As the Angolan defences teetered on the brink of collapse, Castro, seeing over a decade of Cuban *internacionalismo* in jeopardy, decided to intervene. He dispatched an extra 15,000 troops – there were already 25,000 in Angola – including the elite 50th Division which had turned back the South African invasion force in 1975 as it was closing in on Luanda on the eve of independence.

The overall commander was Cuba's most decorated general, Arnaldo Ochoa Sánchez, who a year later was to be executed on charges of drug-running and treason, which many people believed to have been trumped up. By early February the Cubans had deployed around Cuito Cuanavale. Two weeks later they engaged the South Africans in battle for the first time, at least four months after UNITA said they had done so.

On 28 February 1988 my colleagues and I board another Antonov-26 plane to the air base outside the city of Menongue, the point of departure for the front line at Cuito Cuanavale, just 80 miles to the east. Again we endure a gut-wrenching descent to land. The manoeuvre is no mere attempt to impress. The danger of being shot down is real. Courtesy of the United States, Savimbi's men possess the much vaunted shoulder-fired Stinger anti-aircraft missile which can take out jet fighters, much less a plodding Antonov.

The airport is abuzz with the arrival and departure of MiG-23 jets and helicopter gunships and thousands of Angolan troops milling around the tarmac. All through the war, soldiers spend many hours and days sitting around airports, sometimes waiting for orders and sometimes conspiring to steal food arriving on flights sent by the Catholic Church or international aid groups. In later years this latter activity was to become one of their main occupations.

The roar of the war machines is deafening, the fumes and dust stirred up by their engines suffocating. A light drizzle is falling as we board three helicopters, a Russian-built MI-24 gunship, the renowned 'flying tank' used to devastating effect in Nicaragua and Afghanistan, an MI-17 transport and a small French Alouette. I choose the Alouette for the view it affords; its cockpit and passenger area are surrounded almost entirely by glass.

We lift off the runway and speed away just above tree-top level, over the River Cuebe, following a straight path up the road to Cuito Cuanavale. That sinking feeling of impending failure comes after just ten minutes when the 'flying tank' suddenly banks hard and turns around. The other helicopters follow it back to Menongue. Maybe the fighting in Cuito Cuanavale has grown too intense, or perhaps the South Africans have smashed through the FAPLA/Cuban defence. The explanation is rather more mundane. The gunship's radios are not working and the three helicopters cannot communicate with each other. The repairs take 30 minutes to complete and we are soon airborne once again.

A storm centre has intensified to the north and great bolts of lightning split open the deep blue sky. The Alouette flies so close to the ground that it has to rise over particularly tall trees. Down below is a column of hundreds of tanks, armoured cars, fuel trucks and troop carriers weaving slowly in and out of the charred remains of vehicles which have been blown apart by South African jets in strafing runs and UNITA guerrilla attacks. At several points the road is blocked by immense traffic jams, with inevitable crowds of soldiers arguing with each other about how to clear the way. Dozens of tanks are dug in under the trees and behind them are rows of trenches for the ground troops. Every few minutes the MiG-23s scream overhead on their way to the front.

About ten miles from our destination the helicopters slow down and alight on the road. It is not safe to fly any closer to the front. As we land, Wadigimbi, the press centre director cum ex-secret police agent, jumps out of his helicopter, climbs into a waiting jeep and speeds off, leaving the journalists he is supposed to guide standing in the middle of the road. I fear Wadigimbi is having his final revenge on the world's press. What a propaganda bonanza it would be if the South Africans killed a bunch of foreign reporters.

Suddenly groups of young Cuban soldiers manning

anti-aircraft batteries come running out of the bush to welcome their unexpected visitors. A few Angolans from the other side of the road straggle out too. All of them are extremely young, in their late teens or early twenties, some still with peach fuzz on their faces. They are pumped up, still basking in the glow of downing a South African Mirage jet piloted by Major Edward Every nine days before.

They enthusiastically offer an impromptu inspection of their missile batteries and describe how they brought down the Mirage. The South Africans, fearful of the SAM-8 anti-aircraft batteries, are employing a system of flying at tree-top level before pulling up sharply to unload their payloads. 'He passed over once and then came back around again, and when he slowed down to drop the bomb we all fired,' says Corporal Carlos Díaz, a robust nineteen-year-old black gunner from Cienfuegos, Cuba, whose slave ancestors probably came from Angola. 'The Angolan guys on that side say it was their shot, and we think we brought him down. It doesn't matter, because somebody hit that racist jet.' Corporal Díaz says he arrived at the front about a month before, leaving a wife, Julia, and an infant son, Ernesto, back home in Cienfuegos. He admits that he wants to leave Angola as soon as possible, but the renowned Cuban bravado flows in his veins. 'The Angolans are our brothers, and we must help them in their hour of need. The racist South Africans will never take Cuito Cuanavale as long as the Cubans are here. Never.' Fidel would be pleased.

There is still no sign of any transport to Cuito Cuanavale and we are getting anxious and wet. It is still drizzling. A lack of initiative could mean spending the entire day at the same spot. Fifty yards up the road a lorry is emerging from a dirt track on the Cuban side. We sprint towards it and thrust out our thumbs to catch a lift. Miraculously the driver stops, no doubt surprised to see a horde of journalists running his way. We climb on board, immensely pleased with ourselves for hitch-hiking to the biggest battle in recent African history.

As the town comes into view, the lorry stops and the affable Cuban driver, by now laughing hysterically, explains that he is turning off the road to head back into the bush. If we want to go any further we will have to walk. So we climb down and march.

Just as we reach the main army checkpoint, an armoured personnel carrier careens out of a muddy side track onto the road and stops besides us, its noisy diesel engine blocking out all attempts at conversation. The helmeted driver waves his arm, motioning us to climb into the metal beast, but there is not enough room so we hang onto the sides and the top for the ride over the final 500 yards into Cuito Cuanavale.

All the reports that have reached the outside world suggest that Cuito Cuanavale is deserted, except for the 10,000 Angolan and Cuban troops defending the town. All the civilians are either dead or have been evacuated. But as soon as we pull into town, tiny barefoot boys and girls run alongside the vehicle, waving and shouting '*Amigo, amigo*'. Spread across a rolling hill a mile to the south is a village of at least 1,000 wattle and daub huts. Inside the town itself are the remains of a dozen one-storey buildings, with holes blasted through the roofs and whole walls bludgeoned into dust.

The armoured personnel carrier changes its gears violently as it follows the slimy road down to the bridge over the River Cuito. The concrete span has been a key target of the South Africans for the past six months because it has allowed FAPLA to move tanks and other heavy vehicles across on their march to, and subsequent retreat from, Mavinga. It was partially destroyed in early January by a smart bomb launched by a South African jet, but enough of it is still standing to allow foot-soldiers to cross the river.

The drizzle becomes heavier as young Angolan troops loaded with heavy backpacks move back and forth around a major FAPLA logistics base in the flatlands beyond. We gather round in a semi-circle at the water's edge, like school children on a field trip. Major Armindo Moreira clears his throat to explain the purpose of our visit. 'We have brought you here today to show the world that the Angolan army still controls Cuito Cuanavale,' he shouts nervously. 'We are not going to permit the South Africans to take Cuito. We are staying here and the South Africans are going to have to pass over our dead bodies.' Major Moreira keeps looking at his watch as if he might be missing his next appointment. 'The South Africans should begin shelling at any moment. The artillery was very heavy this morning.' I think he is trying to dramatise the moment.

A few minutes after Major Moreira has spoken, an eerie zipping sound announces the arrival of a howitzer shell. The earth rumbles as the projectile hits the ground at least 500 yards away and sends a cloud of dust and smoke into the overcast skies. Thirty seconds later comes a second blast, this time just a few hundred yards away. Apparently we have been seen by a South African forward-spotter stationed on the high ground about five miles north-east of Cuito Cuanavale.

All around Angolan soldiers are fleeing to take cover. The driver of our armoured vehicle revs up his engines and beckons us to move quickly. Another shell lands 100 yards away, just across the river, and convinces us that it is time to go. Several journalists are laughing in excitement at seeing action, perhaps for the first time, and they are visibly disappointed that the class outing is being aborted. The Angolan troops urging us to move are not smiling. They know from several months of experience that the spotter on the hill needs less than a minute to call in new co-ordinates and that the artillery strikes with pinpoint accuracy.

Across the river individual soldiers fire their AK-47s into the air, more out of frustration than anything else since they can hardly expect to hit the howitzers, which are at least twenty miles away. None of their mortars can match the range of the G-5, the South African howitzers which rain shells down upon Cuito Cuanavale and which, unfortunately, are considered among the world's finest pieces of artillery. They have a computer-controlled firing system, and the 43.5 kilogramme shells have a range of up to 30 miles. They deliver fragmentation shells which can detonate ten yards above the ground, sending thousands of steel shards flying in all directions.

Occasionally MiG-23 jets race past in the general direction of the guns. But since the howitzers are hidden in the thick bush, detecting them is quite literally like trying to find a needle in a haystack. There is nothing for us to do but to retreat. The pen might be mightier than the sword, but it is certainly no match for a G-5. I have never felt so helpless, and truly sympathise with the soldiers loosing off aimless rounds from their AK-47s.

The armoured personnel carrier reverses up the hill in a hurry as another shell smashes into the ground where we have just been standing. Shifting into forward gear, the vehicle flees at high speed towards the airport on the western side of town. The shells trail our path. The ground is shaking with each blast now and it is difficult to hold on, especially as the driver is zigzagging violently. The soldiers' purpose in taking us to the airport is to prove that the landing strip, which the South Africans claim to have destroyed, is more or less intact. It is, although huge craters four feet deep in the bare earth all around the tarmac testify to the attempts by the South African gunners to demolish it.

I do not care anymore. I just want to get out of Cuito Cuanavale as quickly as possible. Luckily there is no chance to stop because the shells have become our constant companion, thudding into the ground before the dust of the previous one has time to settle. We return to the main road and the shells are following us up the hill towards town, which is now completely deserted. A few minutes later we lose sight of the river, and the spotter of us. The bombardments stop. Within 30 minutes we are back in the helicopters for the return ride to Menongue above a road that has become one massive muddy traffic jam. Darkness is falling over the lands at the end of the earth when we land in Menongue and set off in search of accommodation.

We stop by the government guest house for a brief meal of beer and cakes. I spend most of my time fending off a Russian cameraman, whom I had stupidly greeted with '*Kak dela, Tovarish*?' ('How's it going, comrade?') and who pursues me for the rest of the evening in the mistaken belief that I speak Russian. I stand through fifteen-minute monologues of Andrei excitedly recounting the day's events, to which I nod knowingly. '*Da, Andrei, da*.'

After our meal, we go to settle in at the only functioning hotel in Menongue, A Pérola do Sul, the Pearl of the South. Functioning is a liberal description of the state of the Pearl of the South. Turning off the light requires unscrewing the electric bulb. I share a room with Jan Raath, correspondent for the *Times*, and Godwin Matatu, the veteran Zimbabwean correspondent of the *Observer*, who is frequently gripped by fits of laughter about the trip. The state of the sheets convinces Raath and me to sleep fully dressed, while Godwin strips down to his underwear. We tell him he is making a big mistake. The bed bugs have a feast that night and poor

Godwin is in a foul mood the next morning.

We have been told to be ready by 9 a.m. to catch a military transport plane back to Luanda, which we are anxious to do in order to be able to file our stories by our late afternoon deadlines. Angry but hardly surprised when no one shows up by 10 o'clock, we begin to walk to the airport. After a mile or so we are within a few hundred yards of our goal when a lorry appears and its driver agrees to ferry us the rest of the way.

Cuito Cuanavale was one of those momentous battles, such as the Tet Offensive twenty years before in Vietnam, in which everyone claimed victory, but which, technically, no one really won. While the South Africans surely got the better of the fighting, they certainly lost the most psychologically. For the first time in the history of southern Africa armies of mostly black soldiers proved that the champions of apartheid were vulnerable, that the time of South Africa's military domination was running out. The town of Cuito Cuanavale instantly became the stuff of legend, a symbol of black pride across the region, in Zambia and Zimbabwe, in South Africa's rebellious black townships and in Mozambique, where Pretoria had trained, armed and funded the RENAMO insurgency that had devastated the country.

Several writers, whose books have glorified the South African performance at Cuito Cuanavale, echoed the complaints of the SADF officers that demands by politicians back home to keep white casualties to an absolute minimum prevented them from mounting a full-scale assault on the Cubans and the Angolans. American generals used to say the same thing about the Vietnam war – if only the politicians would let them do the job properly.

For Fidel Castro, Cuito Cuanavale would go down as perhaps his last great chance to shine as the defender of the downtrodden against the all-powerful imperialists. To make sure everyone understood the point, he delivered innumerable speeches and commissioned a special film on the battle, which invariably portrayed the *comandante en jefe* in the operations room in Havana, personally directing the victory.

The resulting withdrawal of the Cuban forces in return for a commitment by South Africa to pull out of Angola and grant independence to Namibia allowed Castro to bring his soldiers home with honour. The Cuban departure also removed the pretext of a 'communist onslaught' which the government in Pretoria had used with varying degrees of success to mollify Western criticism of its apartheid policies. There was no doubt that the Battle of Cuito Cuanavale contributed to forcing South Africa to look inward and, inevitably, to begin a reform process that led to the unbanning of the African National Congress in 1990 and the first all-race elections four years later.

The Angolan government was happy to have survived the encounter, given that the embarrassing defeat at the River Lomba outside Mavinga had carried it perilously close to the brink of disaster; Savimbi's UNITA movement could also claim victory because it was saved from annihilation.

What Cuito Cuanavale did prove to all sides was the impossibility of resolving the Angolan civil war militarily, although two years later the MPLA once again tried and failed to wipe out UNITA. By then supplies and support from the US government helped UNITA to avoid catastrophe. Washington would not accept the military defeat of UNITA.

In the end the Battle at Cuito Cuanavale helped set the stage for peace negotiations between the MPLA and UNITA. They would come three years later, after stop-go talks sponsored by the Portuguese, the United States and the Soviet Union. On 31 May 1991 President José Eduardo dos Santos and Jonas Savimbi travelled to Portugal to sign the Bicesse peace accords which provided for a ceasefire, demobilisation of their two armies and general elections in September 1992. At the urging of Portuguese Prime Minister Cavaco Silva, the two adversaries, the *donos*, reluctantly shook hands. Church bells rang throughout Lisbon that day.

3 The Road to Huambo

Estoril, Portugal. Angola's left-wing government and its US-backed UNITA rebels have reached a peace accord to end sixteen years of fighting within two weeks. The accord entails a *de facto* suspension of fighting by 15 May and a formal ceasefire signing in Portugal at the end of the month. It provides for Angola's first multi-party election between September and November 1992. 'There were no winners or losers in the talks, just as there were no winners or losers in the fighting. The only winners were the Angola people,' said José Durão Barroso, the Portuguese foreign minister.

Reuters, 2 May 1991

A purple glow peers over the horizon towards a black sky still filled with stars. Dawn is less than an hour away. The wide Portuguese-style avenues of Luanda are silent except for a few stray tramps beginning to stir from their cardboard beds among the heaps of rubbish that cover the street corners and sometimes whole blocks in a patchwork quilt of empty beer cans, muddied pieces of paper and torn plastic containers. A man with a sprinkling of grey in his unkempt matted hair and clothed in a tattered army uniform is singing loudly as he weaves and stumbles barefoot across the Avenida do Commandante Valodia, celebrating a few remaining minutes of freedom before the imminent rush of traffic blows him off the road. For these fleeting moments he is king of Luanda.

An Italian aid worker named Bepe and I climb aboard a white Land Rover to embark on a 500-mile journey down the Atlantic coast to the twin port cities of Benguela and Lobito and then up an escarpment of 5,000 feet to Angola's central highlands, the *planalto*. Our destination is Huambo, Angola's second biggest city, which the Portuguese colonialists had once called Nova Lisboa.

If successful, the drive will take us across the great divide that defines the Angolan conflict pitting the MPLA, with its base among the intellectuals and mixed-race people of the coast and the Mbundu of the north-west, against UNITA, which derives its main support from the Umbundu people of the *planalto*. The Bicesse accords signed six weeks before in May 1991 have made such an expedition possible. The question on our and everyone's minds is: will the peace last?

As we bump along the heavily pot-holed roads of central Luanda, Bepe says he is sceptical because the years of bitter fighting, atrocities and hate cannot not be swept away by signatures on a piece of paper. But I am optimistic, hopeful for an outbreak of good news on a continent seemingly doomed to disaster.

'The people are tired of war, they won't put up with a return to fighting,' I am fond of saying. Bepe rolls his eyes at my innocence and delivers a response that Angolans repeat over and over again: 'But the people don't make the war.'

We both have high expectations that this journey will begin to answer the question. It is said that the road to Huambo has been cleared of landmines but, typically, Bepe is not so sure. I am filled with the confidence inspired by the notion that there is no way to know for sure except by pushing ahead.

The purple glow is being subverted by a soft red light as the traffic heading south out of Luanda increases. A small stream of lorries flows towards the entrance of the 4 de Fevereiro airport past a remarkable sight, a giant opposition party banner stretched over October Revolution Avenue which reads: 'Welcome to the People's Republic of Angola, a country of inequalities, hunger, misery and intimidation'.

That one banner as much as anything confirms the arrival of peace in Angola for the first time since 1961 when black nationalists launched their liberation war against Portugal. Since the civil war erupted at independence and the MPLA declared itself a Marxist-Leninist 'Workers' Party', opposition to the government was considered treasonous. Anyone who attempted to speak out, much less raise posters or banners critical of the one-party state, would have to answer to the Ministry of Interior's dreaded secret police.

The passive regurgitation of the MPLA's infinite wisdom has always been the main role of Angola's state-owned press.

It was among the most mind-numbing in Africa, perhaps second only to UNITA's radio station, the Voice of the Resistance of the Black Cockerel, or Vorgan.

Disappearances and executions had, at times, been common. Few Angolans have forgotten the massive killing spree that gripped Luanda after Nito Alves, a former MPLA guerrilla leader and minister of internal administration, attempted to seize power in 1977. Government security agents retaliated by arresting and executing thousands of people, some of whom were dropped from helicopters into the sea.

This, however, is the new Angola, and at least for the moment people can say what they want. Practically overnight, it seems, Luanda is being swept by a mini-revolution. UNITA officials have even come to town, setting themselves up in the city centre at the Hotel Turismo, where small crowds of curious onlookers gather and stare up in apparent disbelief at the UNITA flag hanging off a balcony next to a parabolic satellite telephone dish. Officers of the two rival armies meeting in a Joint Political-Military Commission (the CCPM), to work out the mechanics of the peace agreement – how to confine their troops to assembly points and to plan for the demobilisation of 200,000 soldiers and the integration of the rest into a new 50,000-strong army – are, by all accounts, getting on famously. Amadeu Neves, an activist in the promising new opposition group responsible for the banner at the airport, the Democratic Renewal Party, sums up the mood when he tells me, 'Angola is beginning from year zero.'

The road south slices through a vast maze of shacks that make up Rocha Pinto, one of the biggest of the shanty towns known as *musseques* which smother Luanda in a blanket of mud-brick, tin-roof dwellings. Down below towards the Atlantic Ocean looms an extraordinary monument to the country's first president, the late Marxist poet Agostinho Neto. Flanked by freshly cleared worksites and covered in scaffolding, the mausoleum resembles a giant rocket, which, despite the $100 million that has been poured into it, is still not ready for take-off. No matter how many times you see them, the mausoleum and the nearby destitute *musseques* remain shocking reminders of the MPLA's brazen neglect of its own people amid its lavish spending on grandiose, never completed projects.

A few miles later is Futungo de Belas, a former beach club for Portuguese army officers, now a huge, modern presidential complex which for the past decade has given José Eduardo dos Santos a quiet, beachfront refuge from the war and Luanda's massive squalor, its routine power and water shortages, its outbreaks of cholera and the fine rancid dust that rises from thousands of tons of rotting rubbish which covers the body with a fetid film. The first psychological frontier comes 50 miles south of Luanda at the River Kwanza bridge. This used to be defended by an anti-aircraft gun which Cuban soldiers, the last of whom had pulled out a few weeks before, wrapping up a sixteen-year *internacionalista* military campaign in Angola, would point at cars and trucks as they made their way across. It was here that the Cubans turned back the South African armoured column in 1975 and ensured the MPLA's dominance in Luanda. Before the ceasefire vehicles travelling to and from Luanda had to pass the bridge before 6 p.m. Anyone who arrived after this deadline was considered an enemy target, and the disciplined Cuban soldiers were under orders to shoot first and ask questions later.

I had the misfortune of reaching the bridge at 7 o'clock one evening in 1989. At the last Angolan military checkpoint before the crossing an army private had warned, 'You are welcome to sleep here, because if you advance any further the Cubans will shoot you.' However unattractive the prospect of sleeping under a truck with a unit of Angolan soldiers, it seemed preferable to running a nocturnal gauntlet of trigger-happy Cuban soldiers. Luckily, a UN food convoy had pulled up at the same time and the team leader agreed to sneak my landcruiser through in the middle of his caravan of some 50 lorries. When he and several UN World Food Programme officials approached the bridge to negotiate our after-hours passage across the River Kwanza, the Cubans fired into the air. 'We told you so,' the Angolan soldier said as he and his mates erupted in laughter. The Cuban sergeant ordered his men to stop firing when he saw the blue UN flags waving. After an hour of discussion he allowed the convoy, with my vehicle concealed in its midst, to pass on to Luanda.

Two years later the only troops to be seen are Angolan, and they are unarmed and undressed. They stand in a row behind a shed pouring buckets of water over their heads. Dawn has just broken. There is not even a checkpoint; the only memento of the Cubans are sketches of a bearded man in a beret on the bridge besides the words: '*Socialismo o muerte! Viva Fidel!*' (Socialism or death! Long live Fidel!).

Wreckage of burnt-out vehicles, metal casualties of crashes or attacks by rocket-propelled grenades, landmines or machine-gun fire, appear on the roadside from time to time, some well on their way to being reclaimed by the unyielding African bush. Further on soldiers and civilians packed in trucks making their way up the coastal road towards Luanda wave as they brace themselves against the early morning cold of the Angolan winter.

Like millions of their compatriots across the country, they are taking advantage of the ceasefire to travel by road for the first time in years. Prior to the peace accord anyone wishing to travel safely from one government-controlled area to another did so by plane, while in zones held by UNITA movement was strictly on foot.

No one ran a bigger risk during the war years than the lorry drivers who were hired by the government to deliver supplies to isolated cities in the war zones. These are men of outstanding courage or insufficient brain power, depending on one's point of view. Aurelio Cardoso has been a driver for 26 years, first for the Portuguese colonial government, then for the MPLA and more recently for the United Nations. He will go anywhere, at any time. For the past three years he has been driving a white Renault lorry and he hates leaving home without it.

'My truck is like my wife. I like to be with her all the time.' His real spouse, Sonía, and their twelve children have begged him to seek other employment. 'My family starts getting quiet in the days before I leave. They are very sad. You never know what is going to happen on the road.' But Cardoso refuses to listen. 'I know all of Angola, I have been everywhere. I'm a long-distance driver and in Angola my profession can be very dangerous, but it's my profession.'

His family has good reason to be concerned. Cardoso has been shot three times, in the stomach, ear and hand in 1974, when a convoy escorted by Portuguese colonial troops came under fire from guerrillas in the northern province of Uíge. He was never able to work out which nationalist movement was responsible for the attack. Even after independence Uíge was a dangerous place to drive. In August 1989, his convoy fell into another ambush, although this time it was clear that UNITA rebels were the assailants. Fourteen lorries were looted. By now he has a well-rehearsed drill to follow. 'When the shooting starts, I climb under the truck between the tyres and hope that God is near.'

Francisco Manuel Leitão said his wife Susana Joaquim Pinto has been pestering him for years to find another line of work. He started driving for the colonial army in 1969 and escaped incident until fourteen years later, when UNITA troops attacked his convoy outside the north-eastern city of Saurimo. A rocket-propelled grenade slammed into his truck, killing a woman and her child. Leitão spent fifteen days in the bush and survived on manioc before another passing convoy picked him up. Five years later he was involved in another ambush, this time on the road to Huambo, my destination, but again he escaped serious injury. 'When I'm sent on one of these jobs, all I think about is the convoy going well. You just think about reaching the end.'

For drivers like Francisco and Aurelio, the coastal road south from Luanda has traditionally been one of the safer routes in the country. Yet all along the way are signs of the huge migrations of people who have fled the conflict in the surrounding countryside. Unfortunate civilians caught between the two armies have left their land in the interior highlands to settle where they can, near cities or the coast. On the outskirts of two picturesque port towns, Porto Amboim and Tsumbe, makeshift mud huts built by the refugees are perched precariously on sandy hillsides. The tree cover has long since been stripped away and consumed as firewood. The onset of the rainy season nearly always brings tragedy, sweeping away entire neighbourhoods in giant mudslides.

The scenery begins to change dramatically when our Land Rover approaches the UNITA-controlled village of Kanjala, about 220 miles south of Luanda. Millions of tiny white, black and yellow butterflies fill the air in an apparent celebration of peace, as thick as the paper in a New York City ticker-tape parade. They are so dense that we have to switch on the windscreen wipers to clear the windscreen of their tiny delicate corpses.

The piles of twisted metal – it is hard to imagine that once they were shiny new vehicles – are much more frequent now that we have reached the rebel zone, often resting beside the huge scorched holes in the road that mark landmine explosions. Freshly dug pits appear in the tarmac every mile or so, greatly slowing the journey, but there is something reassuring about them. They are confirmation that the joint teams of the FAPLA, the government army, and UNITA's military wing, FALA, have been by to scoop out the landmines that had not yet exploded. Bepe's confidence soars.

For most of the afternoon we see no one. Mile after mile of uninhabited bush, testimony to the country's sparse population, just 11 million people in a country the size of Britain, France and Spain combined. Angola is still making up for the ravages of the slave trade which took 4 million people across the ocean to the Americas, to places like Brazil and Cuba. Some of their descendants no doubt came back to fight with the Cuban *internacionalista* brigade, like the soldiers I had met out on that road near Cuito Cuanavale three years before.

By dusk scores of FAPLA soldiers spill onto the road. The more ambitious ones are hoping to catch a lift to the nearest village, while at the sight of our vehicle others simply press two fingers to their lips in a humble request for a cigarette. There is something odd about them. These are the first Angolan soldiers I have seen in the field in five years who are not carrying AK-47s or weapons of any kind. In the fading light, they seem like a defeated army, straggling down the road in tattered uniforms, sometimes even barefoot. Many had been dragooned into the army and lost their youth to the war. Now they are taking the opportunity to return home. With luck they will soon be with their mothers and sisters, perhaps their teenage sweethearts.

At nightfall we pass through Lobito, site of Angola's best deep-water port, and reach its sister town of Benguela, our resting point before climbing the escarpment to the *planalto*.

The next morning we begin the most difficult part of the trip, pushing our Land Rover across a wide sandy plain bathed in a soft orange light and up into the blue mountains beyond. Only weeks before the road up the plateau was barely passable, even with an armed military escort. Twenty miles out of Benguela sits a now abandoned car park where convoys of trucks used to gather to wait for their chaperons, the armoured vehicles provided by the government army to shield them against UNITA attacks along the 200-mile road to Huambo. Strewn along the way are the charred remains of the vehicles which did not arrive at their destination. By the looks of it, many army trucks also fell by the wayside. On this morning, though, motorcycles, lorries with their suspension bent wildly out of shape by Angola's battered roads and even a VW beetle start the assault on the *planalto* unescorted.

At our first major stop at Catengue, about 50 miles inland, groups of women with sacks of fruit sit under a blinding mountain sun waiting for lifts to the markets of Benguela, which for years the isolated peasants on the escarpment had looked down upon as a city of gold. Barefoot young boys in ragged T-shirts armed with catapults are hunting small game along narrow footpaths through a landscape filled with hulking, twisted baobab trees and huge boulders. We are crossing the frontier dividing the hot, muggy coast of west Africa and the cooler highlands of southern Africa.

All along the route clouds of smoke rise from the earth as farmers practise their centuries old slash-and-burn technique to prepare the land for the winter-planting season, the *nacas*. The brushfire haze rolling over people walking around their homes and through crushed cement buildings give the impression that the area has just emerged from a giant explosion. Pedestrians scurry off the road at the approach of our vehicle – they are clearly unused to traffic. Invariably they turn to start waving and cheering as if we are conquering heroes.

At Caimbambo women selling bread and oranges along the road say they doubt that the war is over. 'Will it be like 1975?' a woman named Rosa asks with great severity as she orders her two rowdy boys to hush so she can hear my reply. I cannot say whether the new peace accord will become a repeat of liberation from Portugal, when independence disintegrated into a new civil conflict which drew in troops from South Africa, Zaire and Cuba and pitted the United States, backing the UNITA rebels, against the Soviet Union, the MPLA's patron. I mumble something lame about the people being tired of war, but Rosa is having none of it. She responds as sharply as a strict schoolteacher, 'Papa, it is not the people who make war, but the leaders.' Bepe raises his eyebrows knowingly and nods in agreement.

There is desperation in Rosa's voice. The civil war of the post-independence years has brought immense suffering and hunger to the central highlands. The fertile *planalto*, known as simply the *nano* by early European observers, has not been through such turmoil since the onset of Portuguese occupation at the turn of the century.

The *planalto* is the home region of the Umbundu people, Angola's largest ethnic group, accounting for about 38 per cent of the population. Sitting on a plateau between 4,000 and 6,000 feet above sea level, its mild climate had prompted one nineteenth-century Portuguese settler to describe it as a place of 'perpetual springtime'. It was once a region of vast elephant herds and forests, but they had disappeared over a century ago.

The Umbundu were organised into 22 independent kingdoms formed in the seventeenth century by the merging of the original inhabitants of the plateau and a militaristic people known as the Jagas who invaded from the north-east. The first time the *planalto* felt the presence of the Portuguese was in the middle of the seventeenth century when African and mixed-race *mestiço* traders began venturing out from garrisons in Luanda and Benguela. Umbundu merchants adapted quickly and came to dominate trade in slaves, beeswax, ivory and, from the 1880s until 1901, rubber, sending the goods to the coast in giant caravans of up to 1,000 men, women and children who would stay away from home for up to two years.

Trouble started with the collapse of the rubber boom in the early years of the twentieth century with the establishment of plantations of better quality rubber in the East Indies, South America and the west coast of Africa. The slump coincided with a smallpox epidemic and drought and cattle disease in the south. Unrest grew in the Umbundu kingdoms, especially in the biggest, Bailundo. The arbitrary behaviour of the foreign traders, Portuguese promotion of sales of rum and the increasing failure of the traditional leadership to deal with the encroachment by the Portuguese, mainly *degredado* exiled convicts, merchants and poor whites, including Boer farmers from South Africa, sparked great discontent.

In early 1902, when Kalandula, the new *soba* or chieftain of the Bailundos, was preparing to assume power, a local Portuguese trader accused one of the king's most militant advisers, Mutu-ya-Kavela, of not paying for rum he had bought for the celebrations. In April of that year, the Portuguese military commander known as Capitão Mor arrested Kalandula and Mutu-ya-Kavela launched an uprising. For the first time the Bailundos united with a *soba* of Wambu, the kingdom of modern-day Huambo, and several other kingdoms, raising an army of 10,000 warriors to expel the Portuguese and the traders.

In June Mutu-ya-Kavela called a war council and delivered an impassioned speech demanding reform, justice, economic growth and freedom from the slave trade, which was taking up to 3,000 Ovimbundu (the plural form of Umbundu) a year to plantations in northern Angola and São Tomé. Central to his appeal was a glorification of the prosperous reign of a past Bailundo king, Ekuikui II, and he blamed the growing rum trade for sapping his people's strength. As he told the war council, 'Before the traders came we had our own home-brewed beer, we lived long lives and were strong.' The main targets of Umbundu rage were *mestiço* traders and westernised blacks.

The war lasted only three months. A Portuguese-led force of up to 1,000 African troops using repeating rifles and artillery out-gunned the Umbundu guerrillas, who fought with ancient muzzle-loaders from the great rock outcrops which dominate the landscape. The main rebellion ended in August with the death of Mutu-ya-Kavela, but guerrilla warfare continued sporadically for another two years. Mutu-ya-Kavela's memory survived in Umbundu oral tradition, however, and the Portuguese remained forever impressed with his military prowess. The Governor General of Angola at the time, Cabral de Moncada, described him as 'this brave *caudilho* of black war'.

In the aftermath of the Bailundo rebellion, European immigration increased rapidly and the Portuguese colonial army pacified the once independent kingdoms, including Wambu for the first time. With their traditional way of life in tatters, a new generation of Ovimbundu flocked to both Protestant and Catholic mission schools. The *planalto* became one of Angola's most underdeveloped regions. Thousands of young Ovimbundu were sent first as forced labour and later as contract workers to coffee plantations in the north where the Mbundu and Bacongo people had refused to co-operate with the Portuguese.

Ovimbundu acquiescence to the Portuguese demands earned the wrath of the Mbundus and Bacongos who regarded them as the equivalent of scabs, country bumpkins whose labour permitted the colonialists to exploit the region's best land. When the Mbundus and the Bacongos launched the independence war in northern Angola in 1961, 60,000 Ovimbundu were forced to flee back to the *planalto*.

The Umbundu people were late to join the nationalist struggle against the Portuguese, but when they did so a majority supported the UNITA movement formed in 1966 by a new guerrilla leader, Jonas Savimbi, whose grandfather Sakaita Savimbi had fought in the Bailundo rebellion and lost his status as a counsellor to the ruler of Ndulu as a punishment. If UNITA was to stand a chance of winning the general elections scheduled for September 1992, it would have to win by a decisive margin on the *planalto*.

The first clear sign of UNITA's political appeal in the region comes at the town of Cubal, in eastern part of Benguela province, where a slogan freshly painted in big red letters on a wall reads: 'Savimbi is our choice – Long live peace'. There is plenty of evidence of the rebels' military prowess too, especially near the border with Huambo province. There the wreckage of several hundred ambushed vehicles – cars, buses and military lorries – is lined up almost bumper-to-bumper along a crater-filled dirt track which cuts through vast eucalyptus forests and winds around spectacular jutting mountains.

The pro-UNITA graffiti gradually increases from town to town until it reaches a peak at Caala, where lorries are driving around with Savimbi's photograph plastered on their bonnets and doors. Such displays would have been unimaginable two months ago.

Twelve miles later an abandoned industrial area marks the entrance to Huambo, a mountain city of tall modern buildings whose population has been swollen to 500,000 by an influx of refugees. A crowd has gathered in the morning on the road to inspect the remains of a man who was run over the night before. His flattened skull bears the clear marks of tyre treads. 'Some old men drink a bit and fall asleep on the road,' says Bernardo, a driver from Huambo. 'For years people did not see cars on the road, but now peace has changed that.' In Angola even peace can kill.

Shootings and bombings had plagued Huambo throughout most of the war, ever since Cuban troops helped the MPLA to expel UNITA from the city in February 1976, when Savimbi led the remnants of his guerrilla army back to the bush.

Civilians and soldiers with missing legs hobbling on crutches are a common sight, testimony to the *planalto*'s unenviable reputation of having one of the world's highest concentrations of anti-personnel mine victims. The violence continued right up to the signing of the Bicesse peace accords with a series of civilian killings in a gruesome settling of accounts that took some 50 lives.

The ceasefire has changed everything. UNITA's commander for Huambo province, Brigadier David Wenda, emerged from the countryside and, together with a small unit of soldiers, has taken up residence at the Hotel Roma. Three days after his arrival Brigadier Wenda addressed a public rally of between 30,000 and 50,000 people, leaving no doubt of UNITA's popularity in a city the MPLA had ruled, albeit uncomfortably, for fifteen years.

These are heady days for Huambo. Farmers are enthusiastically readying their fields for the winter planting season and traders right across the region are able to move easily on the roads in and out of town, no longer fearful of landmines, ambushes or onerous army checkpoints. UNITA and MPLA soldiers pass each other on the street with no apparent bitterness and the town's moribund nightlife is beginning to pick up. There is great excitement that the Benguela railway, the Caminhos de Ferro de Benguela, which once linked the copper mines of Zaire and Zambia to the Atlantic Ocean but had been put out of action by UNITA, will start running again. Modern Huambo was born alongside the railway and depends on the transport artery for its lifeblood.

The easy freedom of movement between the former adversaries in Huambo is taking time to trickle down to more isolated rural areas, despite the written promise in the

Bicesse accords that Angolans could travel where they please. To visit a UNITA-controlled town outside Huambo with the International Committee of the Red Cross, I have to obtain written permission from both the MPLA government and Brigadier Wenda.

I find Wenda at the Hotel Roma down near the railway station. After sending messages to UNITA representatives in Luanda and Jamba, the rebels' headquarters in far south-eastern Angola, Brigadier Wenda, a large jovial man who is considered one of UNITA's brightest commanders, orders an aide to type out my journalist's credentials immediately. He is clearly proud that a foreign correspondent must come to him for permission to travel in UNITA's 'liberated' territory. But as we chat about the dramatic changes of the past month and his certainty that UNITA will win the general elections next year, he suddenly changes the subject.

'You will see a lot of burnt vehicles on the road to Alto Hama,' he says gravely. His embarrassment at his own men's handiwork is evident. When I ask him who was to blame for the destruction, he gives the standard UNITA response, one that I hear over and over again – '*guerra*'.

Brigadier Wenda is certainly right about the demolished vehicles. After completing the route the next day, one Angolan driver for the Red Cross guesses that we passed eight wrecks, while another says twenty. I count 58 destroyed cars, trucks and tanks on the 35-mile road to Alto Hama. Such destruction is so commonplace in the region that many Angolans seem not to notice it any longer, as if the rusting hunks of metal are a natural part of the landscape.

In Alto Hama itself, most of the buildings, except the white Catholic church, are in ruins too – the physical price tag of its capture by UNITA forces in March. Rebel soldiers, mostly unarmed, mill around the town centre as the local *sobas*, blowing whistles and shouting, busily set about organising 4,300 families in queues to receive seeds from the Red Cross. There is something eerily depressing about Alto Hama, and it goes beyond the fact that farmers in one of Africa's most fertile areas are queuing up to receive seeds from young Europeans. It is the oppressive sense of UNITA's control over everything.

In news accounts and journalistic shorthand the MPLA

was always referred to as the 'Marxist' party while UNITA, dubbed by former US President Reagan as an army of 'freedom fighters', has been labelled as a pro-western movement struggling for democracy. Such a portrayal had little to do with reality. However much it tries, and no matter how much training its young agents once received from the likes of the East German secret police, the MPLA has never had either the patience or the discipline to match UNITA's totalitarian grip over the civilians under its control.

Commentators often attributed UNITA's rigid mind control, the total obedience of its members to *O Mais Velho* (The Eldest One), as Savimbi is known, to the movement's early links to China. Savimbi and several of his top commanders received their initial military training, as well as weapons, from China in the 1960s. Savimbi has always had an appetite for cultivating a Mao Tse Tung-type reverence among his people. Vorgan radio often refers to him as 'the guide' of the Angolan people. His favoured style of dress, other than military fatigues, is a Mao suit. The rounded Mao cap is standard issue for UNITA soldiers.

But I wonder if UNITA is not a product of the *planalto*'s cultural history. Maybe its methods come from the tyranny which reigned in the central highlands in the seventeenth century when the militaristic Jaga people came down from the north-east and established modern chieftaincies in places like Bailundo, Bié, Huambo, Andulo and Caconda. Their method of recruitment was to kidnap children from neighbouring villages and train them as soldiers. Often they would force the youngsters to attack their own villages or even to kill members of their family to ensure loyalty to the Jaga cause.

Alto Hama itself is a product of more recent history, intimately linked to Portuguese colonisation. It did not even exist until the first white traders came in the late nineteenth century. At the time residents in the area were living at the foot of a mountain about twenty miles to the west, according to the town's senior *soba*, Matos Mwesenge, a father of eight who was said to be, and looked, 100 years old.

'The people were very rich at that time,' he says. 'We were able to grow sorghum, maize and potatoes. There were no roads like today. Alto Hama developed after the first white came into the region. His name was Almeida and he set up a small shop to trade clothes, oil and salt with the peasants in exchange for agricultural produce. Gradually Angolans began leaving their homes near the mountain to live closer to the white trader. That is why the first *bairro* of what is now Alto Hama was called Sansala Almeida.'

Then Mutu-ya-Kavela launched his rebellion against the Portuguese traders and the colonial authorities sent armies from Luanda and Benguela to defeat him. 'The whole region was on fire,' says *soba* Mwesenge. 'The saddest part of it was that most of the troops fighting with the Portuguese were black Angolans. It has always been like that. Angolans killing Angolans.'

Initially Portugal saw Alto Hama as somewhat of a backwater. An administrator and several aides were sent, and troops passed by only occasionally. 'When the Portuguese decided to build the roads to Luanda and Nova Lisboa, that is when they started treating us badly. We were forced to build the roads. If we refused to join the road gangs, we would be beaten, sjamboked [whipped]. The Portuguese made the Africans pay taxes, either by working for them or in the form of food payments. The Portuguese would not let the people carry out their traditional cultural activities. The playing of our drums was strongly forbidden.'

The independence war had little impact on Alto Hama. 'No one was really sure what was going on, but then we heard that the country was independent. We were very happy because we thought that independence meant the people could return to living in their traditional way. They could go back to their old *lavras* [farms]. They applauded and cheered, saying, "The country is ours, the country is free." All the political parties started to come to the area speaking about independence. Everyone was represented. There were supposed to be elections so we could choose our leaders. But in the end they never happened. Then there came *confusão*, MPLA, UNITA, Neto, Neto, Neto, Savimbi, Savimbi, Savimbi,' *soba* Mwesenge says as he flicks his hand and turns his head in disgust.

MPLA and Cuban troops occupied Alto Hama in 1976 and drove UNITA into the countryside. 'The people accepted the MPLA because they had guns, but they never accepted them in their hearts. There was great suffering. The MPLA said they would respect the *sobas*, but the party was really in command. Whenever there was an argument with the *sobas* the MPLA accused us of being UNITA supporters,' he says.

The story of the MPLA's testy relationship with traditional authorities is common throughout the *planalto*. Initially the MPLA saw the *sobas* as backward obstacles to the vanguard-led 'revolution', much as the Portuguese a century before had rightly viewed them as a threat to European domination of trade. Only later, when the UNITA insurgency spread throughout the region, did the Luanda government attempt to cultivate the *sobas*.

'The MPLA were like the Portuguese. They did not let the people live where they wanted. The war against UNITA was getting worse and the MPLA forced people to live near the town centre. They set up control posts to make sure no one left town. That meant we could not cultivate our *lavras*, and the only place we could farm was around our houses. There was not enough land, not enough to eat. There was great hunger during the planting seasons,' *soba* Mwesenge says.

UNITA recaptured Alto Hama in March 1991 and immediately told the town's residents that they could return to their original homes in the countryside. Two months later the Bicesse accords were signed in Portugal. 'The people were very excited when they heard the war was over, but there is still a great scepticism in their hearts. Many do not believe it is true.'

Soba Mwesenge concludes his brief lecture with what is becoming a common question. 'Do you think the war is really over?' I repeat my weak response about how it appeared to me, an outsider, that the people are tired of war. *Soba* Mwesenge, clearly unimpressed by my lack of understanding, shakes his head and says, 'But that is what we do not understand, because the people never wanted the war.'

As the current occupying force, UNITA naturally attracts a great deal of public sympathy among the 25,000 people of Alto Hama which, like every other town in the region, is swollen with refugees. Because the peace accords were signed just two months after the rebels' arrival it appears that many people associate UNITA with peace. The relationship between the *sobas* and the UNITA commander, Captain Rui M'bala seems good. Like most rural guerrilla movements in Africa, UNITA has worked closely with the *sobas*, provided they are obedient.

The local Catholic priest, Tarsisio Kanepa, is in no doubt about whom the residents support. 'People in the area were supporting UNITA because UNITA is largely made up of people from here,' he says. Father Kanepa was trained at the Kalenga mission about 30 miles south-west of Alto Hama and took over the parish in 1976, a year after independence. He decided to flee Kalenga when he learned that the MPLA troops were about to attack the mission because they believed he was feeding UNITA soldiers.

'It was a ridiculous accusation because at the time we did not have enough food for ourselves,' he says. 'The roads were all closed and people came in from outlying villages to the towns. The MPLA told them to come. Sometimes the troops went to round them up, but on other occasions the people came voluntarily because they were frightened of the war.

'There was great tension between the church and the MPLA. The MPLA would not openly stop the masses, but on Sundays they would organise alternative activities to take place at the same time as the church services. Attendance at such activities was an important way of steering clear of trouble with the authorities. The MPLA did not want people going to church because it was against their Marxist ideology. These people have been occupied by both sides, back and forth, back and forth. If UNITA leaves people here will be sad. They are very suspicious of the MPLA. The election campaign could create a lot of *confusão* here. Right now people are most concerned about the lack of clothes and food,' he says. 'Politics do not interest them very much.'

I wander around Alta Hama for a while, seeking to bore my UNITA minders enough to let me speak alone with someone. I find one old man who is clearly not too enamoured with UNITA. João Sandongo is a father of nine who fled from his village near Lunge, about 50 miles east of Alto Hama, with 200 other residents in 1981. He seems very nervous with troops nearby. Sandongo has been drinking the local maize brew, *cachipembe*. Like a robot, he prefaces every remark about his future plans to return home by shouting, 'It depends on the orders of our superiors,' and smiling at the soldiers. They do not return the gesture, clearly irritated by the mocking tone in his voice. When I ask him who attacked his village, which was in an MPLA-controlled area, and killed three of his daughters, he echoes Brigadier Wenda, blaming simply the *guerra*.

During a moment when the soldiers are looking the other way, he confides that UNITA is not, as they had promised, permitting civilians displaced by the war to return to their homes. 'They want us to stay near them.'

Much the same story emerges the next day when I travel out to the MPLA-controlled village of N'gove, about 80 miles south of Alto Hama. Not surprisingly, a dozen *sobas* speak initially against UNITA and in favour of the MPLA government. But there is evident unease in their ranks, as each question sparks agitated grumbling among them. I assume at first it is because their leader is not around and that they are somehow overstepping their authority by speaking to an outsider. Then the second in command, Constantino Chicano, clarifies the matter: 'Look, the people here were taken by UNITA, they were taken by the army, and they never had the power to stop either one. For the people, both armies were the same, and we had no choice but to do what the men with arms told us to do. Armies do not respect tradition, our traditional way of life. We *sobas* lost all our authority.'

The statement has the cathartic effect of a confession and immediately lifts the veil of tension that had settled over the gathering. Suddenly the chiefs start complaining vociferously that neither UNITA nor the MPLA are letting their people return to their homes. This puts the *sobas* in a very difficult situation, they say, because they are losing their people's respect.

Confirmation that the MPLA, like UNITA, still tightly controls the movements of civilians comes from an unexpected quarter, Major Roberto Fernando de Matos, commander of the local government garrison. He is not pleased about it. 'The MPLA party commissariat visited N'gove this month and told the people they could not leave yet,' he says, not hiding his disgust with the behaviour of his political bosses. 'As far as we soldiers are concerned, these people should return home, but the government says not yet.'

Ironically, Major de Matos and his troops have excellent relations with the UNITA soldiers they were fighting until a few weeks ago. Speaking at the operations room in his hill-top command post overlooking the N'gove dam, he describes how the two sides trade food and salt and often play cards and organise football matches. 'The soldiers are very friendly with each other. We have no problems except when one side loses a football match, but that's normal.' And for a soldier defending what once was a Marxist government, Major de Matos is surprisingly religious. The peace agreement is 'thanks to God. It was like a miracle.' He is certain that the ceasefire will not break down before next year's general elections, as happened in 1975. 'If the politicians create a conflict again, the Angolan people and the army would not accept it.' Feeling that finally my optimism has been vindicated, I wish Bepe was around to hear that remark.

4 The Right Future

I come to talk about my brother
About a time of peace
And a time without pain
Without hatred in the eye
Without guns in the hand
About the people in the streets
Whatever their colour
Rising to complete union ...

Angola no Coração (Angola in the Heart)

A giant red banner with the words '*Angola no Coração*' stretched across the back of the 4 de Fevereiro airport comes into sight as my flight from Brazzaville touches down. The plane taxis into the parking area and stops at a spot several hundred yards from the airport building to await the bus to ferry the passengers to the arrival hall. As we board the vehicle three armed plainclothes policemen climb into the bus and gruffly demand to inspect everyone's passports, everyone, that is, except those who are white. 'We are looking for infiltrators,' barks one of the cops. Two groups of young black men instinctively turn away. They fall silent and stare out the windows as the police move in their direction. When the officers approach they hold their Angolan passports in their outstretched hands·and, as best they can, refuse to answer any questions, but the police persist in what is clearly an exercise to determine whether or not they can speak Portuguese. Those who can only speak French are led away for further questioning about their true nationality.

This harsh inspection seems oddly out of place at a time when Angola is two weeks away from holding its first ever multi-party elections on 29-30 September. Freedom of movement and of expression are supposed to be guaranteed, but a police sergeant confides that he and his men are looking for Zairean and Congolese thugs allegedly being smuggled into Luanda by UNITA in case trouble breaks out.

I clear immigration and customs in record time. After years of suspicion of Western reporters Angolan bureaucracy suddenly melts before a journalist's card. It is the first of many signs I will see that the government, the political parties and, most of all, the people believe that the more foreigners there are to observe the polls, the greater the promise that everything will go smoothly.

Some things never change, however. There are no taxis at the airport and I catch a lift into town with a young couple to find a bed and a bath after spending a night on a wooden bench at Brazzaville airport. First, though, I need some local currency, kwanzas, once a difficult proposition in Luanda on a Sunday when the banks are closed. I enquire where I might be able to change money. The couple look at me as if I was stupid. 'Kwanzas? That's one thing that you can find anywhere, at all hours,' Jóia, the plump woman in the passenger seat says through a gap-toothed smile.

When I tell her I have not been to Angola for over a year, she nods knowingly. 'Angola is not like the past any more.' The black market, or *candonga*, has always flourished in Luanda due to the tight exchange controls and the artificially low official rates offered for foreign currency. Since my last visit a year ago, however, the *candonga* has literally exploded onto the streets of Luanda.

The best place to change dollars, I am told, is the Bank of Havana, the name given to a street corner opposite the Cuban Embassy on Che Guevara Avenue. As we slow down a dozen women, some dressed in brightly coloured traditional African cloth, others in tight denim mini-skirts, race towards us waving bundles of new kwanza notes and claiming theirs is the best price. '*Fala bem, amigo,*' ('Speak well, friend') they say. These are the *kinguilas*, a Kimbundu word which translates roughly as 'the one who waits'.

When I first visited Angola in 1986 the official exchange rate was 29 kwanzas to the dollar. Two weeks before the election the street rate was 3,000 and rising. There were two reasons for the change. The government had abandoned most of its rigid currency controls, and many Angolans with money feared the election would collapse into violence.

'The price is high because many rich people are sending their children out of the country, to Portugal or Brazil,' says a young *kinguila* called Preciosa. 'Because of the *situação*, people are frightened and they like the feel of an American dollar.'

Situação is a word symbolic of the radical understatement with which Angolans describe the incomprehensible catastrophes that have blighted their country since independence. To understand Angola one must grasp the concept of *situação*, which, in essence, is a state of mind. In common usage, it is a catch-all word that can mean anything from minor tension to a formal declaration of war or mass starvation, depending on the context. Often in the war zones, soldiers refer to small skirmishes, ambushes or a stalemated battle as a *situação*.

Once the status quo actually shifts for the worse, for example with an eruption of gunfights or rioting, then the *situação* escalates into *confusão*. A *confusão* is to be avoided at all costs, while the prevailing *situação* of civil war and hardship has been the normal state of affairs to a whole generation of Angolans. An entire economy has been built around the *situação*. It has the delightful effect of removing all sense of personal responsibility.

At the Bank of Havana the prevailing *situação* means the exchange rate of the kwanza rises steadily, while the outbreak of full-scale *confusão* will send the price of the dollar soaring. The Bank of Havana is part of a massive financial system made up of dozens of illegal currency markets known collectively as the Street Bank or simply the *tesouro*, the treasury. It operates much like any foreign exchange market in London or New York, with one fundamental difference. While European dealers might speculate on quarterly announcements of a particular economy's growth rate or the budget deficit, in Angola the betting is on whether or not the country is headed back to war. With 360,000 kwanzas, the prevailing value of a crisp $100 dollar bill, stuffed into my pockets, I go in search of a bed.

Hotels in Luanda have always been scarce and exorbitantly expensive, and after checking at the usual spots, the Hotel Tivoli and Le President, it becomes clear that the thousands of election observers from the United Nations and Western non-government organisations, and hundreds of journalists, have taken almost all the beds. I end up at the home of Katia Airola, the Finnish-born woman who works at the Press Centre, who comes to my rescue once again.

For anyone who has visited Angola over the years, walked through its depressingly dirty cities, seen its children frolic in sewage water, watched its people struggle to maintain a modicum of dignity, this is a moment of sheer inspiration. Angola is about to re-dock on planet earth.

Luanda is a giant festival by day. Massive billboards which feature the smiling face of President José Eduardo dos Santos over the MPLA campaign slogan *O Futuro Certo* (The Right Future) are plastered all over the city. White cardboard doves of peace have been placed atop the curious tank statues in the central plazas which the government erected some years ago as monuments to the independence struggle.

Pick-up trucks with loudspeakers blasting merengue and rap music roam the streets, handing out leaflets, baseball caps and T-shirts sporting propaganda from the eighteen parties contesting the legislative and presidential elections. Millions of T-shirts have been printed with party slogans, and one of the first stories I write about the campaign says that no matter who wins the polls, Angolans are probably better dressed than at any time since independence.

The airwaves are filled with party songs, including the MPLA's catchy jingle, '*Angola no Coração*'. Back too is Angola's best known crooner, Bonga, a pro-UNITA performer who has long been banned by the government. Even the state-controlled television station carries campaign advertisements by the opposition political parties, but its news broadcasts maintain firmly in favour of the governing MPLA. Freely available too is UNITA's weekly newspaper, *Terra Angola*, published in Lisbon and edited by a former hardline MPLA propagandist and information officer at Angola's UN office in New York, Raymundo Sottomaior, who, in one of the great ironies of the war, has defected to UNITA. As the director of the national news agency, Angop, the extreme tone of his anti-UNITA diatribes caused even hardened MPLA activists to blush.

By night Luanda is one big party. Hundreds of people mill around the Kinaxixe plaza dancing to live music until sunrise. Business is roaring in the new bars and restaurants that have opened in the once moribund *baixa*, the lower part of the city near the picturesque bay which in colonial times earned Luanda the nickname of the Rio de Janeiro of Africa. Informal markets line the streets of the city centre selling wine, beer and grilled *galinhas*, or chicken, accompanied by spicy *xindungu* sauce, until late into the night.

Anybody who is anybody has to make an appearance at the open-air Bar Aberto, where wealthy Angolans returned from Lisbon, diplomats, UN observers, well-heeled prostitutes, MPLA party officials, and Luanda's *novos ricos*, mix easily in a cocktail of good-natured rowdiness. Here one can sip a cool beer and watch tracer bullets, fired in celebration rather than in anger, soar over the Luanda skyline while chatting with UN military observers or even the president's daughter. From there the young chic will put in an appearance at the Espaço 93 bar before pushing on to the Pandemonium discotheque.

Below the giddy surface, however, all is not well. UNITA troops stationed around the Hotel Turismo, where many party officials are staying near Jonas Savimbi's residence in the posh neighbourhood of Miramar, and outside party headquarters in São Paulo are extremely nervous and aggressive. They are not shy of using their AK-47 assault rifles and grenade launchers to threaten pedestrians and vehicles passing by. They are the law in whole sections of town.

Their macho image is heightened by the huge Chevrolet trucks with tinted windows in which they drive through the city. Most of the UNITA soldiers are young peasant men from the countryside who are both enticed and frightened by Luanda's cosmopolitan atmosphere. They come from a time warp, indoctrinated by the stories of 1975 when the MPLA armed its civilian supporters with AK-47s, the so-called *poder popular*, or people's power, and drove its rivals out of town. They seem to sense a violent clash awaiting them but then do everything possible to provoke it.

Occasionally shouting matches escalate into fist fights, once in a while even into firefights. Five days before the election a convoy of UNITA cars is involved in an accident with another vehicle. Believing the crash to have been deliberate, armed UNITA troops chase the car's driver into the National Radio complex until government soldiers guarding the station open fire. At least six people are wounded and a UNITA driver is killed.

The news from the countryside is worse. Remnants of the government army have been launching mini-rebellions at their assembly areas over the authorities' failure to demobilise them. A freelance British film crew working for the World Food Programme and three UN military observers are held hostage for six hours on 22 September at a government assembly area in Quibala, south of Luanda.

Instead of focusing on demobilisation of its soldiers, the government is re-arming and creating a special anti-riot police force, commonly known as the *ninjas*, a rough bunch dressed in navy blue uniforms, wearing dark glasses and carrying AK-47s and Uzi machine guns. UNITA is reneging on its pledge to demobilise its troops, and is building its own special security force, which like the *ninjas*, numbers up to 20,000. 'A guaranteed recipe for conflict,' is the way Lieutenant-Colonel Roger Mortlock, the New Zealand commander of UNAVEM forces in central Angola, describes the new parallel forces.

The two armies, totalling about 150,000 troops, are supposed to be abolished by election day and in their place a new 50,000-strong army, known as the Forças Armadas Angolanas, the FAA, is to be created. This is not going to happen. By late September the new FAA has just 8,800 troops, and the rest of the soldiers are waiting aimlessly in assembly areas or still under the control of their old commanders. UNAVEM reckons that about one-quarter of UNITA's troops have been demobilised compared to nearly half of the government's army.

UNAVEM does little about it. The UN Special Representative, Margaret Anstee, a British-born United Nations diplomat who had previously been the organisation's under-secretary general, repeatedly complains about the failure to demobilise, but the Bicesse peace accords stipulate that UNAVEM's job is to verify, not control, the process. That is the responsibility of a joint commission made up of representatives of the MPLA and UNITA. UNAVEM is supposed to observe.

'Sometimes it seems that neither side was ever really serious about it,' a British colonel involved in the demobilisation effort tells me.

Both sides are hedging their bets on the outcome of the vote and UNAVEM and observers from the three main countries overseeing the process, the United States, Portugal and the Soviet Union, are well aware of this. Their only option is to announce that the process should not proceed until demobilisation takes place and wash their hands of it. It is a step they are not willing to take. UNAVEM is throwing away the only weapon it has, the threat to pull out of the process.

The international community is in no mood to finance the Angolan peace process any longer than need be, in contrast with its eagerness to finance and profit from the civil war. As the British ambassador, John Flynn, puts it, the world wants to set up democracy in Angola 'on the cheap', to construct a bargain basement new world order.

Officers in the UNITA army are particularly reluctant to send their troops to the new army. The attitudes of the troops from the two sides are completely different. If a government soldier is asked about his plans after demobilisation, he will talk about going home to see his family, enrolling in school or looking for a job. Ask a UNITA fighter the same question and his answer is normally, 'I will await orders from my commander.'

The UN World Food Programme is feeding 75,000 troops in the assembly areas, and its director of operations, Philippe Borel, says that in Cuando Cubango province, *as terras do fim do mundo*, UNITA forces are demanding far more food than they need. 'There is evidence to suggest that UNITA is stockpiling food for any eventuality,' he says a few days before the elections. But Borel feels there is no choice but to continue the food distribution. 'If we stop feeding these soldiers, they will be lost. Then they could become "hunger guerrillas", using their guns to take what they need from nearby civilians.'

There are even bigger problems with the government soldiers who fear that if they are not demobilised by election day, they might never be able to leave the army. So they rebel, march and protest, threatening to turn a serious *situação* into some real *confusão*.

A week before the polls I run smack into their anger during a visit to Huambo as a mob of government soldiers has broken out of their assembly area near Cruzeiro and march through the centre of town firing their AK-47s into the air. They demand to meet an officer who can issue them with demobilisation papers. When they cannot find one they head over to an academy where British, Portuguese and French military instructors are training troops for the new army and start shooting up the place. They are wild-eyed and angry.

'We just want our demobilisation papers and a plane out of here,' screams a soldier named António, an eight-year veteran of the FAPLA who becomes extremely agitated when I ask him to spell his last name and tell me where he was born. 'The government isn't worth anything. They spend all their money on themselves, and if it wasn't for the United Nations we would be starving.'

UNAVEM observers in Huambo, such as Lieutenant-Colonel Mortlock, were not surprised. 'Any conventional force, whether European or African, will collapse if it is confined to assembly points and cut off from logistical support,' he says. 'UNITA, as a guerrilla force, can survive much longer because they were trained to live off the land.'

The most dramatic uprising took place in the northern oil-rich enclave of Cabinda, where hundreds of young FAPLA soldiers went on a rampage in the centre of town killing nine civilians and spraying the home of governor Augusto da Silva Tomás with machine-gun fire. The governor escaped by climbing out of a window at the back of the house and catching a boat south to the port of Soyo. Cabinda was left without an effective government for two days. Government soldiers in Cabinda were especially anxious to quit the army because of a renewal of hit-and-run attacks by the FLEC, the small guerrilla movement fighting for independence from Angola. Two weeks before, the guerrillas had killed two of their officers.

A few days after the rebellion mutinous troops are drinking palm wine in front of the main garrison in Cabinda city. Bedlam reigns. They are sitting on their ragged backpacks, occasionally engaging in fist fights with each other. Many have taken off their shirts and tied red ribbons around their heads. Every time an officer passes by to enter the garrison gates they hurl insults at him.

A tall, fat lieutenant emerges from behind the barracks

wall and with a good deal of arrogance orders them to calm down. They threaten to shoot him on the spot if a truck is not provided to take them to the airport. 'We almost killed the governor, and you are just a little man,' one crazed youngster shouts. They tell me that they have been in the army for years, but they are difficult to pin down on specifics. Some say they are veterans of the Battle of Cuito Cuanavale. They have suffered and risked death for their country while their commanding officers are becoming rich. 'Look at that lieutenant, how fat he is. How come the officers are all fat? None of us are fat, because we have no food. Where is our money, where are our papers?' Another shirtless, shoeless soldier screams, 'Stop this shit. This is shit.' The lieutenant, his arrogant attitude long since faded, scurries behind the gates waving his hands in the air and shouting '*São malucos*' – 'They're crazy'.

5 Beg for Your Life

I reach Cabinda by catching a lift on a plane owned by Chevron, the American oil company which accounts for about two-thirds of Angola's daily production of 500,000 barrels and brings in some $1.5 billion a year. The discovery of petroleum in coastal waters by Gulf Oil in 1966 changed Cabindan history for ever and meant that first the Portuguese and then the independent Angolan government could never let go of the enclave.

Thirty years before the dense Mayombe forests of the region had provided the staging area for the MPLA guerrillas to launch their war against the Portuguese, a war which ended not in the African bush but on the streets of Lisbon when disgruntled officers, worn down by never-ending wars in Angola, Mozambique and Guinea Bissau, staged the April 1974 Revolution of Carnations against the fascist dictatorship. In November that year MPLA guerrillas led by the future defence minister, Pedro Tonha 'Pedale', emerged from the forests and captured the region as Portuguese soldiers looked on. Cabindan independence fighters were forced to retreat.

At Luanda airport I run into João Pokongo, a Cabindan-born journalist working for the state-owned daily newspaper, *Jornal de Angola*, and his photographer Carlos Lousada. My encounter with Pokongo is especially ironic since he had been one of my minders when I visited the province in 1986. Pokongo and another government official ably steered me away from any controversial subjects during that trip, and we spent most of our time out at Chevron's Malongo oil complex where we received an earful from American workers, most of them from Louisiana and Texas, who in their long southern drawls repeatedly accused

Ronald Reagan of being 'full of shit' for failing to open full diplomatic relations with the MPLA government. The MPLA always had a cordial business relationship with Chevron, despite its Marxist ideology and Washington's decision to fund and arm Savimbi's UNITA movement.

Six years on Pokongo no longer hides his pro-Cabinda leanings. It is a sign of the rapidly changing times. We land at Cabinda airport and immediately hail the only taxi in sight. Our first stop is the provincial government building, where several officials make no secret of their support for the Cabindan independence cause, perhaps fearing that their positions in the Luanda-appointed administration make them legitimate targets of the FLEC. But they are just as scared of their own army. The governor is still in Luanda, too frightened to return.

'We are going through a very difficult time,' says one official. 'We don't know whether to run from the FLEC or from FAPLA.'

From there we head to the *Jornal de Angola* office and meet two journalists, both named André, one of whom works for the paper, the other for national radio. After five minutes' conversation it is clear their sympathies too are with the FLEC. I am nursing an ambition to visit the guerrillas in one of their base camps, or at least to interview one of the FLEC commanders who routinely comes to town right under the noses of the authorities, but I am unsure how to broach the subject with Pokongo, whom I still think of as a government stooge.

I finally screw up my courage at a petrol station, not with Pokongo, who I fear might report me to the government, but with André Lubalo, the radio correspondent. For the past hour he has been regaling me with stories about how everyone in Cabinda supports the FLEC, so I pop the question: is it possible to meet them? He just smiles and says he was hoping that I would ask. That night we check into the same cheap hotel in which I stayed six years before and I am convinced that the moist brown sheets – I suppose they were once white – have not been changed since then.

André and his namesake hire a car for the next morning and we leave early to drive north. Pokongo and Carlos come along too and they keep giggling at the prospect of interviewing a certain Captain Bonga Bonga, a former

FAPLA officer who defected to the main armed faction of the FLEC, known as FLEC-FAC, the year before. Captain Bonga Bonga is something of a legend in Cabinda. Two nights before our arrival he walked into the city jail and freed 69 prisoners, including seven FLEC-FAC guerrillas, without firing a shot.

We know the general area in which Captain Bonga Bonga and his men are operating. It is just north-east of Chevron's Malongo oil complex. Our problem is to find a guide who can take us to his base, someone who knows the FLEC well enough to ensure that the guerrillas will not attack us on the way. With the collapse of the FAPLA army, the FLEC has been roaming freely on the main road, ambushing at will. Often such assaults are fairly tame. A typical operation involves stopping buses or trucks, ordering the passengers down before forcing them to walk home and then burning the vehicles.

Other attacks are less benign. Just a week before the FLEC-FAC fighters waylaid a truck carrying a senior Cabindan police officer, Miguel Fernando Nzambi, murdered him and dumped his body in the River Chiloango. A rival faction known as FLEC-Renovada has a more brutal reputation, specialising in cutting off the ears and noses of those they consider to be government agents. They are also fond of kidnapping foreigners and then holding them for weeks or months before negotiating their release with their respective governments. Travelling with someone known to the movement, and even better in a vehicle which the guerrillas know not to touch, is therefore a must.

The Andrés know of such a person. The man turns out to be, of all people, the local administrator, appointed by the provincial government, of the area in which Captain Bonga Bonga operates. On reaching his house we quickly explain our mission. He motions us into his living room, asks his wife to prepare a lunch of grilled chicken and walks out behind the building to hold a whispered conversation with two of his aides. They are to travel ahead of us and announce our imminent arrival to Captain Bonga Bonga.

I suddenly feel nervous about the whole affair, fearing that the administrator could be calling the police to arrest us for attempting to contact FLEC terrorists. For once I am heartened by the presence of journalists from the state-owned media. They would certainly be in far more trouble with the authorities than I would. If they are happy, so am I.

After dispatching the delicious grilled *galinhas* and washing them down with warm Zairean beers, it is time to move. The administrator, who can also ensure our safe passage through any official checkpoints, jumps into his white pick-up truck and leads the way.

Every few miles there are signs of the FLEC's handiwork, burnt-out vehicles resting awkwardly on their sides in ditches. I marvel at the number of destroyed cars and trucks that litter the roads of Angola and think about the fortunes awaiting adventurous scrap-metal dealers in Africa.

About twenty miles north our convoy of two turns off the main road onto a sandy track which winds through gently rolling hills and thick woodlands that mark the edge of the Mayombe forest. It is ideal ambush country. The sand is so deep that our wheels spin freely and our loudly revving engines and grinding gears surely alert any nearby gunmen with questionable intentions. Wide-eyed women and children peer from the backs of their huts in the isolated homesteads which we pass, staring in wonder at the idiots heading up such a dangerous road.

On top of one hill I think that I spot a young boy ducking quickly behind a tree, but then assure myself I am seeing things. Our vehicles are speeding as fast as possible in the difficult terrain when suddenly the brakes lock on the administrator's pick-up and he skids to halt. We narrowly avoid smashing into him.

From the surrounding hills young boys in an imaginative array of uniforms and tennis shoes, some wearing flip-flops, come running towards us pointing AK-47s in our direction. Straight ahead is a 50-calibre machine gun aimed at our windscreen. The administrator raises his left hand out of the window and the boy fighters' tense faces slowly relax. Not a word is spoken as we ease into the 'liberated' village of Bofo.

The armed youngsters are clearly unsure what to do with us. It is not a good sign that they will not accept the cigarettes we offer them. None of their commanders are around, they maintain, and we must return to the city. Then the administrator pulls one of the older boys aside and speaks in earnest tones. The only part I overhear is something about a 'foreign journalist'.

The young man lopes down the road. The administrator looks at us and pushes both hands down as if he is gauging the firmness of an imaginary mattress. Be patient, he is saying. Within minutes the young fighter returns with a much older man dressed in civilian clothes. He introduces himself with a most unsettling nom de guerre, *Pede a Vida* or Beg for Your Life.

After quizzing us with the usual questions about our mission and where we came from, Pede a Vida gladly accepts a cigarette, setting off a stampede among the teenage guerrillas demanding the same. Things are looking up until Pede a Vida explains with exaggerated seriousness that without 'orientations' from his superiors he cannot talk to us. Captain Bonga Bonga has gone north to bases near the Congolese border, he says, and is not expected back until next week.

But we are free to look around. The sights of Bofo are hardly impressive, consisting of a few mud huts, half a dozen scrawny chickens and about 30 teenage troops badly in need of haircuts and a good scrubbing. A three-legged wooden table is brought out from one of the huts together with a couple of jugs of palm wine, a drink I sampled in 1986 and know to be a potent brew, especially in the humidity of the Mayombe forest.

A few mugfuls later Pede a Vida, whose official title is Chief of Operations of the Bofo base, is in full flow, mainly about his personal contribution to the Cabindan independence struggle. 'I organised this unit from nothing, and now we are fighting day to day to annihilate the enemy, the MPLA, to win the sovereignty of our country,' he says. In just a few months, he vows, Cabinda will be free of Angolan rule and the huge sums of money earned from the oil exports will be used to uplift the enclave's 150,000 people. 'Without doubt, we are going to win this war, even if it takes twenty years.'

I believe that the Cabindans have a case, but Pede a Vida does not inspire confidence that the FLEC will defeat the Angolan army soon, regardless of who wins the elections. President dos Santos has offered a limited autonomy plan and an economic package which will increase the share of oil revenues spent on Cabinda from 1 to 10 per cent. The FLEC wants nothing to do with it, and its word carries weight. It has called on its supporters to boycott the general elections, and when the central government attempted to register voters only 16,000 people, mostly government bureaucrats and soldiers, signed up.

The Cabindans base their independence claim on the Treaty of Simulambuco of 1885, which first linked Cabinda to Angola but recognised its special status. The treaty was a desperate attempt by Portugal to consolidate its African empire against encroachment by the French, Belgians and the British during the European 'scramble for Africa' and a bid by the Cabindans to seek refuge from the demands for forced labour by King Leopold's Belgian Congo. Nowadays no Angolan government can afford to cut the country's ties with Cabinda or, more precisely, to relax its grip on the enclave's oil. Cabindan crude provides Angola with over half its foreign exchange earnings.

Luanda's offer of autonomy has won little support among Cabindans, who have seen previous promises come and go while they remain among Angola's poorest people. Even the Roman Catholic Bishop of Cabinda, Dom Paulinho Fernandes Madeca, dismissed the notion when I met him the day before. 'If I asked my congregation to pray for autonomy, they would hate me,' he said at his house across the street from the cathedral. 'They are suffering as never before and they see autonomy as a continuation of their current misery.'

Pede a Vida is deep into his increasingly drunken monologue, to which nobody, not even his young soldiers, is listening any longer. Out of the corner of my eye I see a small wiry man about 40 years of age in a khaki outfit approach and begin talking to two young fighters. They immediately stiffen at the sight of him. After a few moments, he ambles over to the table and with a wide grin says, 'Welcome to Bofo. My name is Bonga Bonga.'

Given my high expectations, Captain Bonga Bonga is a man of disappointingly few words, although apparently an incredibly fast traveller. In order to talk with journalists about the FLEC's strategy and tactics, he says he needs permission from his commanders' base camps on the Congolese border. He fought for FAPLA for two decades before defecting to the FLEC. Perhaps he feels more comfortable playing Robin Hood than returning to the boredom of a civilian existence. Cabinda's conflict is the only war going on in Angola at the moment. For most of his adult life Bonga Bonga has been at war with somebody – first the Portuguese, then UNITA and its South African allies and now the Angolan government for which he once fought.

Perhaps he is expecting a cut of the region's considerable wealth should the rebels succeed in winning independence for what surely would become an African Kuwait. He has little more than platitudes to offer on the subject. 'I came to see that as a Cabindan, I had no choice but to fight the independence of my country. We hope to win the fight this year, but it has to be complete independence.' Substitute the word 'Angolan' for 'Cabindan' and one can imagine him saying the same thing twenty years ago. Out here in the Mayombe forest, though, Bonga Bonga is a petty god, the young soldiers hanging on his every word, ready to follow any order. Maybe one day, one of them will become the new Bonga Bonga, independence for their beloved Cabinda still a distant dream.

After a few more rounds of palm wine Carlos the photographer judges correctly that Bonga Bonga and Pede a Vida are primed to grant permission for a series of 'battle' pictures featuring the young guerrillas walking up the jungle paths in apparent determination to confront the *inimigo*. It is a grand moment for the young lads, their opportunity to pose, faces grimacing with unshakeable determination, in front of the cameras.

Carlos knows his job, putting the teenage boys, one of whom is a tiny thirteen-year-old, through their paces lugging their assault rifles through the banana trees a few yards behind the mud house where their commanders are getting thoroughly drunk. It is a farce, but Carlos is sure the pictures will look good, the first ever photographs of FLEC guerrillas in action to be published by the *Jornal de Angola*.

As we climb back into our cars for the ride to Cabinda city, Bonga Bonga invites us to visit whenever we like.

The next morning he leads his men in an ambush of a bus carrying workers to the Malongo oil complex. He orders them out of the vehicle and then burns it. The workers have to walk home. Chalk up another glorious victory for the cause of Cabindan independence.

6 Final Countdown

With the election campaign entering its final stages the early predictions of the MPLA's imminent demise appear to be premature. The view that President dos Santos and the ruling party, tarnished by a well deserved reputation for corruption and incompetence, will be flattened by the charismatic Savimbi is no longer so common. Only the American government, which has consistently misjudged Angolan politics, holds firmly to its belief that Savimbi will win.

Savimbi's campaign is self-destructing. His speeches have become aggressive and his oft-repeated chant of 'war or peace' appears to many urban Angolans to be an accurate description of UNITA's intentions should the elections not go its way. Dos Santos, by contrast, is striking a statesman-like profile, avoiding criticism of his opponents and focusing on what he will do if elected as opposed to what he has not done since assuming the presidency thirteen years ago. Last year dos Santos appeared to be trying to catch up with Savimbi. Now all indications are that the positions are reversed.

The UNITA campaign is hopelessly ill-advised. Savimbi, breaking the cardinal rule of an opposition politician going into an election, has allowed himself to become the dominant, and usually negative, campaign theme. He is unable to shake off a major human rights scandal which broke in mid-1992 over the execution of two of his lieutenants, Wilson dos Santos and Tito Chingunji, the year before. UNITA soldiers in the cities act like thugs. A common piece of graffiti on walls sums up a popular feeling that the MPLA, responsible for however much misrule, might be preferable: 'The MPLA steals, UNITA kills'.

Nowhere is the tension higher than in the central

highlands city of Kuito. Three weeks before FAPLA and FALA soldiers engaged in a four-hour firelight in the city centre after MPLA supporters ripped the head off a chicken in public — UNITA's symbol is a black cockerel, the *Galo Negro*. The two sides do not even agree on the city's name. The government insists on Kuito, while UNITA prefers Bié, the name of the province and the Umbundu kingdom Bihe, which was conquered by the Portuguese in 1890.

Dos Santos brings his campaign to Kuito on a sunny Saturday afternoon ten days before the election. Hundreds of government troops fill the streets, occupying the airport and the city centre. Thousands of cheering MPLA supporters are having their day unmolested in a city considered one of Savimbi's strongholds. There is hardly a UNITA activist in sight. Dos Santos, a tall, suave Russian-trained engineer with movie-star looks, stands on a wooden podium next to his smiling wife and daughter as the picture of a responsible husband.

Young girls, clearly taken with the handsome president, scream as if a rock star is in their midst. His characteristically soothing voice delivers his speech in Portuguese, not Umbundu, the local language. He makes numerous promises of economic development to bring Angola *O Futuro Certo*, the MPLA's campaign slogan. New tractors are on their way, he says, and so too are cattle from the southern province of Huila. The task ahead is one of reconstruction and economic prosperity for all.

His speech goes down well with the audience, mainly well dressed city folk, with a smattering of whites and a strong presence of the *mestiços* who dominate the city's economy.

It is a typical dos Santos performance, choreographed by a slick Brazilian public relations firm, the same one used by the scandal-riddled Brazilian president Collor de Mello, to project serenity and an image of a calm, caring president. The rally ends with the crowd launching into chants of 'He's already won, he's already won!' as dos Santos is driven away in a Mercedes Benz.

The next day it is Savimbi's turn. This time the airport is packed with UNITA soldiers wearing their Mao caps and carrying AK-47 assault rifles and what look like shiny golden balls, ammunition for their US-supplied M-60 grenade launchers, strapped around their waists and slung over their shoulders like Mexican bandoleros. As I wander around the airstrip awaiting the arrival of *O Mais Velho*, I strike up a conversation with some UN election observers who I guess might provide some insight into recent happenings in Kuito.

A young American woman I meet has been a UN observer in Kuito for more than a month. She speaks no Portuguese and gladly admits she knows nothing about Angolan history. She is surveying the scene, admiring the tough-looking UNITA soldiers, and suddenly announces, 'I like UNITA's style. They're strict, but they're cool too.'

I wonder where the United Nations finds such people for so important an assignment. Many of the UNAVEM military officers I have met are impressive and dedicated, despite labouring under incredibly trying circumstances, but several of the civilian observers, such as this young American, are wholly unimpressive. How can they hope to function as election observers when they know nothing about the country, do not speak the language and think UNITA's style is 'cool'?

When I ask her what she thinks about the 'UNITA style' of rounding up people in the rural areas, packing them by the hundreds into dark railway wagons loaded on the back of lorries and driving them into town for rallies, she says she has never heard of such a practice and walks away in a huff. Lorries hauling railway wagons full of people are all over Kuito that day.

Then Savimbi lands in his Hercules transport plane, piloted by South Africans, and steps out onto the tarmac to give two huge young American men, said to be sons of right-wing Congressmen, slaps of the hand in the high-five style of US basketball players.

By the time he arrives at an overgrown football field in town, a crowd of 25,000 is rocking to the pulsating beat of a merengue band flown in for the occasion. A man at the microphone is screaming '*Nosso galo*?' ('Our cockerel?') to which the crowd responds with a massive '*Voa*' ('It flies') as a line of robust women at the front wiggle their corpulent girths. Gangs of UNITA youths whip up the throng and put on an aggressive display of racing the three-wheeled motor vehicles which the party has handed out to its most militant young supporters.

Savimbi's followers, largely barefoot and with the

weathered faces of peasants making a living on the land, are spellbound by his Umbundu oratory. A new order is dawning, he promises, one that will bring equality and dignity to the oppressed people of the *planalto*. He repeatedly shouts the UNITA campaign slogan, 'new trousers in September'.

Wearing a UNITA baseball cap and a T-shirt stretched across his formidable stomach, Savimbi stands next to Sean Cleary, a former South African intelligence official who has become a key campaign adviser, and the two young Americans, one wearing a Mao cap, shouting '*Viva!*' and pumping their fists into the air like communists of the old school.

Unlike President dos Santos, Savimbi projects an image of an angry man, often placing his fist below his chin and promising to give the MPLA a 'punch' if they cross him. His anti-white and anti-*mestiço* rhetoric is sure to cost him votes in the major cities of the coast, but probably wins him support in Bié and throughout the central highlands where stories of the Bailundo rebellion against the Portuguese traders have been handed down from generation to generation.

As the rally ends, Savimbi, flanked by a squad of security men, literally runs 100 yards through the crowd to his house much like a boxer entering the ring for a championship fight. It is an impressive sight. I cannot imagine a top MPLA official running anywhere, but then lack of fitness does not necessarily disqualify them from holding office.

A young American freelance TV crew, Bob Coen and Amy Merz, arrange a post-rally interview with Savimbi and kindly ask me to join them. Jorge Valentim, UNITA's explosive Information Secretary with a reputation for specialising in disinformation, hands out soft drinks and tapes a UNITA flag to the wall while Savimbi has a quick wash and change of clothes for the interview. The chat is brief, but his final answer is a haunting one.

What would UNITA do if it loses the elections? Impossible, he says. 'If UNITA does not win the elections, they have to have been rigged. If they are rigged, I don't think we will accept them.'

This is not the usual campaign bluster. For once I think Savimbi is speaking from the heart. The years of speeches about democracy and freedom were just words directed at an audience of mainly conservative Americans who had become enamoured with Africa's best known 'freedom fighter'. His commitment to democratic principles was no more real than the Maoist rhetoric Savimbi spouted in the pre-independence days when China was his biggest backer. It all comes down to this: 'If I don't win, I won't accept the result.'

At that point several UNITA security officials rush into the house to announce that they have seized some government vehicles which have just been flown in specially from Luanda and are part of a plot to kill *o presidente*. The cars are over at the offices of the UNAVEM military team which is monitoring the ceasefire. The subject of the dispute is three Range Rovers carrying ten brand new AK-47 assault rifles and 1,000 rounds of ammunition.

General Altino Sapalalo, 'Bock', one of Savimbi's most hardline commanders who lost part of his left arm in an explosion in 1978, is ranting about 'the plot to assassinate *o presidente*'. Two government security men sheepishly explain that they are part of an advance team for President dos Santos who is scheduled to visit a nearby rural area in three days' time. Although it is impossible to say who is telling the truth, General Bock's accusations seem a little flimsy – the government hardly needs to fly in ten AK-47s when its army in Kuito already has thousands of such weapons.

General Bock is undeterred by such simple logic. He orders his men to burn one of the vehicles for good measure. 'It is like this all the time,' says an Irish UN officer who tries in vain to mediate between the two sides. 'At the least sign of trouble, both sides want to pick up the guns and start it all over again.'

As I fly back that day to Luanda in a Hercules transport plane laid on for journalists by UNITA, my mind is filled with images of General Bock's contorted face and with the words of warning Savimbi issued in the interview about vote rigging and at the rally when he had told his ecstatic followers, 'If they provoke me, this is going to get ugly.'

7 Things Fall Apart

A young woman races across the dirt floor of a thatched hut to restrain a queue of people who are stumbling like falling dominoes towards a small alcove. 'You can't look,' she shouts, 'This is a secret vote.' An elderly woman emerges from the cubicle holding ballot papers in her shaking hands and carefully deposits them in a box. As she turns to the crowd, her face erupts in a broad toothless smile. Outside long queues of people stretch across the sprawling village of Mavinga as thousands of Angolans stand silently in the hot sun to do what they have never done before – vote in a general election. The scene at Mavinga, some 800 miles south-east of Luanda, is repeated in countless villages and towns across Angola as nearly 6,000 voting stations open on 29 September. Isaías Celestino Chitombi, the UNITA party secretary in Mavinga, is ecstatic. 'This is unique. It is the first election since the existence of time, since the existence of Angola.'

Every few minutes aircraft are landing or taking off at the airstrip, about twelve miles away, which in the past had served South African transport planes carrying weapons and supplies to thwart repeated government offensives against UNITA. The aircraft used to land at night, guided in by runway lights which consisted of lines of UNITA soldiers holding candles or tin kerosene lamps. The airport sits less than 100 yards from remnants of the old town of Mavinga which was completely destroyed when UNITA captured it in 1980. It is dangerous even to walk down its streets, once lined with orange trees, because UNITA troops have laid anti-personnel mines all over the area. When I walk over to relieve myself discreetly behind one of the buildings, several soldiers run towards me screaming at me to stop. I thank them profusely.

On election day the airstrip has been enlisted in the democratic cause to serve ageing Russian-built helicopters and Antonov transport planes that are working overtime to deliver voting materials to outlying polling stations which are clearly going to open late. This is no surprise, given the massive logistical challenges presented by Angola, a vast country fourteen times the size of Portugal, its former colonial ruler, where the few roads are either in bad need of repair or have been completely destroyed by the war. The United Nations has mounted a last-ditch effort to make the elections possible, calling into service 40 helicopters, nine-fixed wing aircraft, 5 million litres of fuel and 300 pilots and mechanics.

By all accounts the Angolan people, the great majority of them poor, illiterate and living in isolated villages or urban slums, carry out their civic responsibilities with great dignity and patience. The two voting days in Angola are another confirmation that anyone who mouths the much cited cliché that Africans are not ready for democracy is simply ignorant of the facts. African politicians, however, are a different matter.

Some voters have to walk ten miles or more, with babies strapped to their backs. Others hobble toward the polling booths on crutches, their limbs destroyed by landmines or in accidents. Still others wait for several hours before the arrival of voting material at their local polling stations. The 91 per cent turn-out among the 4.8 million registered voters is beyond all expectations. The high proportion of spoiled or blank ballot papers, between 10 and 12 per cent, only confirms the failure of voter education. Incredibly, there are almost no reports of violence during the two days of voting.

The vote goes so well that at the Bank of Havana street market in Luanda, the value of the dollar falls from over 3,000 to 1,800 kwanzas. The 800 international observers in the country, 400 of them from the United Nations and the rest representing myriad foreign organisations, crow that the election has been one of the most successful ever witnessed in Africa. Initially both UNITA and the MPLA praise the polls as free and fair. I keep telling friends that I wished the vote would never have come, that the carnival atmosphere of the campaign could last forever, that no one would be declared the winner and no party the loser.

The election is, many Angolans know, too good to be true. They are perplexed when they hear that immediately after the polls close, dozens of delegations of foreign observers begin packing their bags for their flights back to Europe and the United States without waiting for the results.

Ominous signs begin to appear as soon as the voting ends on the night of 30 September, when a temporary power cut, quite routine in Luanda, shuts down the computer at the National Electoral Council in the centre of town and officials say the software has been damaged. Many polling stations throughout the country cannot begin to count their votes because they have no lights. Thousands of party electoral agents are forced to sleep with the ballot boxes at the polling stations to guard against fraud.

Tension starts to rise on 1 October as thousands of Angolans sit by their radios listening to unofficial results announced by the state-controlled media. The results, mainly from areas where the MPLA is favoured, show President dos Santos with a commanding lead. UNITA's Information Secretary Jorge Valentim and several other party officials hastily call a press conference at their São Paulo headquarters in Luanda and insist that their own party counts show Savimbi leading by a two-to-one margin.

There is growing frustration among UNITA leaders at the power of the state-controlled mass media, something they have consistently underestimated, to carry the message of an imminent MPLA victory. Foreign news agencies report that the results so far are too partial and too distorted by the state media to present an accurate picture. UNITA's Vorgan radio station attempts in vain to assure its listeners that the Black Cockerel is flying high. The battle of the airwaves marks the beginning of a psychological contest that will eventually lead Angola back to civil war.

The next day state radio continues projecting a massive victory for the MPLA and President dos Santos, while Vorgan announces an equally overwhelming triumph for Savimbi. At the Bank of Havana the value of the dollar soars past 3,000 kwanzas. The markets are overflowing with shoppers as thousands of people start hoarding food. A few beachfront restaurants on the Ilha, the thin peninsula jutting out from Luanda, close early. At the posh Afrodisiakus restaurant, an apologetic hostess explains that the cooks have not shown up due to the *situação*. By Friday evening, two days after the election, there is still no word from the National Electoral Council, the sole source of the official count.

At 2.30 on Saturday morning I awake from a deep sleep in a flat lent to me by the International Committee of the Red Cross near the Kinaxixe plaza in central Luanda. For a moment I am confused and do not know where I am. Then my head clears and I go out onto the veranda overlooking the Avenida do Comandante Valódia and lean over the small cement wall to take in the cool of the night. No one and nothing is stirring, the only sound is the hissing of a malfunctioning neon sign down the road.

In the stillness a young man in fatigue trousers and tennis shoes with a red bandanna tied around his head walks up to the plaza. He is carrying an AK-47 assault rifle at his side. He comes to attention in front of the tank monument which has been adorned by a white cardboard dove of peace. He stands motionless for a moment in the middle of the street and slowly bows his head as if in prayer, then thrusts the weapon skyward and squeezes off twelve rounds one by one, at five second intervals. In the quiet, the shots sound like cannon fire. When he finishes the young man lowers the rifle and shuffles down the side of the plaza, past the tank, past the Kinaxixe marketplace and towards a bus stop. Two policemen step out from the darkness and lead him away.

The following day, 3 October, I tune in to Vorgan to hear the staccato voice of Jonas Savimbi. He is speaking the words that everyone is dreading. At one stroke he appears to reject whatever results emerge from the National Electoral Council, to declare that the UN verdict on the elections is null and void unless the polls go his way, and warns that a resumption of war is a distinct possibility. It is the beginning of the end.

Angolan people! For sixteen years we sweated, died, fought and succeeded in imposing the Bicesse peace accords upon the MPLA, which would have guaranteed all Angolans the chance to express themselves freely and to determine their own destiny. All this was done with untold hardship on the part of UNITA militants; of those who, secretly, suffered and died in the São Paulo, Catete Street and Bentiara prisons and were publicly executed in different parts of the country. Today we should have been satisfied that the time had come for us to exercise our right as free citizens conscientiously to vote for the regime and leaders who would lead this country …

It is a pity for me to tell you now that the MPLA wants to cling to power illegally by stealing ballot boxes, beating up and diverting polling list delegates and distorting facts and figures through its radio and television network. I appeal to all the Angolan people to remain serene. I appeal to all UNITA militants to remain vigilant as in the past. At the right time, we will give an adequate response to the MPLA manoeuvres …

UNITA, as a true opposition party, is for change. It is necessary that the regime change, otherwise those who believe that they were born to rule will never again be removed from power, even 50 years from now …

Right now the MPLA is cheating. In all provinces UNITA is ahead both in the presidential and parliamentary results, in a noble and just recognition of those who fought for the country's liberation. I ask you not to listen to the Angolan national radio and not to believe in the state-run television network and instead to wait calmly in your homes, villages and compounds for the results which will surprise not only the world but the MPLA itself …

The National Electoral Council will have to take into consideration that its manoeuvres through the falsification of numbers and tampering with the computers will all lead UNITA to take a position which might deeply disturb the situation in this country …

The National Electoral Council is manipulated by the Futungo de Belas presidential palace and we are not afraid of Futungo de Belas. If Futungo wants the process to halt and the situation in the country to deteriorate, then it should continue telling lies, stealing ballot boxes and distorting the figures. Just as we said in 1975 to the late president Dr Agostinho Neto, 'It is easy to start a war, but to prolong and win it is difficult.' If the MPLA wants to opt for war, it knows that such a war will never be won.

We would like to draw the MPLA's attention to the fact that there are men and women in this country who are ready to give up their lives so that the country can redeem itself. As far as we are concerned, it will not depend on any international organisation saying that the elections were free and fair. It will depend solely on the observation of all Angolans as to whether all registered voters actually voted and whether the ballot boxes were not tampered with or stolen and that everybody has a clear conscience that they participated freely in the act of citizens determining the path to be followed by Angola ...

Angolans resident in Luanda should be calm. Angolans in the north should be serene. Angolans in the central highlands, the western part of the country and the south should be confident. When necessary, we will assume our responsibilities. We would like none of us, be it the MPLA, UNITA or some other political party, to have the courage to plunge this country into war once more. History will never forgive these ambitious men who only derive profits and money and never render service to the people ...

Tonight Angola stands on the brink of another civil war. Restaurants and bars, normally throbbing on a Saturday evening, close early. Traffic is sparse. United Nations officials are labouring to maintain a façade of optimism, suggesting that Savimbi is bluffing, that there is no turning back on the peace process. After all, says one of Margaret Anstee's close advisers at UNAVEM, the Angolan people are tired of war.

I cannot help but think of Rosa, the woman I met on the trip to Huambo the year before, who wanted to know if the peace process would fall apart as it did in 1975. Where was she now? Did she hear the speech, and what must she be thinking? I wonder if she remembered the naïve white man who thought that the war was over.

The next day UNITA officials in Luanda are in a state of panic. Elías Salupeto Pena, Savimbi's nephew and a top UNITA negotiator, is growing more defiant by the hour. Valentim calls another press conference to play down Savimbi's comments and to back away from the charges that the National Electoral Council is being manipulated. But there is no doubt, he says, that the MPLA is stealing ballot boxes and intimidating election officials. 'It was not a declaration of war,' Valentim says, 'but a warning to the government that the people will not just accept any electoral process.'

Partial results announced that night show that President dos Santos's lead is falling as votes from the countryside and the *planalto* start coming in. Most international observers now reckon that he will win no more than 51 per cent of the vote, barely enough to avoid a second-round run-off.

Everything seems to be falling apart. Savimbi announces on 5 October that he is withdrawing his eleven generals from the new unified Angolan Armed Forces, which is still a fictitious body with only 8,800 of its planned 50,000 troops. One of the pillars of the Bicesse accords comes crashing down just five days after the polls closed and before the final results have even been announced.

UNAVEM and the key Western diplomats from the United States, Portugal and Britain are powerless, the folly of their position exposed. They had played down the failure of demobilisation, especially by Savimbi's army, by arguing that everything would come right after the elections, and now that it has not done so they have no fall-back position. The ultimate nightmare is unfolding and the international community appears unable to do anything about it.

Ordinary people in Luanda wonder why the foreigners do nothing to force Savimbi to return to the FAA and are stunned to learn that the most powerful nations in the world are impotent. In Washington the US Assistant Secretary of State, Herman Cohen, issues two feeble statements calling on UNITA to show restraint. He describes UNITA's withdrawal from the FAA as 'an unfortunate step which is not in accord with the spirit or letter of the Angolan peace accords'.

Such light verbal reprimands must be soothing to Savimbi, for they provide the clearest evidence yet that his former backer, the United States, will do nothing to halt his antics. Washington is playing to Savimbi's worst instincts and is breaking the international community's promise to the Angolan people that it would play the role of honest broker. It is impossible to imagine that the US reaction would have been so mild had it been the MPLA rather than UNITA which was threatening to wreck the peace process.

By the looks of him, Salupeto Pena is close to a nervous breakdown. He starts drinking in the morning and by the early afternoon is so deluded that even the mild American criticism angers him. 'Mr Cohen is not an Angolan,' he says, reflecting the xenophobia that has always seethed just below the surface of UNITA's thinking. Now the National Electoral Council must review or annul the election, halt publication of the results and admit that the police had intimidated voters. UNITA has 'categorically rejected the process' and Abel Chivukuvuku, the foreign affairs spokesman, calls the election 'generalised systematic fraud'. The phrase becomes a UNITA mantra, as if its mere repetition will make it fact.

On Monday 6 October Margaret Anstee and diplomats from the key observer countries, Portugal, Russia and the United States, call an emergency meeting of the Joint Political-Military Commission, known by its Portuguese acronym CCPM, so senior military commanders and officials from both sides can negotiate a solution. A shouting match between UNITA and government representatives ensues. 'Some harsh words were exchanged between UNITA and the government but, without painting a rosy picture, there is still room to negotiate,' one of the Western observers tells me afterwards. Naïvely, I believe him.

After 95 per cent of the votes have been counted dos Santos is down to 50.8 per cent to Savimbi's 39 per cent in the presidential race. The National Electoral Council, bowing to pressure from UNITA's claims of fraud and pleas from Margaret Anstee, agrees to suspend the count to double-check the vote.

Late that evening the foreign press corps assembles at UNITA's São Paulo headquarters. Nothing happens for half an hour. The place is jammed with heavily armed UNITA troops and civilians strutting around, occasionally shouting that the press are *mentirosos* or liars. This is a particularly difficult time for UNITA supporters in Luanda, who are being bombarded by the state-owned press telling them that Savimbi is heading for defeat. For them it is almost a religious belief that Savimbi will win. Even supposedly moderate UNITA members, such as economic spokesperson Fátima Roque, cannot conceive of the possibility of an MPLA victory, but now their world is caving in and, as Savimbi promised ten days before during his campaign visit to Kuito, UNITA cannot accept defeat.

The press conference finally comes to order, with

Valentim and Norberto de Castro, for years a UNITA spokesman in Portugal, presiding. After a brief introduction the UNITA officials hold up result tallies apparently proving MPLA fraud. Are there any questions, they ask. A Portuguese journalist raises her hand and asks whether they have any comment on Savimbi's departure to Huambo that day. Pandemonium erupts. UNITA thugs in the driveway outside start shouting abuse at us. Over the din Noberto de Castro hollers, 'We are here to discuss the MPLA's systematic fraud in the elections, not the whereabouts of Dr Savimbi.' The Portuguese journalist retorts that as UNITA spokesmen they are there to respond to reporters' questions, so what about Savimbi's flight to Huambo? The shouts from the UNITA activists outside grow uglier and the conference quickly breaks up with Valentim and de Castro still yelling that they have proof of vote-rigging.

We pour out of the room to make a quick get-away. Several thugs start threatening us, focusing most of their anger on Anita Coulson of the BBC, whom they accuse of being a government sympathiser. There seems little doubt now that a storm of violence is coming. The only question is when it will erupt.

The next day several senior UNITA officials, including General Arlindo Pena, 'Ben Ben', who was to be the joint chief of staff of the new Angolan Armed Forces, follow Savimbi to Huambo. UNITA's brinkmanship is working. Under Western pressure the official announcement comes that the declaration of the election results has been delayed until the arrival of a special mission from the UN Security Council. Savimbi now has the initiative. He refuses to receive Margaret Anstee or any Western envoys in Huambo.

When Herman Cohen tells the House of Representatives Foreign Affairs Africa sub-committee in Washington that, 'I have had private assurances from senior associates of Dr Savimbi in the last day that they will abide by the results,' he seems to be engaging in a heavy bout of wishful thinking.

Savimbi himself keeps the hopes alive, telling the United Nations that he is planning to return to Luanda to discuss the formation of a government of national reconciliation. Ever the cunning military tactician, Savimbi is buying time. UNITA soldiers are abandoning their cantonment areas in their hundreds and, although no one knows for sure, it looks as if they are beginning a general mobilisation for war. The Americans' optimism seems either woefully out of touch with reality or designed to give Savimbi, their former client, time to plan. 'We just heard the news that Dr Savimbi is likely to come to Luanda and accept President dos Santos's invitation,' Cohen says in Washington. 'We feel that there is still time and still grounds for optimism.'

UNITA troops strike the first blow on 8 October by occupying the district of Caconda in Huíla province. The next day Margaret Anstee is standing on the tarmac at the Luanda airport. She is wearing a black dress, appropriate attire for the mood of the moment, and is speaking into her walkie-talkie to UNAVEM headquarters. A UN plane is being prepared to take her to Huambo for her first meeting with Savimbi since he fled Luanda. The strain of the past few days tells on her face. I try to talk to her, but all she says is, 'I wake up each morning not knowing what is going to happen today.'

Margaret Anstee cuts a sad figure that day. She has overseen an almost impossible mandate, her UNAVEM hamstrung by too few resources and too few powers for an operation of such a size. She once likened it to flying 'a 747 with only enough fuel for a DC-3'. Yet for a moment, when the polls closed on 30 September with almost no violence, it seemed that all might go according to plan.

Yet there was more to it. She did not use the power she possessed as the focal point of world opinion and the Western countries, especially the United States, did little to back her up. Everything would work itself out if Angola could get through the elections, they said.

Seeing Margaret Anstee off at the airport is the government's top military man and senior negotiator, General António dos Santos França, better known by his nom de guerre, Ndalu. He is the one man in the MPLA whom Savimbi trusts. General Ndalu had put much effort into negotiating the Bicesse accords and, unlike many of the government's senior security officials, believes profoundly that another showdown with UNITA will spell doom.

Ndalu was in Huambo the day before to see Savimbi and he does not share the international community's stubborn optimism that a deal can be struck. When I approach him he says, 'Things are very bad. We are on the brink of war. We know that FALA is leaving the assembly points and heading back to the bush. They are pulling out and returning to their old bases. At the end of it, Savimbi will not settle for a position in the new government. Savimbi just wants to be the leader.'

Diplomatic exchanges and more calls from Portugal and the United States for restraint fill the 10th of October. UNITA officials like Chivukuvuku and Salupeto Pena are threatening that unless the alleged election fraud is admitted, Angola will become another Somalia. When I ask Salupeto Pena at the National Electoral Council office about the future, he literally drools out the words 'Somaliasation of Angola.' The man is frightening. Savimbi, on the other hand, is attempting to appear reasonable, telling Margaret Anstee that he will respect the election results if an investigation finds that there has been no fraud in the vote. FALA soldiers continue to abandon the assembly points.

The UN Security Council's four-man mission arrives the next morning, a few hours after UNITA forces attack and occupy the municipality of Cacula in the central highlands. Most Western diplomats continue to say that they believe a deal can be worked out. By the end of the day, however, nearly everyone is filled with gloom.

A car bomb detonates before dawn in front of the Hotel Turismo where dozens of UNITA officials and their families have been living since the movement returned to Luanda in June 1991. The explosion blows out several of the hotel's windows. When a lorry full of government police approaches the building a few hours later, UNITA soldiers fire on the vehicle, capture the policemen, take them up to the fourth floor and tie them up as hostages.

When I arrive on the scene with a group of reporters the UNITA soldiers outside the hotel are preparing for battle. We are led to the rooms where the policemen are being held. Suddenly, two shots ring out from the street below and a black car speeds away. Chaos erupts upstairs. A hysterical UNITA woman shoves a couple of us into one of the rooms full of police prisoners. We peer out of a shattered bathroom window to see the events down below. The woman starts screaming, accusing us of breaking the glass, and tries to lock us in the bathroom. We shove our way past the hostages and their captors into the hall, where women are shouting wildly and attempting to herd us into the corner rooms.

Occasional shots ring out in the street and the pack of journalists is too big for all of us to squeeze into the one room with a view. Ominously, the UNITA officials order us to remain where we are. No one is to leave. Hostage-taking has been one of UNITA's favoured tactics throughout the war.

I had stayed in the Turismo in 1986 and knew that the stairs at the back of the hotel lead to a bar on the mezzanine level. So I shout to Julian Ozanne, correspondent for the *Financial Times*, and we run down the escape route. We take a seat at the wide windows at the bar, where in more peaceful times I had sipped coffee, as a dozen UNITA soldiers fan out into the street and take up positions over at the Bank of Angola.

Suddenly they begin firing indiscriminately towards the police headquarters across the plaza, into flats above the Lello bookshop, at anyone or any vehicle that moves. Hundreds of people in shorts and T-shirts, with towels draped over their shoulders on their way to a relaxing Sunday at the beach, momentarily freeze in disbelief before fleeing. One UNITA soldier ducks into the entrance of a building and dances a jig as he unleashes a few bursts of automatic fire before realising that his imaginary enemy is a wooden door. Another fires his grenade launcher three times at the roof of the police headquarters, scoring direct hits each time. A passing police jeep is hit by six rounds before screeching off. Police are hiding in doorways and crouch down behind rubbish dumps a few blocks away. They hold their fire. During the entire half-hour of shooting they loose off only a few rounds.

In the hotel entrance panic sets in. A voice comes crackling across a walkie-talkie with the news that a police armoured car is on its way to attack the hotel. UNITA militants in civilian clothes gather up pistols and AK-47 rifles and run out into the car park. I suggest that it is time to go. We leap down the stairs from the mezzanine and encounter a Portuguese radio correspondent who is standing in the middle of the hotel lobby with tears streaming down her face. She has just come from an assignment in Sarajevo and is clearly still suffering from shell-shock. I ask her if she wants to leave, and she says yes. So we take her hand, hoist our pathetic little white press cards in the air and walk briskly out of the hotel, angling to the right across a line of UNITA soldiers and down an alley to the area controlled by the police. Incredibly, no one stops us.

Having deposited our shaken Portuguese colleague at the press centre three streets away, we head over towards a police station on the Marginal, the wide seafront avenue which rings Luanda's picturesque bay. The armoured vehicle which the UNITA soldiers at the hotel are fearing has arrived. Heavy police reinforcements have taken up positions a block from the front of the hotel, but their commanders seem in no hurry to advance. They are holding back. 'Negotiations,' one disappointed officer scoffs.

We hustle back to the hotel just in time for the arrival of a UNITA brigadier in a truck with 30 soldiers. He immediately orders the troops to cease fire. 'Be calm and we will sort this problem out,' he shouts. Moments later General Renato Mateus assumes command. 'We had nothing else to do but to defend ourselves,' he says in between barking orders to aides rushing around with walkie-talkies. 'After the bomb they came to attack again, and we are going to defend ourselves to the last.'

After two hours of negotiations agreement is reached on a ceasefire and an exchange of the police hostages for 35 UNITA prisoners held by the government for violent offences committed during the election campaign.

Considering the scale of the shooting, the death toll of five is relatively light. One of those slain was a middle-aged man I find lying in a pool of blood on Frederick Engels Street behind the hotel. He is wearing trousers rolled up to his knees and pink flip-flops. I walk up to two UNITA soldiers on the street corner, one with a 30-calibre machine gun and with a belt of bullets strapped across his chest, and inquire as politely as I can why they had shot the man. 'He had a pistol,' the one with the big gun says stiffly, his eyes constantly shifting back and forth. So where is the gun now? The two look at each other nervously and after a pause say that they gave it to their commander who is somewhere in the hotel. Fifty yards away a small crowd of teenagers has gathered, and they are outraged when I tell them what the UNITA soldiers had said. 'Look at his shirt, the bastards shot him because of the MPLA T-shirt,' says one. 'We saw everything. The man was going to the beach just like us.' The crowd of teenagers glare at the UNITA soldiers across the road with hate in their eyes.

*

Pik Botha, the South African foreign minister, arrives in Luanda to help bring peace to the country his government has done more than any other to destroy. In the end he fails in his quest, but all the while Pik Botha is an outrageous specimen to behold. Pik might be white and of Afrikaner stock, but he is just as much an African as his 'black brothers'. According to Pik, Europeans and Americans, the United Nations and the Russians do not understand Africans as the Afrikaners do.

All previous mediation efforts have failed. Margaret Anstee has had no luck and repeated American statements urging Savimbi to abide by the results of the elections have been ignored. The special mission from the UN Security Council that arrived in Luanda for a four-day visit on the morning of the Turismo Hotel shoot-out has little to show for its efforts except another ineffectual statement expressing 'grave concern' at acts of violence and warning that a resumption of the war will be met 'with the strongest condemnation of the international community'. Now it is Pik's turn and he is relishing the limelight: there is nothing more pleasing to an Afrikaner leader than to be called in to sort out the problems among squabbling blacks.

When Pik announces he is going to Huambo to see Savimbi, all the journalists in town scramble to accompany him. A South African correspondent for the Argus Newspaper Group arranges a seat on Pik's jet through his contacts with the South African mission to Luanda. He tries to throw Ozanne and me, and no doubt others, off the trail by telling us that anyone wanting to travel with Pik is supposed to show up at the airport. He is lying. In fact, we are supposed to meet at the South African mission, but in our blissful ignorance we turn up at the VIP lounge at the airport and wait for Pik.

At the mission's office in town, meanwhile, the journalists with the correct instructions are told there is no more room because several Angolan government officials are to make the trip too. Not surprisingly, the government representatives fail to arrive, so when Pik pulls up next to his jet he invites us aboard. We are asked to sit in the rear of the plane while Pik huddles with his advisers in the front to discuss strategy during the hour-long flight.

After landing we join the South African delegation in

several Land Rovers for the short ride to Savimbi's grand Casa Branca residence. Dozens of UNITA soldiers armed with grenade launchers and AK-47s stand around the house, and the dirt road leading to it is blocked off. In theory, the MPLA government still controls Huambo, but its authority is superficial at best. UNITA soldiers already reign supreme throughout most of the city.

Pik and his delegation of four advisers take their seats in the spacious living room with a host of top UNITA officials, including Jorge Valentim, who is looking even more agitated than usual. After a few minutes the doors to the entrance hall open and Savimbi comes bounding down a majestic staircase and rushes into the room. The handshakes and greetings are warm. 'I can listen to you because you have been my friend and you have never betrayed me like the others have betrayed me,' Savimbi tells Pik. It is an obvious reference to the United States, which once welcomed him into the White House and proclaimed him a 'freedom fighter' but is now demanding that he accept defeat in the elections. Pik basks in a glow of attention and the favourable comparison with the United States. 'You have touched me,' he tells Savimbi.

For many years Pik has been one of Savimbi's greatest defenders and his government has repeatedly sent the South African Defence Force across the Namibian border to save UNITA from annihilation. UNITA owes much of its current military strength to Pretoria, just as the MPLA has a huge debt to the Cubans and the former Soviet Union.

South African troops first entered Angola in June 1975 when they took up positions in the far south near the Ruacana Falls. In September that year Pretoria launched Operation Zulu, which sent a motorised column sweeping up the Atlantic coast. In October South African military instructors began training UNITA troops at Silva Porto, the colonial name for Kuito, in Bié province. By November the Operation Zulu forces were within 100 miles of Luanda. Their invasion had provoked a massive deployment of Cuban troops on 7 November when Fidel Castro countered with Operation Carlota, which forced the South Africans to retreat.

In return for support from South Africa Savimbi betrayed his former allies in the Namibian independence movement and provided the South Africans with intelligence on the South West Africa People's Organisation (SWAPO). Since then South Africa spent millions of dollars on arms for UNITA and sent its troops to fight side by side with Savimbi's troops in faraway places like Cuito Cuanavale and Mavinga. It had set up 32 Battalion, a hodge-podge of Angolans, South African officers and a sprinkling of mercenaries, to help UNITA intensify its war against the MPLA. Many actions claimed by UNITA were actually carried out by 32 Battalion.

All that is history now. South Africa withdrew from Angola four years ago, and is well down the road to negotiating an end to centuries of white domination, establishing a democracy that will surely see the leader of the pro-MPLA African National Congress, Nelson Mandela, elected as the country's first black president. Namibia has won its independence from South Africa and a SWAPO government is in power in Windhoek.

Now Savimbi is in trouble. As the discussions begin we are asked to leave the room and await a statement at the end of the meeting. There is not much to do but sit out on the veranda and listen to the tales that Pik's bodyguards tell about their various trips around the world with the foreign minister. They are in particular awe of the Japanese, and especially their highly efficient railways. 'At this place we were waiting for a one o'clock train, and so when one arrived at 12.59 we started to board it, but we were told this was not our train,' one remembers. 'At 1 p.m. exactly ours pulled up. It was incredible.' 'And the cars,' says another 'there are no old cars in Japan, everything is new.'

An hour or so later one of Pik's aides steps out on the veranda and motions us to come into the meeting. Pik explains that during the talks Savimbi revealed evidence purporting to document his allegations of vote rigging. 'I thought it was important for the press to hear this, it is very interesting,' Pik says.

Then he turns to Savimbi and asks for a guarantee that UNITA will not resort to violence. 'You have my word and you know me well,' Savimbi responds. The ever explosive Valentim, none too pleased with the tone of the conversation, keeps jumping up from his seat like a naughty school boy, shouting, 'But UNITA will never accept fraud, never!' Pik appears to be growing impatient with Valentim and Savimbi flashes him a look which clearly means 'sit down and shut up'.

Would Savimbi be willing to meet President dos Santos, Pik asks, and Savimbi responds with a firm 'Absolutely'. Savimbi then says, 'What I am asking you to do is convince President dos Santos that he needs us to bring the country together, that unless he takes us into account, the country will never be unified again.' Savimbi is issuing threats again, but Pik either does not understand them, chooses to ignore them or, more likely, conspires with them. A smile creeps across his face. 'There is international support for this concept as a solution in this country,' he says. 'I cannot create miracles, but I will try,' says Pik.

On the plane back to Luanda Pik is in a buoyant mood, one that is enhanced by a considerable amount of whiskey. Pik has his eye on the blond stewardess serving him rapid-fire drinks, stroking her hand every time she brings in a new glass. When he sees that we have spotted his shenanigans, a grin sweeps across his face. What Europeans and Americans fail to understand, he says, is that Africa is really not ready for democracy. 'The democratic culture is just not there,' he says. It is an incredible claim for a leader of a white minority government which has jailed Nelson Mandela, the nation's true leader, for a quarter of a century.

South Africa will lead the way in Africa, perhaps the world, he maintains. Just look at the country's success in international sport. When I remind him that South Africa's national football side has just been pummelled by the Nigerian team, he shakes his head and says, 'I was really crying for the boys.'

Yet, crude as he might seem, Pik should never be underestimated. He has been involved in several spectacular diplomatic coups, such as the Nkomati non-aggression pact with Mozambique and the troop withdrawal accords which brought independence to Namibia and the Cuban withdrawal from Angola. He is confident that in Angola he is on the brink of scoring another diplomatic success. 'I smell another one,' he says.

Unfortunately, Pik's sense of smell is probably not as acute as it used to be. Savimbi has never been the obedient puppet that both the South Africans and the MPLA always made him out to be. He treats allies like transients, useful as long as they further his cause and to be disposed of when they no longer serve their purpose. If the South Africans are not prepared to give their unqualified support to Savimbi's charges of vote-rigging, perhaps they too have outlived their usefulness.

Arriving at Luanda airport, Pik asks us to stay on board until he has spoken to the crowd of waiting reporters. He is starting to worry about how it will look back home when word gets out that he left the South African reporter behind and instead took two foreign journalists to Huambo. After all, Afrikaners are none too keen on foreigners, especially British newspaper correspondents. It is a useless request since everyone knows we left with Pik.

Later that evening, Pik goes to the presidential palace at Futungo de Belas to brief President dos Santos. He also holds a meeting with the Security Council mission and Margaret Anstee at the bar in his hotel, which is commonly known as the Love Boat. This is a converted Cypriot ferry, the *Westminster*, brought to Luanda harbour because of the shortage of hotel space in the city. He shocks the United Nations officials by delivering a loud lecture about how South Africans understand Africa better than anyone else because Afrikaners are themselves African. All this in the bar of the Love Boat. Margaret Anstee is not amused.

Pik is a show unto himself, sometimes to the delight, sometimes to the horror of the hotel managers. On one occasion, after too much to drink, he boards a small boat with an outboard motor and cruises around the harbour in the middle of the night. On another he gets into a foul-mouthed shouting match with a deputy down a satellite telephone line, which other hotel residents cannot help but hear.

After finishing supper Pik goes on the prowl, stumbling around the restaurant in pursuit of startled waitresses. At a private bar which the hotel management puts at his disposal one evening, Pik takes a drink from the blond stewardess on his jet, grabs her behind and says with a boyish grin, 'I'd like to doodle that one.'

In the end, Pik's diplomatic foray into Angola proves no more successful than anyone else's. The MPLA loses patience with Pik's antics, increasingly concerned that he is, in fact, encouraging Savimbi to take a hard line.

The day after Savimbi gave his word to Pik that he would eschew violence, UNITA troops forcibly occupy the municipality of Andulo in Bié province. The former commander of the FAPLA troops in the area is killed and local government officials disappear.

I am awoken from a deep sleep shortly after midnight on 15 October by massive explosions which rock Luanda in waves of rolling thunder. Window panes and doors rattle from the concussion. The vibrations shake the ground. The world seems to be coming to an end. The skies over the southern part of the city erupt into a display of exploding light and thousands of the city's residents pour out into the streets to see what is happening. Whole families pack their bags within minutes and are on the road fleeing their homes for fear that a tremendous battle is under way.

There is something oddly comforting in the enormity of the blasts. It seems impossible that either the government forces or UNITA could bring so much firepower to bear in one battle. Nothing I have seen or felt, even at the Battle of Cuito Cuanavale four years before, remotely compares to the sheer force of the booming discharges. After 45 minutes or so the noise begins to die down.

The next morning I travel out to the scene of the blasts on the road south from Luanda at an open air arms depot about a mile from UNAVEM's headquarters. Government soldiers strolling around the wreckage say that the night before UNITA fighters stationed at a nearby motel had crept up and fired rocket-propelled grenades into the area to ignite the magazine containing the air force's bombs and rockets. Torn metal and pieces of bombs are strewn all over the area. The depot itself is still smoking by the time I arrive. Soldiers gingerly walk along the wall of the containment area, which is about as big as a football pitch, and warn that it is dangerous to approach too closely. There is no telling how long the munitions have been sitting in the open air, or how much deterioration the explosives have suffered from the rain or the salty air rolling in from the sea which is only two miles away.

If the attack is intended as a piece of psychological warfare, it certainly works. Tension in Luanda is ratcheted up another notch. UNITA officials later deny involvement in the explosion, but it fits a pattern of attempts to deprive government forces of its heavy ammunition stores. UNITA had dynamited an arms depot in the south-eastern city of Menongue on 5 October, and the government accused UNITA troops of destroying a munitions depot in Malange six days after the Luanda blasts. It is one more indication that full-scale fighting is on the way.

On 17 October, after repeated delays, the National Electoral Council announces the official election results, despite strong objections from UNITA, which feels that its claims of fraud have not been properly investigated and wants the entire election annulled. President dos Santos wins 49.57 per cent of the vote compared to 40.07 for Jonas Savimbi, with UNITA sweeping the *planalto* by huge margins and also winning in Benguela and Cuando Cubango provinces. The MPLA defeats UNITA in the legislative elections by 53.74 per cent to 34.1.

The final results are remarkably similar to a 'quick count' conducted by UNAVEM at a sample of 166 polling stations which projected results within 0.3 per cent of the final tallies for dos Santos and 2 per cent for Savimbi.

That same night, Margaret Anstee issues her verdict:

> The United Nations considers that while there were certainly some irregularities in the electoral process, these appear to have been mainly due to human error and inexperience. There was no conclusive evidence of major, systematic or widespread fraud, or that the irregularities were of a magnitude to have a significant effect on the official results announced on 17 October. Nor, in the view of their random nature, could it be determined that such irregularities had penalised or benefited only one party or set of parties.
>
> I therefore have the honour, in my capacity as Special Representative of the Secretary-General, to certify that, with all deficiencies taken into account, the elections held on 29 and 30 September can be considered to have been generally free and fair. The United Nations urges all Angolans and all Angolan political parties, as well as the international community, to respect and support the results of this stage of the electoral process. A further certification will be made after the second round of the presidential election.

*

My editors at the *Independent*, like much of the world's media, are growing bored with the Angola story and they ask me to travel across the continent to Mozambique so I can carry out a magazine assignment about a team from International Committee of the Red Cross that is opening up mined roads near the headquarters of the RENAMO rebel movement. I hate to leave Luanda as the story is still unfolding, but I confidently advise them that Angola should remain fairly calm for at least several weeks.

The previous month in Rome RENAMO and the FRELIMO government of President Joaquim Chissano had signed a peace agreement ending their seventeen-year civil war. Many of the Red Cross workers whom I had met in Angola are rushing over to Mozambique to provide assistance to hundreds of thousands of civilians who have been trapped behind the battle lines for over a decade. Much of the UNAVEM equipment in Angola is earmarked to be shifted over to Mozambique for a similar operation. According to some reports, Margaret Anstee is to be named as the Special Representative in Mozambique to oversee a replay of the Angolan peace process.

My trip with the Red Cross begins in Mozambique's central port city of Beira, where, by chance, I run into my old friend Bepe, the Italian aid worker with whom I travelled to Huambo the previous year. Over dinner one night I sketch out my thesis that a deal can still be worked out in Angola, that a return to civil war is not inevitable. Bepe flashes his knowing smile and asks how I can still hold to such optimism. The reports he is hearing suggest that full-scale war is imminent. A week later, deep in the Mozambican bush, I hear on the shortwave radio that Bepe's prognosis is accurate.

Reports from UNAVEM field bases show that by mid-October UNITA forces are on a war footing Dozens of local government administrations are forced to flee after being attacked by UNITA troops or receiving death threats.

As UNITA's foreign affairs spokesman, Abel Chivukuvuku, wrote to Savimbi at the time:

> It is also important at the same that we keep open the channels of communication and negotiation, that where we supposedly lost the elections there should be a demonstration

> of popular support ... there should be a demonstration of UNITA's military force, like in Benguela, Huambo, Bié, Moxico, Kuando Kubango, Uíge, Malange, where the MPLA should be chased out of all the municipalities and remain restricted to the capital cities, and for the world to know that if a conflict is unleashed, we will begin from bases near where we were on the 1st of May 1991.

By 20 October history is repeating itself. The government begins distributing arms to civilians, mainly demobilised soldiers, MPLA activists and unemployed street thugs. The MPLA used the same tactic, known as *poder popular*, or people's power, on the eve of independence when it handed out weapons to supporters in the *musseque* slums around the capital.

Seventeen years later, with its army collapsing and UNITA forces gobbling up the countryside, the MPLA again reverts to *poder popular* to ensure its survival. So blatant is the arms distribution exercise that Angolan workers at one British aid organisation ask their director if he too wants some AK-47s.

By this time, the British embassy is considering withdrawing all British citizens from Angola. The United Nations, however, has still not been put on alert status. Over the next few days Luanda is remarkably calm, apparently vindicating the UNAVEM view. International non-governmental organisations (NGOs) hold a meeting with UNDP's chief of security, Albert Fawundu, on 23 October to discuss plans for an evacuation. When they tell him they are pulling out their foreign staff, he laughs at them. The NGOs ask if UNAVEM has any plans for evacuating international relief workers in case of an emergency. It is a question which UNAVEM never answers.

The relative quiet prompts the British embassy on 25 October to consider bringing back the non-essential staff it has evacuated when it went on Phase II alert. Then heavy fighting again breaks out in Huambo. UNITA troops attack the radio and television stations and attempt to occupy the governor's palace. On the second day of fighting UNAVEM's Lieutenant-Colonel Mortlock brokers a ceasefire. In Luanda UNITA negotiator Salupeto Pena, under sharp questioning by a reporter from the state-run television, suggests that the journalist will speak with a more civil tongue once UNITA takes control.

Government supporters are growing impatient with President dos Santos's failure to act against what they regard as UNITA provocations. A senior FAA officer tells the director of an international NGO, 'This guy is a *mutilado*, we just have to convince him when to do it.' Early in the morning of 30 October that same NGO director receives a telephone call from a friend in UNAVEM to say that there are widespread rumours that major fighting is about to erupt. Early that day eleven people, including three Portuguese, are gunned down in Cassenda near the airport.

UNITA officials later claim the Portuguese were armed, although some witnesses say they saw UNITA soldiers throw several guns into their car after the shootings took place. Heavy gunfire breaks out that evening in what the government charges was an attempt by UNITA to seize the airport. The MPLA never provides hard evidence to back up this claim.

The next morning, 31 October, war explodes in the capital in what later became known as the battle for Luanda. By the end of the three days of clashes, UNITA has been driven from the city and among the thousands of casualties were its vice-president Jeremias Chitunda and its top negotiator, Salupeto Pena, Savimbi's nephew. UNITA's military commander, General Arlindo Pena, 'Ben Ben', fled Luanda and was on the run, and the 36-year-old foreign affairs spokesman, Abel Chivukuvuku, was under arrest. Both his legs were broken. Some estimates put the number of dead in Luanda at 2,000. Angola was back at war.

8 People's Power

> I was standing on the ridge over in Miramar one day after the confrontations in Luanda. There was this well dressed woman asking a policeman why the police had not burned down the shacks there on Boa Vista where mainly Umbundu people from the centre of the country live. The policeman said he could not do that because these were people's homes. The woman said, 'They are not people, they are only Bailundos [Ovimbundu].'
>
> Pepetela

For the moment it seems impossible to return to Angola. The 4 de Fevereiro airport has been closed during the three days of fighting in Luanda, and all international airlines have cancelled their flights. The airport authorities are allowing only UN planes to land. My one hope is the World Food Programme (WFP), which is continuing its shuttles to Windhoek in Namibia, to evacuate non-essential UN personnel.

On 5 November I reach Philippe Borel, the WFP's French director of operations in Angola, by telephone at his home in Luanda. The line is faint, but his shaken voice indicates the horror that he has witnessed sweeping through Luanda. As usual Borel immediately grants permission for me and several other journalists to make the journey if we can reach Windhoek in time.

Our Antonov-26 cargo plane from Namibia lands in Luanda the following afternoon to a welcoming committee consisting of a few WFP airport workers and a host of soldiers and security agents. Thousands of empty AK-47 cartridges litter the tarmac, and several planes have been raked by machine-gun fire. Since the airport is effectively closed, there are just a couple of soldiers and one immigration official to check our passports. I am reminded of my first visit in 1986 when the immigration authorities consisted of two illiterate teenage soldiers. Luanda airport has come full circle and the giant *Angola no Coração* banner stretched across the building seems like a joke in very bad taste.

Even more burnt-out cars and piles of burning rubbish than usual fill the city's streets. War has come to the capital for the first time since independence. Groups of women armed with giant brooms move down the wide avenues sweeping up mounds of broken glass, thousands of empty cartridges, bits of discarded UNITA uniforms, ripped-up party flags and torn-up posters of Jonas Savimbi's earnest face. The headline on that Friday's *Jornal de Angola*, 'The War Continues' is, unfortunately, an accurate summary of the situation.

We make our way to the Hotel Le President, where a state of depression reigns. The European management has emptied all the money from the safe, gathered up most of the room keys and fled to Europe, leaving the gallant Angolan staff to keep the hotel open under trying circumstances.

Le President has always been highly overpriced for the service it offers. The month before I had found a cockroach in a bowl of onion soup and, when I complained, the waiter dutifully removed it and returned with another bowl from the same pot. Sheepishly I explained that I o longer had an appetite for onion soup. A few days later, when I told the hotel manager how disappointed I was to find that onion soup was no longer on the menu, he said, 'Oh, we ran out of cockroaches.'

The Angolan staff search through their set of master keys and find some rooms for us. As my colleagues and I are settling in, two men appear at our doors identifying themselves as officials of the Ministry of the Interior, surely from the secret police. They want to know how we entered the country since all international flights have been cancelled. When we explain that we came on a United Nations flight from Windhoek, they look at each other blankly and promise to return if they have any further questions. We never see them again.

The brief visit by the secret police sets the tone for the changes which have taken place in Luanda in the past month, sliding from the heights of euphoria of the country's first elections back to the paranoia for which the MPLA has been responsible for years. It does not take long to find out why.

Only a handful of foreign journalists were in Luanda during the three days of fighting, and most of them were evacuated immediately to São Tomé before they were able to discover precisely what was taking place. For the most part the outside world initially accepted the explanation given by the state media that government security forces together with the civilian population had mounted a heroic defence against a UNITA attempt to erase its electoral defeat by staging a coup d'état against the MPLA. But once in Luanda it is hard to accept this thesis. There are ample signs of what one senior United Nations official describes as the 'wholesale butchery' of UNITA supporters by the government police and armed vigilantes.

I set out first to visit UNITA's São Paulo headquarters where so many press conferences and meetings with UN officials and foreign diplomats had taken place the month before. The building has been smashed into piles of blackened ruins. Parts of it are still smouldering. On its façade large red letters proclaim that its fate had been decided by *poder popular*.

Poder popular also left its mark on Savimbi's once elegant house in Miramar and the Turismo Hotel, where dozens of UNITA officials and their families had huddled against an onslaught of AK-47s and mortar shells. Both buildings are burnt-out shells. The heavily armed UNITA troops, whose arrogant and aggressive presence had been so evident just days before, have all disappeared; they have either fled the city or ended up face-down in the streets.

Whole areas of the city, especially Miramar, where many foreign diplomats and oil companies such as Texaco have their residences, have been looted. Armed vigilantes, known as *fitinhas* because of the red bandannas they wear on their heads, helped themselves to thousands of dollars' worth of food and medicines stored in UN warehouses. The government, in the person of deputy Foreign Minister Johnny Pinnock, astounded the heads of UN agencies in

Luanda by asking for additional international aid, partly to cover the loss of goods stolen by the vigilantes and the police. The government, he maintained weakly, was unable to control *poder popular*.

It is true that UNITA's behaviour in Luanda infuriated the civilian population, an outrage I had seen in the eyes of those teenage boys three weeks before when UNITA soldiers gunned down the man strolling to the beach just because he was wearing an MPLA T-shirt. UNITA's policy of brinkmanship and occupying the countryside had panicked a government whose army had all but disintegrated.

However it is also becoming clear that *poder popular* was hardly as spontaneous as the government makes it out to be. Ten days before the battle of Luanda the authorities had handed out weapons to demobilised soldiers, MPLA activists, indeed to almost anyone who would take them. If UNITA was planning to stage a coup d'état, as the government claims, how is it that the only offices, residences and hotels to be destroyed all belong to UNITA? The damage to government installations is remarkably light.

The story of the battle of Luanda which I am able to piece together makes clear that the government's claim of a UNITA coup plot was designed as propaganda to cover up its decision to strike back the only way it knew how.

It began at dawn on 31 October, a day after the murder of the three Portuguese at Cassenda and only hours after the shooting at the airport. Luanda had reached the point of spontaneous combustion. The police threw up roadblocks throughout the city and on the major roads leading out of the capital. Heavily armed UNITA troops virtually took over Miramar, the wealthy residential suburb overlooking the bay of Luanda. The city centre was an armed camp, with UNITA troops surrounding the Turismo Hotel and *ninja* anti-riot police deployed around their headquarters two blocks away.

UNITA was hoping to stage a march from the northern suburb of São Paulo to the centre of town, but the government refused permission on the grounds that it might spark off violence. This was to be UNITA's first demonstration since the elections and as Abel Chivukuvuku, UNITA's foreign affairs spokesman, later remembered, was designed, 'as a kind of pressure for the negotiations'.

In the early morning hours of that first day, a UNITA truck was ambushed on the road to the airport and set alight. The vehicle was still on fire by the time Dr Neville Ndondo, the Zimbabwean ambassador, passed by at 7 a.m. on his way to drop his family and the embassy's non-essential personnel at the airport to catch the morning flight to Harare. Forty-five minutes later shooting broke out in front of the Rádio Nacional complex when a UNITA car drove by at high speed and opened fire.

Chivukuvuku telephoned British ambassador John Flynn to say that he would be unable to attend a lunch that was to bring together the principal UNITA officials, including the top negotiator Salupeto Pena and vice-president Chitunda, and the government army's chief of staff General Ndalu, deputy Foreign Affairs Minister Venáncio de Moura and deputy Minister of the Interior Francisco de Piedade Nandó, Margaret Anstee as well as several ambassadors. 'John, I told him, it won't be possible for me to be there because something's wrong. There's tension in the city ...' Flynn agreed to try to organise another meeting the following week. Margaret Anstee arrived for the lunch and remained trapped there throughout the battle for Luanda.

General Higino Carneiro, the government's top military negotiator, held a meeting at 10 a.m. with representatives of the three observer countries, Portugal, Russia, and the United States, at the CCPM offices in the city centre. He presented a list of complaints against UNITA, including its continued push to occupy the countryside, drive-by shootings at the airport and the First of May plaza and the imprisonment of several government army officers in Huambo. The government's patience was wearing thin, he announced, and the authorities had given arms to the public to prepare for any eventuality.

Government and UNITA delegations headed by Nandó, whose Ministry of the Interior had been distributing arms to civilians, and Salupeto Pena, Savimbi's nephew and right-hand man, met at the CCPM an hour later. Nandó repeated the government accusations, insisting that the wounded in Huambo be evacuated and that UNITA explain why it had attacked the diamond-producing area of Cafunfo in the north-east of the country.

Salupeto Pena responded by accusing the government of

engaging in games and denied that UNITA had attacked Cafunfo. The *ninja* anti-riot police, not UNITA soldiers, were instigating violence there. UNITA activists were being killed and wounded, he said, and several party cars had been destroyed. 'Our forces will not shoot first,' he promised. Salupeto Pena denied that UNITA troops riding around in trucks had been involved in drive-by shootings, saying there had been no witnesses. A senior US military official who attended the meeting had witnessed at least two such incidents.

Oscar Monteiro, the Portuguese ambassador, suddenly asked the meeting, 'Are we or are we not going to war?' Everyone should declare their intent, he said. Nandó claimed that the government was not planning to go to war. Salupeto Pena said that UNITA harboured no warlike plans, but asserted his movement's right to respond if attacked. Salupeto Pena said he had received reports that six UNITA offices in the central city of Malange had been destroyed. Monteiro asked both sides for a commitment to protect foreigners. Salupeto Pena described UNAVEM as a positive force and said that UN officials should move to where UNITA could guarantee their safety. No one took his suggestion seriously.

Concern was rising at the US Liaison Office, effectively the American embassy, in Miramar. The United States said it was planning to evacuate non-essential personnel if it did not receive guarantees of foreigners' security by 3 p.m.

By this time Dr Ndondo, the Zimbabwean ambassador, had reached his home in Miramar from the airport. The drive, which normally takes fifteen minutes, had taken him three hours because he was stopped constantly at roadblocks. He sat down to lunch and for reasons of safety was planning to move to the Le Presidente hotel later that afternoon. He was alone except for his cook and his guard.

At about 1 p.m. several government police officers attempted to detain UNITA's General Renato Mateus near the airport. Many observers pinpointed this moment as the beginning of the battle for Luanda. As Abel Chivukuvuku remembered it, 'I would not say he was arrested, but some of the police entered his car and said, "Let's go to the provincial police headquarters," close to the Hotel Turismo. He was driving and the police were in the back seat. He didn't say anything to the police officers but, when he arrived near the Turismo, instead of going to the police headquarters he turned to the Turismo and got out. Then the police started firing and the soldiers in the Turismo fired back. Those were the first shots.'

Heavy gunfire exploded around the Hotel Turismo as General Carneiro and Ben Ben of UNITA came down from their offices on the second floor of the CCPM building at 1.50 p.m. Ben Ben left after agreeing to resume the meeting at 4 o'clock.

Fighting quickly spread to the outskirts of the city and heavy explosions could be heard all over town, including in the southern area near the Futungo de Belas presidential palace. At 3 o'clock national television went off the air after UNITA saboteurs dynamited the main broadcasting tower in Miramar. Rádio Nacional announced that UNITA soldiers had tried and failed to capture police headquarters near the Hotel Turismo. Civilians were advised to avoid the area.

A government helicopter flew over the Miramar area for the first time at 3.10 p.m. Heavy shooting started at the Hotel Trópico on the Avenida do Comandante Valódia where a number of senior UNITA officials were staying. UNITA soldiers, reverting to their hostage-taking ways, began rounding up any foreigners they could find in the Miramar area.

At 3.35 p.m. General Carneiro returned to the CCPM for the meeting he had scheduled with Ben Ben. This was as clear an indication as I could find that at least some elements within the government were not intent on liquidating UNITA, as Savimbi would later charge. If they had been, would General Carneiro, one of the MPLA's top military men, have returned for negotiations with Ben Ben?

After Ben Ben failed to turn up, General Carneiro telephoned General Ndalu who reported that he had spoken to a hysterical Salupeto Pena who was threatening to take foreigners hostage. 'I have five ambassadors,' Salupeto Pena screamed into the walkie-talkie. 'Go ahead and shoot us.'

Over at the CCPM office the police guarding the building were standing in the street. A UNITA soldier in a building up the road shot dead one of the policemen. One of his colleagues responded by firing a rocket-propelled grenade through a window of the sniper's building.

By 4.20 p.m. pro-government forces were engaged in an

all-out offensive. Three mortar shells hit the Hotel Turismo, sending up plumes of thick black smoke. Savimbi's house in Miramar, where most of the top UNITA officials, including Ben Ben, Salupeto Pena, Chitunda and Chivukuvuku, were staying, came under heavy mortar fire. Army troops, police and *fitinhas* were attacking a motel near Futungo de Belas on the edge of the Rocha Pinto *musseque* where dozens of UNITA soldiers and their families lived.

At about 5 o'clock several UNITA soldiers and a civilian arrived at Dr Ndondo's official residence and ordered him to come with them to Savimbi's house. This was for his own protection, they said. 'I knew it wasn't for my safety because the government had no reason to kill me. I was the accredited ambassador to this country. I told them I didn't want to go, but they insisted. There was nothing I could do.' He and his cook and guard were taken to Savimbi's residence, three houses away from his own. He was put alone in a room on the second floor. 'The house was shaking badly from the explosions. I think there were shells from 120 mm mortars falling all around.' No one said anything to him. An unarmed guard stood outside his door.

Also taken by UNITA troops at this time were two Bulgarian embassy employees and David Chambers, a Briton working for Hull-Blythe, and his Bulgarian-born wife Eleonora. Chambers said they were abducted at gun-point from the Swedish ambassador's residence in Miramar.

At 5.30 p.m. the Hotel Turismo was still on fire and there was heaving fighting in Miramar. The personnel at the US Liaison Office went into hiding in the laundry room and under the main office building. Mortars continued to pound the Miramar area and there was heavy shooting around the Sagrada Família church near Rádio Nacional.

Chivukuvuku recalled heated conversations at the time between Salupeto Pena and Ndalu on walkie-talkies. 'Salupeto was agitated and he was drinking a little bit. Ndalu was saying, "You're doing things," and Salupeto was saying, "You're the one who's attacking! I'm monitoring your orders and I don't understand what you're doing. How can we solve this? You're the one who must tell everyone to stop. I'm just defending myself." '

Later that evening UNITA troops attempted to take the American diplomats hostage. They scaled the wall of the US compound and demanded that the Americans follow them to Savimbi's house. They threatened to break down the door of the laundry room where several of the diplomats were hiding. The soldiers said that the Americans would be safer in Savimbi's house.

By this time the US military command at Stuttgart had been alerted to the potential hostage situation and began preparations for a commando operation to extract the Americans. Cohen, the US Assistant Secretary of State for African Affairs, telephoned Savimbi's house in Miramar.

'We were in the basement,' Chivukuvuku said. 'Bombs were falling, and the military officers were really nervous. Someone called us and said that Cohen was on the line and wanted to speak to Salupeto. This was at about 10 p.m. But I saw how Salupeto was. He was really nervous and he couldn't really have a positive conversation. Instead of calling Salupeto to the line, I called Chitunda, but Cohen wanted Salupeto. At that moment I understood that Cohen was worried about the possibility of foreigners being held – that's why he wanted to speak to Salupeto and not to Chitunda. He said, "I can negotiate a safe passage." Chitunda said, "No, it's not a question of having a safe passage – the question is really to help stop the fighting." Cohen insisted. Chitunda said, "Call everyone, call Futungo [the presidential palace] to help us stop this." Cohen said, "I'll call later, but I want to speak to Salupeto."

'Half an hour later Cohen called again. This time he insisted on speaking to Salupeto. I said, "Chitunda, you're the one who must speak to Cohen, not Salupeto – he's very nervous, he's out of control." But this time Salupeto went to the phone and they started having a discussion. Salupeto was telling Cohen that, "You're also responsible for this because you're the ones who really played into the hands of the MPLA." Cohen said "OK, keep cool, we'll try to do something, I'm trying to call Futungo but they're not answering." ... He was warning Salupeto not to harm foreigners.'

Chitunda later recalled the incident in his diary, which government supporters found when they overran Savimbi's house.

'Cohen is calling insistently,' he wrote, 'to warn us of the negative consequences of UNITA capturing Americans in

Miramar. The US government can be of more help if the Americans are left where they are and not touched by UNITA ... And already there is a Briton, together with Bulgarians and Zimbabweans, who were taken from their diplomatic residences to Miramar in the hope that with foreigners/diplomats here, the government would hesitate from bombarding and leaving us to die with them. But the government might think differently, and in the process we would be even more badly burnt internationally.'

Fighting resumed early on Sunday morning when intense shooting and explosions could be heard around the airport. At 6.30 a.m. a US diplomat announced on a private radio channel that UNITA was prepared to open talks to end the fighting. Blasts and gunfire swirled around the United Nations building in the city centre. Just before 7 o'clock Margaret Anstee, still at the British embassy, called Portuguese ambassador Monteiro to report that the International Committee of the Red Cross had received a message from UNITA's police chief, Brigadier Madaleno Tadeu Chipa inside the besieged Hotel Turismo. He asked for help in evacuating dozens of seriously wounded and 36 women trapped inside the building. Monteiro said that the government had agreed to stop the fighting, as had UNITA, but that it needed time to contact its leaders.

Minutes later police de-activated a bomb inside the Adventist Church in Luanda. The device was timed to go off when the church would normally have been full of worshippers.

Heavy fighting erupted three hours later around the UNITA headquarters in São Paulo, and there were clashes near the cemetery in Miramar. Groups of *militias populares* were seen heading down the road from the cemetery towards the Kinaxixe plaza. A UN security official announced on the radio that it was no longer safe for UNAVEM vehicles to be on the road because the *milícias populares* believed UN cars were transporting UNITA personnel.

Margaret Anstee spoke on the radio channel at 8.15 a.m. the next day, saying that she was finding it difficult to negotiate a truce. At that very moment six shells landed in the Alvalade area and heavy explosions continued there for the next hour. The bodies of dozens of UNITA soldiers were lying in the streets of Alvalade.

At 9.35 a.m. seven UNITA soldiers arrived at the gates of

the US Liaison Office threatening to invade the compound and take hostages if the bombing of UNITA positions continued. A guard at the compound reported that the UNITA soldiers 'were lost'. They suspected that someone in the compound was in contact with the MPLA forces and was urging them to bomb UNITA. The guard was ordered to tell the UNITA soldiers that all the Americans had gone to the Le President hotel.

At 10 a.m. American officials at the US compound advised the seven UNITA soldiers by radio not to violate diplomatic territory. 'Savimbi and [US President] Bush will not like it,' one US official was heard to say.

At about this time two UNITA generals, Adriano Makevala Mackenzie and Zacarias Mundombe, contacted the government authorities to say they wanted no part of what was going on. In effect, they surrendered.

'The tanks were closing in on Miramar,' Chivukuvuku recalled. 'At that time Salupeto was ordering people to try to flee from where they were and go to private houses to see if they could find somewhere to hide.

'He called Chitunda and me and said he thought things were very serious. His view was that by midday we might be killed. They would close in with tanks. His decision was that we should try to leave. It was the only way, rather than waiting to be killed. "How can we leave?" I asked. "It's impossible. I would prefer to go to the embassies." "If you feel that's best, let's go to the embassies," he said, "But how will we do so?"

'He said, "You go with Chitunda and try to get to one embassy. Ben Ben and I will go to another embassy." Then I understood that he wanted to get rid of us. He didn't believe in the idea of going to embassies. Chitunda and I left. We tried to go to the residence of the Nigerian ambassador but there was no one there. Then the Italian embassy. There were already tanks there so we couldn't go further. We went towards the US compound. "Let's go to the US compound," I said. "No, I can't go there," he replied. He thought it would be humiliating for him to go to the US compound.

'We jumped over some walls and arrived in what I thought was the house of the French ambassador, but later I realised it was the Chevron house. We knocked but everything was closed. We found a small room at the back. It was about 11 a.m. We started talking. Chitunda asked me if I had ever been in such a difficult situation. "No," I said. "Before when I've been in trouble I've more or less known how to get out of it." But this situation was hopeless. Then he started writing. I looked around the room and found some beer. We drank a beer and slept a little bit. The fighting continued.'

At midday Rádio Nacional announced that the situation was under control but warned the public to stay indoors. At 12.35 p.m. Ben Ben arrived at the gates of the US compound saying that the government was bombing UNITA positions throughout Luanda and that the United States should ask them to stop. US officials reported that British ambassador Flynn was in contact with General Carneiro and Savimbi. Ben Ben said he wanted to talk with General Carneiro and asked for his telephone number. Salupeto Pena spoke to the US compound on the radio: 'See what you can do. They're bombarding us ... they want to expel us from Angola.'

'Engineer, we're working on it,' replied a US official known as Mohawk. 'Ben Ben will talk to Higino [Carneiro] and Savimbi to the ambassador. I hope we can drink a glass of champagne soon as this country needs peace.'

'Yes, this great country is going down and it should go up,' Salupeto Pena replied.

'No,' said Mohawk, 'we're doing all we can. That's why we are here.'

'OK,' said Salupeto Pena.

At 1 p.m. Ben Ben called General Carneiro and began discussing how to implement a ceasefire. Before ringing off Carneiro said he would get back to him. For the next several hours he tried to call Ben Ben but could not get through.

By 4 p.m. the shooting and mortar explosions were dying down. UNITA now occupied the whole Miramar area, though government forces were nearby. The US Strategic Command in Stuttgart stepped up preparations to send American commandos into Angola to extract the diplomats from the US compound. At least two operatives boarded a plane to Brazzaville to begin organising the operation.

'At 5 p.m. I listened to the news on Radio France Internationale,' said Chivukuvuku. 'It reported that Salupeto and I were dead. If they are already saying that I was dead, it meant that I could die. It was serious. By 6.30 p.m., after starting to listen to the Voice of America, I heard footsteps. We were worried. I tried to look through the door. Chitunda went into the bathroom. I realised they were Chitunda's bodyguards looking for us. I asked them what was going on. By then our radio batteries had faded.

'They said, "Salupeto and Ben Ben have gone. They've left and by now they must be arriving in Caxito. We've come to pick you up so that we can leave also." Chitunda decided that we should go. We jumped over the walls again until we arrived at Dr Savimbi's house. Everything was chaotic. Brigadier Katopesse, the top military official there, was confident that Salupeto had arrived in Caxito. Then he said to us, "Chivukuvuku and Chitunda, I'll put you in the picture. The situation is really terrible. You have three alternatives. If you feel that you were safe where you were, you can decide to stay there. That's option one. Option two: if you want to follow Salupeto and Ben Ben, fine. We have the cars here, I'll give you an escort and you can leave. It's dangerous but it's your decision. If you want to go on foot with me, that's option three. So, those are your three alternatives – just decide." '

At about the same time the guard at Savimbi's residence approached Dr Ndondo, the Zimbabwean ambassador who was being held hostage 'for his own safety'. 'They said I had to come downstairs because it was too dangerous to stay on the second floor. It was clear that this was a big lie. They wanted me downstairs so they could pack up their belongings. Then they came to me and said, "You can go." Just like that. I could see a couple of whites [the Chambers] through the door. The white captives were found to be useful. I think they were being brought to Salupeto Pena who was preparing to leave. By the time I went back upstairs to get my things, everyone had disappeared.'

When Dr Ndondo returned to the entrance of the house, Salupeto Pena and Ben Ben had taken Chambers and his wife Eleonora and fled. He asked some UNITA soldiers to escort him, his cook, his guard and another guard from the Swedish embassy back to his house. They refused. 'That was the first time I was really frightened, because I knew that government tanks were surrounding Miramar. When the government force came I knew that they wouldn't ask questions about who we were, they would just shoot. I said to myself, this is serious. We made our way to the maternity hospital and spent the night there.'

Two years later Abel Chivukuvuku, the UNITA foreign minister before his capture during the battle for Luanda, recalled that moment during an interview in the Hotel Tivoli in central Luanda where he was being held by the government under a loose detention order.

> Chitunda said we should leave by car. 'That's impossible, Chitunda,' I replied. 'How can we leave by car? We'll be killed. Let's go back where we've just been and see what to do.' 'No,' he said, 'you go back if you want, but I'm leaving by car.' I went back to my house and got a bullet-proof vest that my wife had bought for me in New York. I had never used it before, but I put it on that day.
>
> I came back and told Chitunda, 'OK, I'm coming with you, but we're going to die.' We got into Chitunda's car. The driver and one of Chitunda's bodyguards were in the front; Chitunda, myself and another bodyguard were in the back. There were cars with bodyguards behind and in front of us. We drove out of the compound and to the road going to Roque Santeiro and Caxito. The firing started as we reached the road. It was horrible. The shooting came from all around us. I couldn't think – instinct took over. The driver had the car's lights off, but there were barriers in the street so he turned the lights on because we were bumping into them. This made it worse because then our attackers could see their target. At one point my leg felt very, very cold. I didn't understand what was going on, but I had been shot. The driver kept on going when suddenly I felt that the car was out of control. The driver had been killed. The car went off the road and struck a house.
>
> I turned to ask Chitunda what we should do. He was leaning forward and not moving. I could see that something had happened to him. I was not sure if he had died or was wounded, but he wasn't moving. I decided to jump out of the car because it was still being hit by gunfire. When I tried to stand up I realised that my legs were broken. I had been shot in both legs. I crawled along the ground until I got to a house where I found a family lying on the floor. 'Please,' I told them, 'I am Chivukuvuku, I am very badly

wounded and I want to hide in here.' 'Fine, our son,' they said, 'just stay here'. Outside the fighting continued and then I realised that one of Chitunda's bodyguards had followed me. A few minutes later he took out his pistol and I shouted, 'Hey don't do that!', but he shot himself in the head. I couldn't understand why he did that – maybe he was wounded, maybe he was thinking that he would be taken prisoner.

The shot warned our attackers that someone military was in the building. Then the *poder popular* people began to close in. The owners fled and I was left alone in the house. I decided to go to one of the bedrooms where I lay under the bed. Then I heard someone say, 'They're here, they're here, shoot them!' I took the bullet-proof jacket off and then my shirt, which I tried to tie round my legs. I had no feelings at that point, I was really out of my mind. I couldn't even follow what they were saying.

Then I heard someone shout, 'Let's burn the house!' Another voice said, 'I'm going to fetch petrol.' 'No, no,' I said to myself, 'I can't allow myself to be burned alive.' I realised that I would have to negotiate with these people, but how was I going to speak to them? I listened to hear someone who sounded responsible. I heard a name, João Mulato, and decided to call out to him. 'João Mulato,' I said, 'this is Chivukuvuku, I want to talk to you. Come here.'

'No, no,' he said, 'it's a bandit.'

'Cool down, João Mulato,' I replied, 'cool down. I am Chivukuvuku, an unarmed civilian. Let me talk to you.'

'No, no. First I have to see if you're really unarmed. Stand up and I'll look through the door.'

'I can't stand up, I'm wounded. Please just come in.'

'No, it's up to you,' he said, 'if you can't stand up we'll burn the house down – the choice is yours.'

'Fine,' I said, 'wait a moment, just cool down. I'll make an effort and come back to the living room. I'll stand up there and you'll see that I'm unarmed.' I made a great effort. I came back to the living room saying to myself, 'Well Chivukuvuku, just stand up on whatever is left of your legs if you want to save your life.' I made an enormous effort to pull myself up at the wall. 'OK,' I said, 'look at me.'

Then they said, 'We're coming, we're coming.' They crashed through the door and about eight of them came in.

They searched me and saw that I was unarmed. Some of them started beating me and others were demanding money. 'Where are the dollars? We want the dollars,' they shouted.

'I haven't any dollars,' I said, 'look at what's in my pockets. That's all I have – and no dollars.' The group was split. Some of them wanted to kill me, but because of the dark the others still weren't sure who I was. They said, 'If he is Chivukuvuku then we won't kill him, but if it's someone else we'll kill him.' Then they brought in a lamp and saw that it really was me. 'How could this happen, Chivukuvuku?' they said, 'you're a nice person. It's all so sad.' Some of the younger ones were saying, 'No, the girls like Chivukuvuku a lot, we've got to kill him.' But there were some responsible ones, like João Mulato, who said, 'No we can't kill him. Let's take him prisoner.'

So they took me away. Some were still beating me in the back. We walked a little bit but I was bleeding and said, 'I'm tired, please let me rest.' They allowed me to rest. The ones who wanted to kill me started pushing me into the street while the others started firing into the air and began to run away. Then someone arrived who looked really horrible. He was drunk or on drugs, he was armed and also carrying knives. He started shouting at everyone and said that he was a cousin of mine and wouldn't put up with what they were doing to me. If I died, he would kill whoever was responsible. I had never seen him before. From that moment on I had no more problems.

Then I was taken to police headquarters in Sambizanga. I was put in a room with one officer inside and another who stayed outside. They both had radios. The one inside had the key to the door. Because they were afraid that someone would come and harm me they agreed that the one inside would not open the door unless he received proper instructions. Then he informed someone, I suppose it was General João de Matos, that I was there, and he got instructions that someone would be coming to take me. They would send tanks to take me to the hospital. Then we heard the police sirens outside.

The officer outside said that the police had arrived to fetch me but the one inside said, 'First let me ask a senior officer if these really are the people who were sent to take

Chivukuvuku.' The report came back that they had sent tanks and a general, not the police. So the young officer inside said that he would not open up because these were not the people who had been sent officially. We heard some shooting and then the cars left.

The officer said, 'You see, if I had handed you over to those people they would have taken you off and killed you. Maybe they intercepted our radio communications and know you're here.' Later on, around midnight, the tanks arrived. The one outside radioed and said that the tanks had come. He opened the door. General Faísca, who knew me, was there. We greeted one another. 'This is all very unfortunate,' he said, 'how come we're fighting each other like this? I've come to take you to hospital on orders from João de Matos.' He spoke to the young officer and said that he was going to take me away. The young officer said, 'I was told that a general was coming and that tanks would arrive, but first let me radio to let them know you've arrived and so they can give me orders to hand Chivukuvuku over to you.' The general felt that he had been insulted by a young officer and they spent half an hour arguing. Finally, I said, 'Faísca, you're a friend of mine and you can see that I'm wounded. Please, just let him call so that I can leave this place.' The young officer called and then said, 'Yes, you can take him.'

Faísca took me to the tank and we drove to the hospital. A colonel who had been sent by João de Matos was waiting there to arrange everything. The doctors were also waiting for me. That night I had my first operation.

By then army tanks were in position for an early morning operation to extract the foreigners, especially those in the American compound, from Miramar. In Stuttgart the Americans had decided to suspend plans for a commando operation.

At 6.30 a.m. on 2 November the tanks began moving into Miramar. Thirty minutes later Rádio Nacional announced that the government had regained control of Luanda airport and the cities of Lubango and Huambo. At 7.50 a.m. Margaret Anstee reported that a ceasefire was supposed to have started at midnight, but she knew that it could not take effect because of severe communication problems.

At 8.25 a.m. Portuguese and Brazilian Hercules planes were circling the airport to evacuate Portuguese nationals. Shooting broke out at the airport an hour later. Looters entered Savimbi's residence in Miramar at 10.30 a.m. and a few minutes later the Hotel Trópico was surrounded and evacuation of the wounded began. UN officials making their way to the airport reported seeing dozens of bodies on the road.

By late morning General Carneiro arrived at the British embassy in an armoured car to pick up Margaret Anstee so that she could fly back to UNAVEM headquarters in a helicopter. General Isidro Wambu of UNITA and José Pedro of the government toured the city to calm down the fighting.

The 1 p.m. news on Rádio Nacional reported that there had been shooting in Benguela until midday. Huambo and Lubango were reported calm with both sides involved in negotiations. 'There are still tensions, pockets of desperate UNITA soldiers shooting at random. People should stay at home; the people should consider UNITA people as human beings who should be respected. No one should take justice into their own hands,' the radio announced.

In the early afternoon looters were roaming Miramar, sacking the Texaco house and nearby diplomatic residences. Shortly afterwards police began patrolling the streets telling people that the situation was under control and asking them to stop shooting. The three tanks in Miramar pulled back and headed for First of May plaza.

At 8 p.m. Rádio Nacional announced that the public should keep out of embassy grounds. No one should hurt foreign diplomats or damage their property, it said. 'The Angolan people should, as usual, be generous but firm and help respect foreign property.'

The next morning, on 3 November, Rádio Nacional reported that Luanda was calm. Police had the situation under control. Some UNITA generals were in custody and were negotiating with the authorities, it said. A 7 p.m. to 6 a.m. curfew was imposed for three days. The radio quoted a call by US Assistant Secretary of State Cohen for the urgent formation of a government and the holding of run-off elections. By 8 a.m. private cars and civilians began circulating on the streets. Later that morning Rádio Nacional called for a halt to looting and ordered all government forces back to their quarters. The battle was over, but the

Angolan civil war was just starting again.

Five days later Margaret Anstee and Western diplomats are still desperately seeking to negotiate a nationwide truce. UNITA has continued its drive to occupy the countryside. UNAVEM reports confirm that UNITA has captured 57 of Angola's 164 municipalities, and it is apparently in effective control of another 40. A confidential map produced by the Defence Ministry shows well over half of the country in UNITA's hands. UNITA troops force UNAVEM observers out of the Cafunfo diamond-producing areas and the hydroelectric complex at Capanda on the River Congo. They take 70 Brazilians and Russians hostage.

UNITA had pushed to within 35 miles of the capital by capturing the town of Caxito, the capital of Bengo province, and then moved a step closer by taking Porto Quipiri.

On 8 November I join three carloads of journalists heading north out of Luanda on the questionable mission of visiting the UNITA forces in Porto Quipiri. It is a trip which several of my television colleagues will come to regret.

When we reach the last government checkpoint on the bridge over the River Bengo at Cacuaco, I, as the driver of the lead car, climb out to tell the local army commander what we are planning to do. 'You want to visit UNITA?' he asks in disbelief. 'Well, we won't stop you, but I can't guarantee your safety. I warn you – those guys are crazy.'

Fifteen minutes later we descend the rolling hills which lead into Porto Quipiri, a deserted sugar-producing town situated on the River Dande. As we slow down at the entrance to the town, a dozen UNITA soldiers stand dumbfounded for a moment and then begin running across the bridge over the Dande which they had blocked by positioning two giant earthmovers and piles of torn-up chunks of the tarmac.

We emerge from our vehicles with our hands in the air holding our little white press cards to show we have no weapons. The soldiers immediately regain their composure, draw a couple of pistols and approach us, angry at first that we had not informed them of our arrival. There was really no way to get in touch with them, we explain. They make a surprising comment. They had been expecting us yesterday. 'You're the United Nations, right?' asks a young man who appears to be in authority. Well, no, in fact we are a group of journalists. Their faces fall in disappointment. A visit by UN officials could bring a modicum of respect, we can see them thinking, but journalists are merely a nuisance.

The soldiers motion us over to sit on the side of the road under the shade of some trees. They dispatch one of their number off to their base somewhere to the north of the city with our request to interview someone in authority. They say we should wait. No filming, no pictures, no interviews until the commander gives the word.

As the minutes tick by the mood of our hosts deteriorates markedly. UNITA soldiers like clear-cut orders, and when there aren't any their nerves fray rapidly. They become particularly agitated when a Portuguese TV crew starts to film a UNITA soldier eating from a tin plate. We are trying to portray UNITA in a primitive light, they claim. The cameraman is an irritatingly arrogant man wearing a red bandanna and a camouflage flak jacket whom we instantly nickname Rambo. Despite the restriction on filming, Rambo carries on, secretly he thinks, but everyone knows what he is doing. He keeps starting arguments and the soldiers' mood continues to sour.

About two hours after our arrival, the soldier sent off to find the commander returns with fresh orders. 'You can return to Luanda, but all the cameras must remain behind.' Not surprisingly, the three television crews, including a Brazilian team which had come straight from the airport, debate the issue strenuously, but theirs is a lost cause. Surely they can leave their film behind and take the cameras, we protest, but the commander has said that everything is to remain behind. Orders from headquarters. A crowd of soldiers raise their weapons to stress the point. Rambo is going ballistic, shouting that the camera is his personal property and it cost many thousands of dollars. He is not helping his case. UNITA soldiers rarely disobey orders, and telling them how much his camera is worth does not seem the best of strategies.

After some final futile pleading we return to our cars, leaving UNITA in possession of $200,000 in television and camera equipment, almost enough to start their own television production company. When we reach the government checkpoint at the River Bengo, the local commander chuckles as he listens to the woeful tale and says, 'I told you they were crazy.'

By this time, rumours are rife about a killing spree of alleged UNITA supporters under way in the *musseque* shanty-towns surrounding Luanda. The government radio is saying that the *ninja* police throughout the country are involved in mopping up operations against UNITA soldiers. The name given to this exercise is *limpeza*, or cleansing, and it is also known as a *caça homen* or man-hunt.

Diplomats speak of an estimated 40 killings a day, but no one knows for sure. So I find an Angolan who can translate from Umbundu into Portuguese and together with a British colleague drive out to the Kikolo *musseque* on the northern edge of the city where there are many Ovimbundu migrants from UNITA's *planalto* stronghold.

The central open-air marketplace is tense, with dozens of families living on the ground next to the homes of people they know. Groups of women and children are lying around in a pitiful state, with meagre piles of belongings by their sides. After wandering around for a few minutes, we find a young man who is prepared to tell us what has been happening. We can call him Jorge, but he will not give us his full name.

Jorge is 24 years old and moved to Luanda from Bié province as a teenager. He is a teacher by profession and was an election worker at the local polling station. Since 31 October five of his friends have been dragged from their homes at night and murdered, he says.

'Every night we lock ourselves in our homes and hope that no one comes looking for us. After dark cars and trucks arrive with armed men, some in civilian clothes but others in police uniforms. We know when they've arrived because they shoot into the air to frighten everyone. Then they go from door to door hunting their victims. Usually they have someone from the neighbourhood, a spy, to tell them who is an Umbundu. When they find someone from the south, they break down their doors and rob them. Sometimes they kill them. There is a lot of settling of accounts going on. And the people the government gave arms to are using them to steal. They have a perfect excuse now. What is going on here is tribal rivalry. Anyone from the southern part of the country is suspected of being a UNITA supporter. If you're Ovimbundu, you're UNITA.'

They came for Jorge one afternoon. 'Some *ninjas* and *fitinhas* came to my house and said I had to go with them. They took me to the local police station. They were saying that I was a UNITA supporter and I knew they were going to kill me. There were other people inside who were screaming because they were being beaten. The only thing that saved me was a piece of paper I had proving that I had worked at a polling station during the elections.'

Jorge says it is dangerous for him to be seen speaking to foreigners, so he soon asks us to leave. Perhaps we should visit the São Pedro da Bara *musseque*, which is about a mile away overlooking the sea. He hears there have been many disappearances there too.

São Pedro da Bara is filled with the same depressing atmosphere. A school in the neighbourhood has been burnt out, and pro-MPLA slogans are scribbled on its walls. A couple of young toughs stand by eyeing us suspiciously and ask our translator what we are doing there. Visiting his family, he says.

We wander around the dusty alleyways for a few minutes, buying a couple of Cokes from some young girls and chatting amiably in the hope that the young men will become bored with us. Then we ask if there is anyone who has been having problems. An old man shakes hands and exchanges pleasantries before inviting us back to his hut. He has watched several of his neighbours being dragged from their homes down the dirt road at night on their way to the Fortaleza prison on top of the hill about a mile away. 'Many of us want to go back home to the south but the police at the checkpoints won't let us leave,' he says. 'We're trapped.'

The old man suggests we visit his friend Arlindo a few houses away. He too has a story to tell. When we enter his one-room brick house, Arlindo is in his underwear lying on a thin, dirty mattress on the floor. His left foot is covered in bloody bandages. Arlindo, the father of two girls, is originally from Huambo but came to Luanda ten years ago looking for work. In the afternoon of 2 November, while the fighting was winding down, he went to his niece's house to see if everyone was all right. The police stopped him in the road. 'Take off your shoes,' they said. Then one of the policemen pulled out his pistol and shot him in the foot.

'They do that so you can't run away. They said I had to walk with them to Fortaleza, but in a way I was lucky. Because my foot was hurting so much I had to walk very slowly. Someone told my niece what had happened and she came running after me. She knew some of the police and was able to convince them that I wasn't a UNITA supporter. They let me go.'

As Arlindo is relating his story, a boy of four and a girl of seven arrive at the house. They have been staying with him for the past week since their father, António Luís Bongo, a building worker from Huambo, was taken away by the police. He has not been seen since.

Another Umbundu man limps into the house. He too has been shot in the foot by the police but escaped arrest. He is worried. The day before he was involved in an argument at a bar with a fisherman who is a local MPLA activist. 'We were arguing and then he told me, "Your mouth is going to condemn you. We've already buried seven and you are going to be the eighth." '

If these stories are true, there must be corpses. There are said to be graves of UNITA supporters, especially around the slopes cascading down from the Miramar suburb, but we have not been able to locate any. Several of the people we interview in the *musseques* say they have heard of UNITA activists being murdered at the Camama cemetery on the southern outskirts of Luanda, just a few miles from UNAVEM's main complex.

From the outside the Camama cemetery looks quite ordinary. It is a huge rectangular space surrounded by a five-foot high cement wall. When we reach the graveyard it is nearly deserted. Inside we can see a handful of mourners in the distance walking among rows and rows of tombs. We call in at the office by the main gate and speak briefly to the cemetery director, asking for permission to look around. He suggests that we find one of the gravediggers to take us on a tour.

As we are milling around the director's office wondering where to begin, two men put down their tools and begin to make their way towards us. On their heads they wear plastic goggles and masks hang around their necks.

They start speaking to us in what at first seems to be an

incomprehensible language. My British colleague, Sam Kiley of the *Times*, asks me several times to translate, but I say I am still trying to comprehend the gibberish coming out of their mouths. After a few minutes I realise that they are in fact speaking Portuguese but in a very incoherent form, beginning sentences in the middle of previous ones, arguing among themselves. They seem hopelessly drunk.

I am beginning to understand Armando, the taller one, while I write off verbal contact with his more rambling partner, Elías, who repeatedly looks to the skies as he babbles on. Not only are they intoxicated, they appear to be stark raving mad. After they tell us their story, however, I cannot blame them, and end up feeling that they are among the sanest people I have met in Angola.

'Come this way, hurry, hurry, you must see this,' Armando's mate Elías keeps yelling at us, urging us ever faster towards the west wall of the cemetery. 'Don't listen to him,' says Armando, 'I'll show you everything that happened here.'

We stride along the path towards our still unknown destination about 100 yards away. I detect movement, a scurrying among the graves we pass. Closer inspection reveals small tunnels the width of a beer can. There are tiny passageways everywhere among the tombs – rats are burrowing into the graves.

Armando and Elías lead us to an isolated spot next to a mound marking a grave just beside the wall. A piece of a UNITA flag is lying on top of the tomb and a stick is protruding from the earth. The smell of rotting flesh is powerful, but comes only in waves, somewhat mellowed by a strong breeze. 'They brought two women and two men here and shot them right there,' says Armando. 'They were standing against the wall and they shot them.' Who shot them? I ask. 'The police.' There is no doubt that this has been the scene of an execution. We count over 30 bullet holes in the wall.

Elías is still babbling away about how he can tell us anything we want to know about the graveyard, or at least that is what I understand him to say. I turn around for a final look at the grave. Only then do I realise that what I took to be a stick jutting out of the top of the mound is, in fact, a human leg. Someone planted it like some form of perverse cross.

'Come on,' says Elías, 'there's more, much more to see.' I stand frozen to the spot, now babbling to myself, asking the others if they have seen the leg. It is a silly question. How could they have missed it? Perhaps my eyes saw the leg at first, but my brain has been fighting to ignore or to redefine it.

We walk to the eastern side of the cemetery, with Armando telling us how Elías and he have buried a number of people who were executed by the front gates. 'We watched one morning as riot police drove up in two trucks, threw seven tied-up people out of the back and just shot them here in the cemetery.' Over on the right there are three dead men and up there on the left are a couple more women. 'Those bodies were in really bad shape, remember Elías?' 'Oh yeah, that one woman, remember? She didn't have a face.' Now I am on their wavelength, understanding every word they say as if they speak the purest Portuguese imaginable.

They lead us through a giant hole in the eastern wall towards a freshly bulldozed patch of earth. Another human leg marks the spot where four more people fell to the police guns. AK-47 cartridges lay all around two separate shallow graves about 20 yards apart.

As we walk back to our car Armando points out the little building where he and Elías sat watching the killings. It is where they normally eat lunch and take their breaks. He appears to have something on his conscience. 'Elías and I are war veterans. We were FAPLA [MPLA] soldiers, and we fought all over the country. We didn't want to fight in the war but when we signed on for our compulsory military service we thought we were fighting for the fatherland. After we were demobilised they gave us this job. But what we've seen here has made our minds confused. I feel sick by what we have seen. My mind isn't right any more.'

It is then that Armando reveals there is more to see. 'There's a much bigger grave, but we have to take the car.' I feel I have had enough for the day and want to return to Luanda and have several stiff drinks. But Armando is insistent, and if he is willing to relive the horror that is troubling his mind, I cannot duck the responsibility of seeing it too. It is the least I can do. Perhaps the tour he is taking us on is a form of catharsis.

Armando and Elías direct us down a sandy road and tell us

to take a left-hand turn. Five hundred yards away there is a huge pit flanked on either side by mounds of earth. Again empty rifle cartridges litter the ground, and dozens of torn military uniforms are scattered amongst soiled UNITA election campaign hats. 'The police brought many people here, maybe 30, shot them and buried their bodies. They brought a big bulldozer to cover them with earth. You can see the tracks.' Vomit swells in my throat. On the higher ground behind the pit there are bootprints and thick circular pools of what looks like a mixture of blood and human excrement. Afterwards the corpses were pushed forward into the depression below and the bulldozers were brought in to erase their memory forever. The turned up soil is covered in black blotches of dried blood. The overwhelmingly powerful stench confirms the presence of human remains below.

As we enter our car and drive away, neither Kiley nor I speak for a few minutes. Both of us have seen corpses before, massacres being an increasingly routine part of the job for reporters in Africa, but one never gets used to it.

After a while the images of blood and legs and rats begin to fade, and I am left with the deep impression of how courageous Armando and Elías were. They knew the risks they were running. They had seen what the police were capable of but they were determined to tell someone about what had happened. I returned to Luanda and duly filed my story to the *Independent* and *Washington Post*. My editors were pleased with the scoop and news of the graves was broadcast on the BBC.

Within 24 hours everyone in Angola and listeners around the world hear the news that foreign journalists have found a mass grave in Angola and proved beyond all doubt that the government's security forces were responsible for summary executions. Yet our role in the affair has been the easiest part. Two Angolan gravediggers, their minds bent out of shape by witnessing the atrocities, showed the real courage and were sufficiently brave and outraged to demand that the truth be known.

The evening after the news breaks I receive a telephone call from a man who says he works for the Defence Ministry. 'Are you *Senhor* Karl Maier?' he asks. Yes. 'I am calling about your story on the graves at Camama cemetery.' Yes. 'Can I ask how you received information for this story?' I explain that I had visited the cemetery and had seen the graves. 'But these bodies you saw were the ones we cleaned up from the streets of Luanda to stop possible epidemics, is that not right?' Well, no, in fact I found bullet holes in the walls and spent rifle cartridges all over the ground. Witnesses say the people were shot there. 'Are you sure about that?' he asks in an increasingly aggressive tone. Yes, quite sure. 'Do you have more information which you plan to write about?' he asks. At this point I like neither his tone nor the direction this conversation is taking. May I ask your name, *Senhor*? There is a pause. 'You can call me Bravo,' he says. You work at the Defence Ministry? Another pause. 'Yes.' Well, can you give me your telephone number? 'Well we're checking into your information and I'll call you if there are any additional questions,' he says. 'Good night.'

For the first time in Angola, I am truly frightened. The streets are full of police, probably many of the same ones who had executed people during the battles in Luanda because they were allegedly UNITA supporters, or simply came from the wrong part of the country and spoke the wrong language. The following morning I contact a Portuguese cameraman and a British correspondent of a rival newspaper to the *Independent* and guide them out to Camama so that others will publish the story. I do so for selfish reasons, hoping that if more reporters cover the story, Bravo and his employers will take less note of me. Armando repeats his tour of the day before. We find Elías near the cemetery gates. He is face-down, asleep in a stupor.

9 A Shout to the Heavens

The battle for Luanda ignited a wave of urban clashes and massacres of unarmed civilians that continued for the next three months and saw UNITA crushed in key cities such as Benguela, Malange and Lubango. So horrific did the *limpeza* campaign become that even two years later a Canadian doctor working in the Lubango central hospital refused to speak on the record. He recalled watching government soldiers enter a UNITA building, immediately execute a teenager and then force another to lie on the ground as they emptied the magazines of four AK-47s into him. 'His body danced with death until it became like jelly,' he said.

Others were outraged enough to speak out about the human devastation left in the wake of *limpeza*. Only later did I come across a remarkable letter written by Father Adelíno Simões, a Roman Catholic priest, detailing the effects of *limpeza* in the town of Viana, a short distance inland from Luanda.

Senhor
Administrator of Viana Municipality 30 November 1992

For the record, I, Father Adílino F. Simões, the head of the Catholic Church in Viana, come with all due respect to inform your Excellency about certain crimes – heinous crimes that 'shout to the heavens' – committed in this Municipality of Viana beginning on the 30th of October.

On 1 November six men of the town council were taken from their homes and shot on the spot in the plaza at the town council. All were of Umbundu ethnicity. Reason: for being UNITA. Many know who committed the act.

Also on 1 November, at 6 p.m., in the zone of Capalanga,

three brothers were killed: Adriano Ricardo Mulenga, 24, Aurélio Ricardo Mulenga, 20, and Hilário Ricardo Mulenga, 16, of Umbundu ethnicity. They were shot in their own backyard by two policemen accompanied by armed civilians in the presence of their mother Antónia Manuel and two younger brothers. Reason: for being UNITA. Many know who committed the act.

On 2 November two more people of Umbundu ethnicity, were shot in the plaza at the town council. Reason: for being UNITA.

Also on the 2nd the old man João and two nephews, of Kikongo ethnicity, were taken from their home on Rua Hoji ya Henda near the electricity office; afterwards they were forced to put on UNITA shirts, taken near the wall of the Sisters Mercedarias de Caridade, near the church, and shot there. It is known who committed the act.

On the 3rd it was the turn of *Dona* Alice and *Dona* Madalena, well known and thought of throughout Viana, also of Umbundu ethnicity. As some people surrounded their homes at about 1 p.m. others were at the square watching the operations. They were taken and shot, they say, behind the cemetery on the road to Calumbo. Reason: for being UNITA. Many know who carried out the act.

Also killed on that day were Manuel Kaoko, the son of Adriano Chimbombe and of Domingas Nacambo, taken from his home and killed in a ditch beyond the factories by a policeman and civilians coming from the town council. Reason: for being UNITA.

António Sousa, son of António Canhanho and Emília Chicumbo, taken from a house in which he had sought refuge, dragged along the ground, pulled by a car, then taken in the car, they took him and went to search his house. He was found dead on the road that goes to the town council. Reason: for being UNITA.

Fernando Barros, resident of the town council area, of Umbundu ethnicity, was taken from his house. While he was desperately trying to prove his innocence – that he was not UNITA – he was thrown to the ground and killed with two machine-gun bursts next to the barbershop at the entrance of the town council. Friends took his body away in a wheelbarrow and buried him.

On the night of the 3rd I went to the police station to

request that measures be taken to stop the man-hunts and the sackings that were occurring. The panic among the Umbundu people of the town council was enormous; some had to sleep outside their homes. Nothing concrete happened.

On the morning of the 4th I again went to the police station to reinforce the request and make known the anguish and panic in which many lived. We saw no concrete action taken.

On the 9th I had occasion to speak with *Senhor* Administrator about what was happening. I saw your sadness and held your promise to do everything possible to 'demand responsibilities' and re-establish calm.

At four in the morning on the 11th three armed civilians took from their own homes in the Morro de Areia neighbourhood Justino Cahumba, Manuel, Firmino Matete, Inácio and José, all of Umbundu ethnicity. José was killed immediately, the others were taken and killed in the Sapu area, in a house under construction. Their bodies were found two days later.

On the 16th the man-hunt was still continuing in Capalanga. It is said that twelve people were killed in this neighbourhood.

On the 17th I was informed that the man-hunt began in Calumbo on Sunday the 15th at 3 p.m. Six people were killed – Zacarias Catulumba, Evaristo Chitengue, Laurindo, Eduardo, Cesário – and two were wounded by machetes; two bodies were thrown into the River Kwanza. All were of Umbundu ethnicity. At this moment no Umbundu can be found in the Calumbo area.

Also on the 17th we were informed that the catechist Vitorino, of Umbundu ethnicity, resident at kilometre 33 on the Catete road, was taken by armed civilians. We don't know of his whereabouts.

On the 18th I was informed that Fernando Manuel, of Umbundu ethnicity, resident in the Bita zone, was taken away in a car by the police on the morning of the 5th. We do not know of his whereabouts.

I want to still remember all those people who were 'held up' and threatened with death, all those who were beaten, all those separated from their property, all those who had to sleep away from their homes ...

Everything that occurred is a 'heinous' crime, because everything was committed in the open air, with 'protection'. Those that went around hunting the adversary were doing so triumphantly, in the plain light of day, and they remain unpunished.

Senhor Administrator, everyone knows that this is not all. This is only an indication of what happened in Viana. And Viana has been profoundly 'stained'. It is necessary to clean this 'stain'. When will justice be done?

I am not a witness in these cases. But it is easy to confirm them to the point of correcting details that are not exact. Many know who the executors were. Many know who was behind commanding everything. Many know who gave the cover.

When I, Father Adílino, the head of the Catholic Church in Viana, speak of these crimes, some think I am carrying out the politics of or defending UNITA. (On other occasions, others said I was defending the MPLA.) No. My job, as representative of God and the Church, is to state the truth, to denounce errors and to defend the oppressed. I cannot 'see' a human being with eyes of the MPLA or of UNITA. I have to see a human being with the 'eyes of God'. And the human being, created in the image of God, is sacred. No one can do him harm. No one can kill him. Who kills is evil. Whoever that might be (MPLA or UNITA). It is God who decides.

It is necessary that everyone repent the crimes committed and see, as much as possible, the evil caused to their neighbour. The hour will arrive in which we will also appear before the tribunal of Christ and each one will be judged according to the good or ill committed while living.

I know that to write all this is to run 'risks'. I have already been advised to be careful. But it has to be. The truth cannot be smothered. Crime cannot triumph.

I write this that at least for the record.

I will give copies to other authorities.

With the most respectful compliments.

Father Adílino F. Simões
San Francisco de Jesus parish
Viana

10 The Good Life

Although the United Nations and many Western diplomats still refuse to admit it, civil war has returned to Angola. If I did not believe it before, the visit to the Camama cemetery outside Luanda has convinced me. Once people start planting legs on top of graves and butchering hundreds of people because they belong to a certain political party, come from a specific region or speak a particular language, then it is time to face facts. Angola's democracy, like its independence seventeen years before, was born in blood.

UNAVEM, while remaining up-beat about the diplomatic prospects for a settlement, is voting with its feet. Of the first 203 people evacuated by the World Food Programme planes to Windhoek, 92 are UNAVEM officers and soldiers. The Angolan people know what is happening and UNAVEM is not kidding anyone but itself. Marrack Goulding, a special UN peacekeeping envoy, has flown in from New York in another attempt to negotiate peace but it has become a black comedy. When Goulding travels to Huambo, Savimbi keeps him waiting for six hours before meeting him. When he leaves the country after six days on 12 November, he issues a grossly understated assessment of the situation. 'There is not much time left. The country is in crisis and the peace process is seriously threatened.'

It is at such times that I feel like wringing the United Nations' collective neck. Peace process seriously threatened? The peace process is dead. I wonder what Armando the gravedigger would say to such nonsense.

While the MPLA and UNITA engaged in their final shoot-out in Luanda, the two sides have negotiated mini-ceasefires in much of the rest of the country and in some cases continue, albeit uneasily, to live and work side by side while plotting for the eventual day of reckoning. One of those places is the central coastal city of Benguela. I decide to make it my next destination.

By this time most of the country's roads are closed and travelling from Luanda to the provinces means, inevitably, a visit to the World Food Programme offices and a meeting with Philippe Borel and his chief logistician, David Schaad, an American born to missionary parents in the northern city of Malange who has returned to work for the international aid effort.

The World Food Programme is flying all over the country, taking food aid to cities which otherwise would be totally cut off from the outside world. So with Borel's permission I board an Antonov-12 transport plane a few days later.

Benguela is in a relatively privileged position to receive food and supplies because it is just fifteen miles south of Angola's best deep-water port, Lobito. Most of the port workers in Lobito are Ovimbundu and UNITA is particularly strong there. Benguela, once the main transit point for the slave trade and the importation of Brazilian rum which had sparked the Bailundo war at the turn of the century, has long been an MPLA stronghold with a heavy mixed-race population. In both cities fighting had broken out in early November as it had in Luanda, Malange and a number of other cities. The only difference is that when a truce was finally called, neither side had won. A tense calm, as journalists are fond of saying, reigns in the area.

The Antonov lands between the two cities at the air force base at Catumbela, a town that had sprung up at the turn of the century as a stopping point half-way between Lobito and Benguela for Ovimbundu traders from the *planalto*. Catumbela is split about 50-50 between MPLA and UNITA supporters.

I am met at the airport by the WFP base manager, a Cuban exile named Alfredo, whose drooping eyes and long hawk-like nose resting on a sagging moustache gives him a perpetual look of sadness. Alfredo is a man of very few words, but when he does open his mouth there emerges a remarkable form of Portuguese laced with a thick Cuban accent, instantly recognisable by the characteristic rapid fire gobbling of all consonants in sight. The Cuban form of Spanish is among the more difficult accents to decipher.

Understanding Cuban Portuguese is almost an art form.

As we ride in his WFP landcruiser towards Lobito, I learn that Alfredo has been working for the World Food Programme in Angola for seven years and that he is not planning to return to Cuba until 'Fidel and the Communists have been thrown out'.

Alfredo points out the sights of the recent battles on the outskirts of town, the odd burnt-out car here, debris of a smashed building there. Damage is heaviest in the centre of town, where looters, mainly *ninja* police and armed pro-government vigilantes, the *fitinhas*, had ransacked dozens of buildings. The World Food Programme itself lost eleven railway cars of maize and two warehouses full of relief items. In the centre of Lobito and on the peninsula jutting out from it the streets are still filled with broken glass from the sacked shops. 'There was more stealing than fighting,' says a Portuguese manager of the British firm Woods International Company which lost $2 million in stolen equipment. 'The police were handing out weapons to anyone who would take them – teenagers, women, children, anybody – and they took advantage of the *confusão*.'

This was obviously one of the rare cases in which civilians profited from *confusão*. The sacking of homes of the wealthy in Luanda, the UN warehouses and the shops had been repeated in Lobito and, I soon discover, Benguela. *Poder popular* had found its purest form.

Alfredo provides a car and a driver for me and my colleague, Sam Kiley, for a tour of the battle sights in Benguela. Pikoko, our driver, knows both cities well. When the fighting broke out in early November, he immediately enlisted in the pro-government vigilante forces and he is fond of relating in great detail each skirmish he was involved in.

The residents of the modern sector of Lobito, he says, share a nightmare that the poor, mainly Ovimbundu families in the tightly packed slums of Bela Vista, a giant *musseque* carved into the sandy bluffs overlooking the city, would one day come down in their thousands in a virtual invasion force. 'Bush people' is how he describes them. 'We had to fight for our families. They wanted everything we have here, the good life.' I do not really see what is so good about the life in Lobito. The city is badly run down, there is rubbish all over the streets and no one except the very rich can survive on their daily wages. Even the marsh where the flamingos rest in the evening stinks from the pollution. But in Angola everything is relative and Lobito must seem like a heaven compared to the dusty maze of mud and brick hut settlements of Bela Vista. 'We will never let those bush people come and take what we have,' Pikoko says.

Pikoko reckons we should see the governor of Benguela province, Paulo Jorge, a man of mixed parentage who for years has been one of the most popular and hardline Marxist members of the MPLA. I remember that at a party congress in 1990 Jorge won more votes for the Central Committee than President dos Santos. It was Jorge, Pikoko says, who ordered the distribution of weapons to the vigilantes.

As we drive from Lobito to Benguela, we pass acres and acres of abandoned sugar-cane fields which women from the area are farming haphazardly in small plots, probably providing enough food for their own families and maybe a little more for sale in the market. It seems a great waste that so little effort is going into developing land like this.

Governor Jorge has always been one of the few senior MPLA officials who is comfortable with the press and it takes only a few minutes for his secretary to show us into his office in the huge government building in the centre of town. I find the interview very disappointing for, although articulate, Jorge simply mouths the standard MPLA charge that UNITA had restarted the war because it lost at the polls. I do not doubt the allegation, but there is no hint that a solution can be found, that the MPLA, flush with electoral victory, can be even the slightest bit magnanimous.

'Facing electoral defeat, there was only one road open: to take power by force. It is very difficult to predict what Savimbi and his close aides will do because his whole strategy has been based on military force. Losing the election cost him credibility with his own people, and the only way to get it back was to take power by force,' Jorge says. Then again, he is in an embarrassing position since UNITA had in fact carried Benguela province in the polls. UNITA is arguing that for there to be peace it should be allowed to govern the provinces it won. If that happens, Jorge will be out of a job.

What about the looting? Was it not irresponsible to hand out weapons to anyone who asked for them? Jorge insists that the arms distribution occurred only after the battle was engaged and that the looting was on a much smaller scale than it appears. 'We did arm the civilians, mainly demobilised soldiers, once the fighting began. Those we armed were all volunteers who presented themselves to the police.' That is not the way others we talked with in Lobito see it, I say, but he insists, 'That is our policy.' Then we ask him about an increasing media campaign, with no evidence to back it up, alleging that the South Africans have resumed aid to UNITA. Jorge's explanation is frank and carries an ominous warning. 'The reason for this campaign could be to keep the population mobilised because we do not know which way the war will go.'

Fear of which way the war is going has convinced everyone over on Rua Celestino Madeira in Benguela not to sleep in their homes anymore. UNITA maintains one of its biggest offices a block away. 'They're just on the next street and we're scared that they will come knocking at the door at night,' says Lila, a mother of six. Her hands are shaking as she describes her return to her two-storey house after the fighting subsided. 'I found two corpses right at my gate. My son, Ricardo, was still out, and when I saw the bodies I started crying because I thought one of them was Ricardo.' Lila is particularly worried because she and her children are *mestiços*. João, her husband, is white. Many mixed-race Angolans in Benguela feel they are special targets of UNITA, an anxiety fuelled by Savimbi's anti-*mestiço* diatribes.

Shortly after the fighting in Luanda the government released a series of captured confidential UNITA documents which included one entitled 'the whites and *mestiços* of the MPLA'. UNITA's anti-white, anti-foreigner propaganda has always had an ironic twist to it, as Savimbi has never showed any qualms about receiving aid from South Africa's white minority government or from the United States. UNITA officials often denied charges of black racism, but it was there. Among the documents released by the government was a letter written by the foreign affairs spokesman, Abel Chivukuvuku, which consistently referred to western governments as 'the whites'. The sentiment was probably a legacy of the Bailundo war at the turn of the century when Mutu-ya-Kavela united several Umbundu kingdoms in an attempt to drive out the Portuguese and *mestiço* traders. Most of the people the Bailundo warriors killed in the uprising were westernised Africans and *mestiços*.

João grew up among the trader community in Bié on the *planalto*, is fluent in Umbundu and feels he has an explanation for UNITA's apparent xenophobia. 'You have to understand that the Ovimbundu have felt oppressed for the entire century. They had great chiefs and were a proud people. But after the Portuguese occupation they were at the bottom of society. They felt like the slaves of Angola. Their sons were sent to the coffee plantations in the north, and others came to Lobito to build the port. Perhaps that is where the great hatred comes from.' Lila has a much simpler explanation. 'They call us the children of Agostinho Neto, our first president, because he had a white wife.'

Contact with Luanda and the outside world is nearly impossible, although we find one private company with a satellite telephone. Our editors inform us that the news agencies are reporting that Luanda is under threat of imminent attack by UNITA from the north and, while neither orders us to leave, there is the distinct impression that we would look pretty silly sitting in Lobito when Luanda was attacked. The BBC is repeating the news agency reports so we ask Alfredo about the next flight back. Two days' time, he says.

That evening we are at a bar at the far end of the Restinga peninsula where Pikoko and his mates regularly meet up for drinks. After a few rounds someone asks us when we will be returning to Luanda. We explain our dilemma and then ask jokingly whether they know of anyone who has a car we can drive for them to Luanda. Someone speaks up immediately.

The idea sounds better in theory than reality. The country is almost on a war footing and we will have to cross UNITA territory *en route* north, and every Angolan we ask about it says we would be crazy to travel by road. Alfredo is strongly opposed.

But the rumours of war win out. By 7 o'clock the next morning we are Luanda-bound in a blue Ford Cortina. This is the same road I travelled shortly after the signature of the Bicesse accords in 1991 for the journey from Luanda to Huambo. Then peace was dawning over the landscape and now, just eighteen months later, it is collapsing. The road out of Lobito is nearly deserted, with only a handful of vehicles willing to take the risk. Thirty-five miles north of Lobito we cross into the UNITA-controlled territory at the village of Kanjala, which is clearly discernible by the UNITA party flag hanging on a piece of string across the road.

No one is manning the checkpoint. We beep the car horn and five barefoot young men come running down from one of the huts, taken aback by the sight of a car. The commander of the group is the only one wearing a UNITA T-shirt. He approaches the driver's side and asks me for our documents and permission to inspect the vehicle since, after all, this is UNITA territory. By all means, I say, and ask him about the military situation in the area. 'Tudo tranquilo' – everything calm – he says. No incidents? 'No, no incidents. UNITA has everything under control.' That's fine. The inspection is over but the young men are lingering, not giving us the final go-ahead to leave. Anything else? I ask. 'Well, there was one thing. Do you have a cassette for us?' Luckily there is an old unmarked cassette in the glove compartment. We offer it to them. 'I'm not sure what it is,' I say, 'but I listened to it once and it was good.' After a quick handshake we are off.

The road beyond Kanjala has not changed much since I passed through in the opposite direction in 1991. Carcasses of cars and trucks blown up by landmines still litter the area, although there are fewer of them and they are a bit rustier than I remember them. The tarmac is in better shape too, the fruit of repairs carried out during eighteen months of peace. There are scarcely any people around, however, even in the handful of villages we pass through.

The ride is largely uneventful until we reach the next checkpoint at Tsumbe. This is a remarkable sight. MPLA and UNITA police, the same forces that had tried to annihilate each other in Luanda, are working together, checking car papers and inspecting passing vehicles for weapons. When they come to us the government police give the car a thorough going over. They discover a used television which the car's owner had slipped into the boot for his relatives in Luanda. The policeman wants proof, a receipt or document of some sort, that we are transporting the television legally. If we cannot produce some paperwork, he says, the television will have to remain behind. I argue for several minutes, pointing out how old the television is, the thick dust on it, the broken volume knob, but the MPLA policeman will not relent. The UNITA cop stands to the side, having a good chuckle over the debate, occasionally chastising his counterpart. 'You're an idiot,' he says, and the MPLA policeman responds, 'No, you're the real idiot.'

When I am about to hand over the television, more than anything to escape what could become a serious fight, I tell the policeman that I am prepared to leave it behind provided he gives me a receipt to say that the television is being held at the Tsumbe checkpoint. 'You have to understand that otherwise the owner will think I stole it,' I say. The cop looks uneasy. His UNITA counterpart chuckles openly. He will have to consult his superior. Fine, I will talk to him too. We walk over to the tower, climb the steps and enter an office. When the policemen explains what I have said, his boss breaks out laughing, realising that his bluff has been called, and says I am free to go with the television.

That is as close as we come to trouble. We cross the River Kwanza bridge in the early afternoon expecting to find Luanda surrounded by a cordon of tanks and soldiers, ready to repel the expected invasion we have heard about on the BBC. There is not a tank or soldier in sight. We drive straight to the Ilha beach, where everyone in Luanda seems to be, and have a lunch of grilled fish at the Surfo restaurant.

In Luanda there is little to do but await the latest statement from UNAVEM about its continuing efforts to negotiate a ceasefire. The key question is, what is Savimbi's price for ending the fighting? He writes to the United Nations on 17 November accepting the election results, but he goes on to describe the polls as 'recognisably fraudulent and irregular'. His FALA army is continuing to gobble up the countryside, and the letter mentions nothing about disarming UNITA soldiers or about withdrawing from the 60 per cent of the country they have occupied since the elections. The MPLA is in no mood to make concessions either. It moves ahead to set up a new government and offers UNITA one ministry, Culture, and five vice-ministerial posts.

The only thing to do is to try to reach Huambo and interview Savimbi. The problem is how to get there. There are no planes to Huambo except for an occasional flight carrying Margaret Anstee on another vain attempt at negotiations.

A private charter company finally agrees to fly there for about $4,000, so two Portuguese, a Briton and I, set out for Huambo on 20 November in the hope of discovering Savimbi's intentions. We telephone UNITA's offices in Washington and Lisbon requesting that they pass on a message to Huambo that we are on our way, but we know the chances of sitting down with Savimbi are slim.

Our despair grows when we arrive at Huambo's airport. It is completely deserted, except for a couple of air flight controllers in the tower. Luckily, one of the few Portuguese businessman who has not fled the city, curious at the arrival of our aircraft, pulls up in a small truck and gives us a lift into town. The city is divided. UNITA troops control most of Huambo, while the MPLA holds the centre of town around the party headquarters, the governor's palace and the post office. The governor himself had bolted the week before.

We quickly check into the Hotel Excelsior and meet up with two reporters from the Portuguese daily newspaper *Público* who have been waiting there for several days with the same goal. We join their Savimbi interview vigil. A trip down to the UNITA office wins a promise by several officials that they will put our request to Savimbi if they can find a way to pass him a message. Savimbi is in hiding, moving several times a day for fear of his life, and no one has seen him for days.

Brigadier Armindo Urbano, one of UNITA's few white commanders, pitches up at the hotel to keep an eye on us. His advice is to wait and for several hours we do so. The hotel restaurant is serving lunch of a sort, pork and beans from an ancient tin with rice. Only masses of hot pepper make it bearable. The waiters, a depressing lot in white uniforms that have not been washed in weeks, offer us some wine from the hotel's dwindling reserve. We hold off, knowing that we will need it later. Brigadier Urbano, whose nom de guerre Chasanya means 'hot' in Umbundu, gives us a long rambling interview about his glorious career with UNITA and his prediction that one day Savimbi's FALA army will overrun Angola. 'FALA is probably the best army in all of Africa,' he says over and over again. Chansaya is incredibly arrogant, but a useful contact. Two things emerge clearly from the conversation: UNITA is planning to capture Huambo and our hopes for an interview with Savimbi are misplaced.

At that point, while my colleagues stay at the hotel to await word of a breakthrough, I wander over to the UNAVEM camp behind the post office to see if I can find Lieutenant-Colonel Mortlock, the commander of the UNAVEM's central region base, whom I had met just before the elections. Lieutenant-Colonel Mortlock is one of the brightest, most conscientious military officers UNAVEM has sent to Angola. On the eve of the elections he rightly warned that the failure of demobilisation would likely spell disaster. He personally negotiated ceasefires to halt firefights which broke out several times in October. On one occasion he had to go to Savimbi's house in the middle of the night to fix a truce while the UNITA leader was still in his pyjamas. On others he had to comfort the MPLA governor, Baltazar Manuel, who would come running to him for safety at the least sign of trouble.

When I enter his tent at the UNAVEM camp, depression is written all over his face. He does not see any way of avoiding a final confrontation in Huambo, and must know that when it comes he and his unarmed UNAVEM soldiers will be trapped. It has been impossible to see Savimbi in recent days, he says, and the quality of his advisers is poor following the killing of UNITA vice-president Chitunda and Salupeto Pena and the capture of Chivukuvuku and eight FALA generals in Luanda.

Too many of his best men are unavailable, and he is getting conflicting advice from those in the peace camp and those in the war camp, he says. Those in the war camp, such as General Altino Sapalalo, 'Bock', the one-armed UNITA general who had acted like a lunatic on the day of Savimbi's campaign rally in Kuito two months before, are clearly in the ascendant.

Lieutenant-Colonel Mortlock sums up the dynamic. 'After sixteen years of civil war, what dominates in Angola is the single-option response: if you don't like something, you point a weapon at it.' I ask Lieutenant-Colonel Mortlock how I might be able to make contact with Savimbi. He does not rate my chances as high. He is meeting a key UNITA commander, General Augusto Wiyo, later that day, however, and suggests I come along to put my case to him.

I walk back towards the hotel, through the central square where the governor's palace and the MPLA party headquarters stand abandoned. Government control of the city has collapsed. Nearly all of the international aid agencies have packed up and left for security reasons. One that remains, Belgian Médecins sans Frontières, is deciding whether or not to quit after one of their workers, André Pascal, was murdered at his home by gunmen apparently trying to steal his motorbike.

I find my colleagues sitting around or sleeping and they have had no news from UNITA about a possible Savimbi interview. We have a few hours to kill before General Wiyo will be arriving at UNAVEM, so we head off in search of the Bishop Francisco Viti. There is no transport around. Fuel is in short supply because tankers will not risk the trip from Lobito, so we walk. At the bishop's house a nun says he might be at the seminary, but she does not know for sure.

We walk back across the park and arrive just as the bishop is climbing into his Land Rover. He refuses to give us an interview, saying that he cannot speak to the press given the country's delicate political *situação*. 'I am in mourning for the country,' is all we can get out of him.

This is becoming one of the most costly and non-productive trips I have ever embarked upon and I am concerned about how I will explain the expenses to my editors.

At the UNAVEM camp Lieutenant-Colonel Mortlock is emerging from his meeting with General Wiyo of UNITA and Colonel José Walter Jorge, the government's negotiator, when we arrive. Little progress has been made and all three men know there is not much they can do to halt the violence except to negotiate local ceasefires here and there. The bigger decisions rest with Savimbi and the MPLA government in Luanda. General Wiyo promises to send our request for an interview with Savimbi through channels, but he admits he has not seen *O Mais Velho* for several days. Colonel Jorge and General Wiyo agree that the situation is slipping beyond their control. Civilians on both sides are arming themselves. Troops under their command are growing impatient.

'There are many small incidents, very localised, and we are doing everything to stop the shooting,' says General Wiyo.

'There is a lot of settling of accounts, nothing really organised. You have uncontrolled elements in UNITA and the government, and then outright delinquents. The politicians must reach an overall settlement, and then you can begin to solve the military aspect. A small number of guerrillas with just 100 rounds of ammunition can set off events that will devastate the whole country.' But what if Savimbi says that the war is on: will General Wiyo agree to return to the bush and resume the civil war? 'I lost my whole youth to sixteen years of war, and the last thing I want is to to see it start again.' It is a heartfelt response, I think, but then again he does not answer the question. He does not have to. If Savimbi says fight, General Wiyo and thousands more like him will fight.

After three days it is clear that there is no use waiting any longer for the interview. It is not going to happen. Margaret Anstee, the representative of the UN Secretary General, has been turned down too. We find a working telephone and make a call to Luanda to request that our plane come to fetch us.

The next morning as we drive to the airport a band of little barefoot children bounce up and down on the metal blades of a Russian-built MI-8 helicopter sitting in a nearby field. The helicopter was shot down during the previous month's round of fighting because it had flown too close to Savimbi's residence, the so-called Casa Branca or White House. When it crashed, UNITA soldiers beat up the two Russian pilots but left its Swiss passenger alone. Luckily for him, Savimbi had studied in Switzerland before deciding to return to liberate the Angolan people from their misery. The sight of such an expensive war machine falling under the control of the youthful crowd, at least from dawn to dusk, symbolises the anarchy and utter waste that reigns in Angola.

We reach the airport a few minutes before the plane is to land. A group of UNITA officials and UNAVEM soldiers pull up as well. The landing of a plane in Huambo is becoming one of the city's sole sources of entertainment. The buzz of the aircraft's engines grows louder overhead, but there is no sign of it approaching the runway. It is circling. 'If there is no one in the control tower, the pilot will not land,' a UNAVEM officer says casually. We beg him to use his portable radio to contact the plane, but neither he nor the UNITA officials know the correct frequency.

My colleagues and I scramble up the stairs to the control tower, frantically turning dials and knobs and screaming down the radio sets that it is safe to land. One of the *Público* journalists barks down the radio, 'This is Huambo control tower, a group of journalists are in control of the tower, we authorise you to land, I repeat, it is safe to land.' The pilot either does not hear us or thinks that everyone in Huambo has gone mad. He circles the airport three times and heads back to Luanda.

That evening we make another call to Luanda to inform the charter company what has happened and to beg them to send the plane again, whether or not anyone is manning the control tower. The plane arrives the next morning.

By the end of November Margaret Anstee organises the last serious attempt inside Angola to negotiate a ceasefire and return to the Bicesse peace accords. A day of talks on 26 November in the southern port of Namibe produces a new peace deal that commits both sides to a nationwide ceasefire, a halt to all offensive troop movements and agreement on expansion of the UN role in the peace process. The deal lasts three days. UNITA forces capture the northern provincial capital of Uíge and the nearby air base at Negage on 29-30 November, just as Savimbi is announcing on UNITA's Vorgan radio that his movement is prepared to join the cabinet, but only at senior levels. Savimbi later claims that he did not order the attack on Uíge, but in a movement as disciplined as UNITA it is difficult to believe him.

Whatever the truth, any hopes for a negotiated peace are dead. The MPLA government launches a counter-offensive at the end of December. By early January UNITA has been pushed out of the cities of Benguela, Lobito and Lubango. The battle for control of Kuito erupts on 6 January. Two days later the final showdown in Huambo, which Lieutenant-Colonel Mortlock had feared, begins.

I fly down again to Lobito and Benguela on 16 January and find that the *limpeza* campaign which pro-government forces employed with such telling effect in Luanda was again under way. In the Bela Vista slums above Lobito Ovimbundu residents are locking themselves in their homes at night for fear of falling victim to what they call 'silent bullets'. Vigilante groups are using silencers on their rifles in the hunt for UNITA supporters, they say.

UNITA offices and houses in Lobito have been pounded into rubble by shelling. In Benguela UNITA troops dynamited the central market, and government forces did the same to the UNITA headquarters. Both sides carried out summary executions. Bulldozers were brought in to scoop up hundreds of bodies that had been left rotting in the streets. Among those killed was Ricardo, the seventeen-year-old son of Lila and João who lived on Rua Celestino Madeira in Benguela. The last time I saw Ricardo, two months before, he was wearing a Che Guevara beret.

By now UNAVEM has closed 47 of its 61 monitoring stations around the country and the evacuation of UN military personnel is continuing. On 20 January Margaret Anstee agrees to see a group of reporters to give her assessment of the situation. Not surprisingly, it is decidedly down-beat. She laughingly suggests that she is spending much of her time waiting for telephone calls and the voice she wants to hear is Savimbi's. Angola is on 'a tragic seesaw. When one side is up they don't want to talk and when the other is up, they don't want to talk.' She admits that the UN mandate is 'increasingly irrelevant'.

Margaret Anstee looks exhausted and she is growing increasingly bitter about what is generally perceived, unfairly I believe, as her personal failure in Angola. While both the government and UNITA 'were playing their games', she says, 'Nobody wanted to know about something that was going to cost money.' UNAVEM's limited mandate meant that when the demobilisation process failed in the run-up to the elections, there was nothing it could do except to employ verbal persuasion. 'One could say, with the lessons of hindsight, that the UN should never have accepted the mandate.'

11 I Meet Jesus

> Talks between the Angolan government and the rebel movement UNITA under United Nations auspices in the Ivory Coast capital, Abidjan, have reached stalemate following a UNITA announcement that it will not withdraw from the towns and villages it has occupied since restarting the war last October.
>
> *The Guardian*
> 14 May 1993

> President Bill Clinton yesterday recognised the government of Angola, reversing fifteen years of US support for its opponents. The change in US policy comes after the government won elections six months ago while rebel forces, formerly backed by the US, returned to the battlefield.
>
> *The Independent*
> 20 May 1993

Jesus is an Angolan. I find him working in Luanda's main hospital, the Josina Machel, caring for women and children who have been shot, stepped on landmines or otherwise been maimed in some hideous way. It is hard to hear Jesus' voice over the din of women and children moaning on the cement floor of the orthopaedic ward as they struggle to cover up their amputated limbs and bullet-torn bodies with strips of clothing and blankets. It is hard to see Jesus clearly through the smoke rising from dozens of tiny cooking fires tended by women preparing lunches of maize, rice and dried fish for their stricken relatives. The hospital has no food for its patients. I find it difficult to look Jesus in the eye.

Jesus is what the patients at the Josina Machel hospital call Emilio de Jesus, a nurse in his mid-twenties who spends his days trying to ease their suffering without the aid of antibiotics, painkillers or proper dressings. Even Jesus admits that it is an impossible task. 'The conditions are so bad that it's depressing to work here.'

The hospital receives few medicines or bandages, not nearly enough for all the patients, despite donations worth millions of dollars from international aid agencies. 'I cannot explain it,' Jesus says. 'We send down to the pharmacy for medicine, and they say there is none.'

Jesus is not exactly lying, but he certainly is not telling the truth. He and all the nurses know precisely what happens to the donations from the aid agencies. They arrive safely at the Ministry of Health, but then they are sold to the black marketeers, the *candongueiros*.

Any medicine imaginable can be bought at Roque Santeiro, the sprawling open-air market on the northern edge of Luanda. Many of the medicines are clearly marked 'not for resale'. The same words are to be found on sacks of maize and tins of cooking oil at Roque Santeiro and at smaller markets in cities throughout the country. One painkiller cost 30,000 kwanzas, about 75 US cents, in September 1993, a huge sum even for those Angolans with jobs. 'The only thing to do is go to Roque Santeiro,' Jesus says, 'but none of these patients can afford the prices.'

When I ask another nurse, Pedro de Oliveira, about the lack of medicines, he is more forthright than Jesus. 'I think you should address that question to the Minister of Health.'

A child's scream pierces the air. A nurse and the mother of a little girl who had been shot in the back by gunmen while sleeping at her home in the central city of Malange are trying to change her bandages. The tape is tearing off huge strips of rotting skin from her back and the infection is getting worse. The nurse says that she will probably die.

These people at the Josina Machel hospital have been abandoned, left to die in filthy conditions, like a chamber of horrors, Jesus says. Everyone has forsaken them, the government, the world, perhaps even God.

In the men's ward Augusto Jocinto is lying on a piece of cardboard covered by a blanket stained with pus seeping out of the stump that was once his left leg. He is shaking so badly that he can hardly form complete sentences. Augusto was airlifted from the eastern city of Luena four months ago after a landmine ripped his leg off while he was searching for some manioc in an abandoned field.

Did he not know that there were mines around? 'Yes, but I had no choice. I have a wife and a baby son and we had no food. We knew there were mines, but our stomachs were empty.' Augusto does not have any money to buy medicines or proper bandages. He has no idea what has become of his wife and son.

As I rise from my knees, Jesus looks down sympathetically, not at Augusto but at me. I imagine he is thinking, 'Silly foreigner, you just don't get it, do you?' As we part, Augusto says, '*Bom trabalho*,' – 'May your work go well.'

Next to him on the floor is Mateus Kotinho, a carpenter from the south-eastern city of Menongue, the site of the airport I passed through *en route* to the Battle of Cuito Cuanavale five years before. Mateus is waiting for an operation on his right leg. The bone was shattered by a bullet when UNITA rebels attacked his neighbourhood on the outskirts of the city. He was flown to Luanda in the hope that conditions would be better in a hospital just 500 yards from the plush National Assembly where deputies spoke for hours about the government's commitment to the people.

Now Mateus wants to get out of the Josina Machel hospital, out of Luanda, as soon as possible. At least in Menongue he has relatives to bring him food. Here he is at the mercy of the *candongueiros* and free-market economics.

Mateus certainly wants the war to end, but electoral campaigns and voting are a different matter. Angolans have had the stuffing kicked out of them and the wind of democracy has gone with it. 'This is what voting brought us,' he says, pointing to his leg. 'This democracy just brought us an even worse war.'

There are those for whom the war, the economic chaos, the *situação*, is a far more attractive enterprise. Luanda's new elite, the so-called *novos ricos*, are getting on splendidly. In the year since the elections, Angola imported $500 million worth of new vehicles, according to the *Jornal de Angola*. Volkswagen Passats are particularly popular among FAA officers, while senior MPLA officials hanker after Audis. Four-wheel drive landcruisers are almost standard issue for the dozens of UN and non-governmental aid agencies that have set up shop in the city. All for a good cause. Ruling, defending and feeding the *povo* can be an expensive business.

The twelve months since Angola's first democratic elections have been among its most tragic since independence, possibly since the end of the slave trade. Famine is threatening two million Angolans. The civil war has seen the most intense fighting ever. The United Nations describes it as the worst conflict in the world. The violence, starvation and sickness it causes are killing hundreds of people every day.

In the city of Huambo thousands of people died in the 55-day siege UNITA launched in January to capture the capital of the central highlands. Most of the city is in ruins. Now bombing raids by government jet fighters are apparently trying to finish off the job. About 100 miles to the east, the city of Kuito is under siege, pounded almost daily by UNITA mortars and artillery. Thousands more civilians are dying there.

A Wild West atmosphere reigns in Luanda. Armed robbers, usually dressed as police or FAA soldiers, specialise in car-jacking and house-breaking. The real police hang out on the streets harassing any car they can flag down, more often than not acting like roadside bandits.

Margaret Anstee retired as the UN Special Representative after sponsoring two unsuccessful rounds of peace talks in Addis Ababa and Abidjan, Côte d'Ivoire. Her replacement, Alioune Blondin Beye of Mali, was appointed on 28 June 1993 and immediately took up where she left off, shuttling between Luanda and Huambo attempting to set up a new round of negotiations. The UN Security Council continued to wring its hands and demand that both sides stop the violence.

By this time the focal point of the starvation threatening Angola is the central city of Malange, which cannot receive UN emergency food airlifts because when the United Nations drew up a list of target sites in July, it was considered too dangerous for planes to land there. But this is September and it is safer. Caritas, the Catholic relief agency, is bringing in food and none of its planes have been shot down. No matter, Malange is not on the UN list.

Savimbi holds the Malanjinhos, as the city's residents are known, in particular contempt. Malange, in the strongly pro-MPLA heartland of the Mbundu people, was the site of some of the bloodiest massacres of UNITA soldiers and activists in November 1992. UNITA troops have encircled the city and planted a belt of landmines to ensure that no one can get out to farm the surrounding land. From time to time they shell the centre of town with mortars. A city with a population of between 200,000 and 300,000 people is slowly starving to death.

I reach the city courtesy of the World Food Programme, which is effectively ignoring UN restrictions on flying there by saying that its planes are working for Caritas. By now the death rate is about 100 people a day. Government security forces are engaged in sporadic battles with each other and civilians over the little food that is arriving.

As soon as our cargo plane taxis to a stop in front of the airport building, dozens of young soldiers, many of them barefoot, gather silently at the edge of the asphalt. Armed troops, their superior uniforms indicating that they are from a different unit, surround the aircraft as if they are protecting an armoured car delivering money to a bank. The stevedores begin throwing sacks of maize onto the back of UN lorries.

Occasionally one of the maize bags splits open, spilling the precious grains onto the tarmac. Suddenly the young soldiers in rags run towards the plane and scoop up handfuls of maize before armed soldiers beat them away with whips. Then another tries his luck, and another, until one of the guards fires a few rounds into the air as a warning. Amid the chaos the stevedores grab handfuls of maize and stuff it into their pockets and strips of cloth tied around their waists. Once the unloading is finished a crew member sweeps out the maize powder and grains onto the ground before returning to Luanda. Tiny boys, out-sprinting the destitute soldiers, run over and skid to their knees, using their nimble fingers to pick out grains of maize from the dust and pebbles.

Several colleagues and I catch a lift into town with a WFP landcruiser which promptly delivers us to the governor's guest house. One of the workers there sends a message to the government's social welfare agency, known as MINARS. Journalists are not allowed to visit Malange unless they have the approval of the governor, Flávio Fernandes, the former

Minister of Health.

Within half an hour the local MINARS director, Conceição Araújo, arrives, clearly irritated that journalists have come to Malange unannounced. Malange is run like an MPLA-controlled town of years past, complete with minders. Journalists always have to be accompanied by government officials and several local reporters lest they see anything which might embarrass the government, especially the governor. Araújo explains the thinking behind the policy. 'Journalists are always accompanied to make sure they get the right information. Otherwise, they might leave with the wrong impression.'

The first stop on the programme is lunch at the LAM bar and discotheque, which is run by one of the Governor's business acquaintances, a certain Laurentino. We say that we are not hungry and have little time to spend on lunch. Araújo and her delegation look at us in horror. We might not need food, but they certainly are not prepared to forsake theirs. Soup and chicken and a choice between Coca Cola and Lone Star beer, straight from Texas, are on offer. By this time I realise that it is going to be a long day struggling with the bureaucracy and the MPLA's desire to monitor our every movement. I take soup and a Lone Star. Make that two Lone Stars, I say after one of the government security agents, a minder for our group, starts telling us about how great the disco is at the weekend.

Perhaps I am too arrogant, too impatient to see the hungry of Malange, to write a dramatic story, but eventually it dawns on me that these are ordinary people who are embarrassed at the state of their city and that they are attempting somehow to create an impression of normality. Maybe that was why Jesus, the nurse in Luanda, did not want to talk about government corruption and the betrayal of his people. Maybe he was not trying to hide anything after all, but was simply ashamed.

After lunch Araújo provokes me to come as close as I ever have to exploding when she insists that we go to her apartment for a coffee and to discuss our plans in Malange, that is, our *programa*, a word I had not heard in Angola since well before the 1992 elections. By the early afternoon, we have been in one of the worst areas of starvation anywhere in

Africa, perhaps the world, and our sole accomplishment has been to drink a few Lone Star beers and a cup of decaffeinated coffee. Before independence Angola was a world-class coffee producer and Malange was just to the east of the plantations, and we have just been drinking instant decaffeinated coffee imported from Europe.

Finally we are off towards the hospital which, ominously, also bears the name Josina Machel, like that in Luanda where Jesus works. Soon after our arrival we discover there is a problem. The hospital director is not around and outsiders cannot visit in his absence. One of the hospital workers explains that journalists have to be accompanied to make sure they get the right information ... Yes, yes, I have heard all that before, but we are here, Malange is facing a major crisis and how is the world going to know about its plight unless journalists can see it for themselves?

As the debate is winding down and our hopes are dwindling, the hospital director, Joaquim Neho, miraculously arrives on the scene. Neho takes charge and begins the tour. We can see anything we like. We go first to the orthopaedic ward to speak with some landmine victims. The ward is another chamber of horrors, but at least the patients have beds and are not sleeping on the floor as they were in Luanda. There are a dozen people with one or both of their limbs blown off by mines. All are women.

I speak to Ana Maria Luís. She was wandering half-starved around the fields outside town looking for manioc last month when her left foot detonated a mine. Now it is gone. When we ask the others what happened to them, they all have similar stories. Hungry, looking for food, stepped on a mine. Only one woman became an amputee as the result of a shooting. There is silence as she describes her attackers as government policemen. One of our minders, the security man who had been enthusing about the LAM disco, interjects. It was not exactly a policeman, but the 'enemy'. Neho loses his patience with the man. 'Look, when the police go around shooting people they are just as much the *inimigo* as UNITA. There is no difference for the people. Both are the *inimigo*.' The security man makes a feeble attempt at a reply, but Neho dismisses him with a click of his tongue. 'For the people, they are the same.'

What does the hospital need to treat the amputees?

'Everything,' Neho replies. Water and electricity supplies have been cut off for months. There is a severe shortage of bandages, linen, and, of course, food. 'The biggest problem is the lack of antibiotics. The shortage is really serious. The people have no money to go to the *praça* [market] and purchase the medicines.' So there is medicine in Malange? 'Yes,' says Neho. But not in the hospital, only at the *praça*? 'That is correct.' But are not these medicines donated by the international aid organisations for the hospital? 'Yes.' So how come the medicines destined for hospitals end up in the market? A most uncomfortable pause. 'I think you should direct that question to the governor. He would be in a better position to answer such a question.' Unfortunately, when we try to interview him later, the governor says he is too busy.

Neho suddenly brightens. But the governor came to the hospital yesterday and promised that there will soon be drugs for the patients. 'I am more confident now that the governor himself has said that the medicines are coming,' he says.

Across the courtyard in the children's ward are 60 youngsters suffering from anaemia and kwashiorkor, the protein deficiency disease which sends off the alarm bells for severe malnutrition. In the grounds behind the ward, women are cooking maize and beans in battered and blackened tin cans. Caritas brought the food over this morning. Dozens of the children are virtual skeletons. The hospital staff say they might not survive the month. 'There are hundreds of children like these all over the city but they can't make it to us,' says Neho. 'We should be feeding them six or seven times a day but there isn't enough food. We're lucky to provide one meal a day. Last month we had to close the kitchen for a week.'

The worst children I see are members of the Baptista family. Esperança, a little girl of four, and her three-year-old sister Gelsa are crying. Josué, aged one, has his mouth open in agony but sound comes out only occasionally, and even that might be from the flies buzzing in and out of the facial cavity. Their mother, Maria de Fátima João, sits on a bed with her skinny arms around all three, somehow trying to smother their hunger pangs with human warmth. I ask her how the family ended up in such a state. 'Soldiers attacked my house last December and took all our food, all our clothes, everything we had. My husband has disappeared. Since then I haven't been able to find enough food for the children.' Which soldiers attacked the house? She does not answer. Can you tell me which soldiers attacked your house? Her eyes, worried, flash from side to side. 'Troops,' she says. UNITA troops? 'No, troops like the ones you see in the city.'

The sun is setting by the time we leave the hospital. Araújo, who by now has warmed to us and we to her, escorts us back to the magnificent government guest house where we are to stay the night. The city is safe, Araújo and other officials assure us, but it would be better if we stayed indoors. I figure they are just saying that to keep us from seeing anything that might lead to erroneous conclusions. After supper we plan to walk to the LAM discotheque for a Lone Star beer or two.

A few minutes after we leave the dinner table, however, heavy shooting breaks out. It is unlikely that UNITA troops are involved, since they are at least seven miles away. This appears to be a routine gunfight among the various warring army and police factions that make the centre of Malange so dangerous at night. It goes on for ten minutes or so and much of it quite close to the LAM discotheque, so we decide to stay in that evening and watch a video, a real treat in Malange. Most of the city has no electricity but the governor's guest house has its own generator.

The next morning we are driving around the city deciding what to do when we see a crowd of several thousand people queuing outside the Pope Paul VI Apostolic Centre. Caritas is about to start distribution of the maize with which we flew in the day before.

The crowd starts pushing and shoving violently as the distribution begins. The weak are jostled to one side. Little children are separated from their mothers and burst into tears. Young men barge to the front. A handful of police officers start beating people over the head with belts and rubber hoses as the mass of humanity presses against the steel gates at the centre's small entrance. The cops are fighting a losing battle. A pregnant woman is smashed into the gates, the eyes of an infant strapped to her back widening in terror as it is squeezed against her. Maria José Fernandes, an elderly Portuguese Caritas worker, struggles to bring order to the swarming mass. In between shouting in her thin voice,

Fernandes explains the panic. 'This is their first time here and they're afraid they'll be left without food.'

More shouting for order. Fernandes has been living in Malange for 30 years. So how bad is this famine? 'This is the worst hunger I have ever seen here. Dozens and dozens of children are dying each day.' But this is only the beginning. 'The rainy season has started now, and no one can plant because of the fighting and the mines. The hunger we're experiencing now could be minor compared to the famine that's coming.'

It was. By the time the UN agreed to allow the World Food Programme to start a massive airlift to Malange in November, the death toll had risen to 250 per day. A senior official at the American embassy in Luanda said that the United Nations had 'the blood of many people on its hands'.

The UN was vulnerable on the Malange issue and Blondin Beye, the UN Special Representative, knew it. When he granted an interview to me and colleagues from the *New York Times*, the *Washington Post*, Associated Press and Reuters television, I asked him about the charge made by several UN and foreign relief agencies that the refusal to permit World Food Programme airlifts to Malange had cost hundreds of lives. He exploded in anger. Such charges were baseless and were made by 'fifth columnists' in the aid community, he shouted. The question and Blondin Beye's emotional response effectively ended the interview.

I return to Malange in January 1994, two months after the United Nations has launched massive airlifts of 140 tonnes of food a day to the city. The death toll has dropped dramatically, although tens of thousands of emaciated people shuffle into makeshift feeding centres every morning. Adults and children in the worst shape are receiving three meals a day from foreign relief agencies such as World Vision and the Irish aid agency Concern, as well as Caritas. Anaemia and kwashiorkor are still widespread, but the number of landmine victims coming into the Josina Machel hospital is falling. With the arrival of food aid people no longer have to brave the mine fields in search of manioc. 'There is no comparison with the situation late last year,' says Fernandes of Caritas. 'But the war continues, the landmines still encircle the city and the farmers cannot plant their crops. So if the food stops coming, the famine will return.'

For some, the scars of famine and war will not disappear with the resumption of aid flights. Lila Gomes leaves her home at 6 o'clock each morning with her three-year-old daughter to reach the Cangambo-2 feeding centre run by Concern three hours later. I meet her one afternoon just before 3 o'clock, her usual hour of departure to make the journey back to her house by sunset. Nightfall normally wins the race. Although her home is in one of the nearby shanty-towns, the reason the journey takes her so long is obvious. She has no right leg.

Her journey into a personal hell began in early 1991, several months before the Bicesse peace accords were signed in Portugal, when a unit of UNITA troops rampaged through her home village of Mangange, about one day's walk from Malange. She is Mbundu, a member of the ethnic group which mainly backs the MPLA, and her father's side of the family was local royalty. Her maiden name and that of the village are the same. Her elder brother, António, was the local village *soba*. 'The morning after the attack, we found António in his home, hanging by his neck from the rafters. They had slashed him with knives so that the blood would run out of his body. That is when my family and other villagers decided to flee.' For three days they mourned António before burying him. Then they left.

When they reached Malange, they had nowhere to stay and nothing to eat. But Lila, her husband and her three brothers managed to rent a small house. When the war restarted in 1992, UNITA was driven out of town but laid siege to Malange, cutting off its residents from their farmlands and sowing the belt of landmines to imprison them in the city. The government army laid another belt of mines to keep UNITA out.

When the famine came in 1993, Lila, like thousands of others, had no choice but to scavenge for food. 'We had no land to farm in Malange, so we went to the sisters at Caritas for help. But there was not enough food for all of us, so I began going out into the fields to search for more.' By October the family, like the rest of Malange, was starving.

On 18 October Lila wandered out into an area called Gazetta about three miles from the city. She was searching for manioc. 'We knew there were mines around, but we were hungry. I was walking with four other people along the footpath, but I was the only one to hit a mine. I passed out and was carried by my friends to the hospital. But after two months I asked to leave because there was no one to take care of the children. The children had no mother to fetch wood for them, and no one else was arranging for their food. The doctors said I should go to Luanda to have the bone cut off, but I have no money.'

I interrupt her. What bone? I immediately regret my curiosity. She gingerly lifts up her blue dress to reveal a blood-tipped bone sticking out about four inches from a stump which is all that remained of her thigh.

Her husband has left her. 'He said I was not a woman any more.' Her daughter often asks her why she does not have two legs like other people. She and her three brothers, ranging between seven and twelve years old, receive some bags of maize from Caritas, but she is selling most of it to pay for the rent on her shack in the shanty-town.

There is no bitterness in Lila's voice as she relates her tale. She says that her hospital experience has convinced her that she wants to become a doctor. When she finishes talking, she thanks me for listening. She has to get moving, otherwise she will reach home after dark and there is danger in the streets.

Even when things are improving, Malange is one of the most horrible places I have ever seen. Every once in a while UNITA gunners fire a few random mortar rounds into the city. A few days before I was there in January mortars scored direct hits in some densely populated shanty-towns, wounding several dozen people and killing an Angolan nurse who worked for Concern. The city reeks of corruption and pain.

Relations between the local authorities, especially the police, and the aid agencies are worsening. On one occasion a group of soldiers hijacked a truck hired by Concern, threatening to shoot the driver unless he handed over the keys. On another a drunk police officer walked into Concern's Cangambo-2 feeding centre, where I interviewed Lila, and sprayed the building with his AK-47. World Vision also had to suspend its operations temporarily after one of its Angolan workers was murdered.

'The level of theft by the soldiers is just terrible. They rob and rob,' says Fernandes of Caritas.

No one could accuse governor Fernandes of being idle, though. While dozens of people were starving to death each day in the city which he governed, he and his family flew to Paris for the Christmas holidays.

12 The Dogs of War Can't Dance

It is one year since the elections. I am often struck by a bout of nostalgia on those steamy weekend nights in Luanda when all thoughts turn to having a cool drink in one of the city's outdoor disco bars where, just for a moment, the repertoire of dance tracks makes it easy to forget the misery of the refugee camps, the queues of hundreds of people waiting for bags of maize, the little boys begging in the streets for money to buy bread, the women and children who have had their legs blown off.

A little over a year ago Luanda nightspots such as the Bar Aberto, Espaço 93 and the aptly-named Pandemonium were scenes of celebration of the new-found peace and Angola's first democratic elections. There was a delightful mix of young Angolans, white Angolan-born Portuguese who had returned from Lisbon with money to burn and a wide assortment of international aid workers and UN military and political officials who were there to help usher in the new democracy.

I keep returning to such places in an attempt to recapture the moment, but I almost always leave in disappointment, the wink of optimism in Angola now gone forever. The young upper-class Angolans, many of them children of the wealthy officials of the formerly Marxist MPLA, are still around, but most of the white Portuguese have gone back to Lisbon, their flirtation with the new peaceful Angola simply a bad dream. The number of UN workers, especially UNAVEM troops and officers, is also much reduced. In their place there is a new breed of international expert – the gun for hire.

One weekend in November 1993 I decide on a late night trip to the Bar Aberto, the most chic bar for the city's *novos ricos* during the elections, but now on the brink of closing for good. Apart from several depressed-looking prostitutes dancing over in the corner, the place is largely deserted. The only customers are a couple of beefy types who strike up a conversation. When I ask them what line of work they are in, they pause and say, 'We work for Ango-Segu, a private company which provides security for the Angolan government.' What kind of security? Protecting business installations, oil complexes, diamonds, that sort of thing, they say, increasingly testy. I ask whether they carry weapons. One of the two, a huge man, the size of a rugby player who has watched more matches drinking beer than he has played, pats a bulging black waist pouch, the kind bikers and joggers wear, which is tucked under his formidable belly.

Suddenly it dawns on me who these guys are. Rumours are circulating in Luanda about foreign soldiers working in the pay of the Angolan government, but I have yet to run into any. I think I have just done so. I ask them where they are from. They say that they are South African, although one has a British accent and the other is clearly an Australian. I ask them if they were in 32 Battalion, the unit of Angolans and foreign mercenaries which was trained by the South African Defence Force and once fought alongside UNITA against the MPLA government in the name of resisting the 'communist onslaught'. No, they say with little conviction, but they have mates who used to be in it. 'Did you guys happen to know Philip Smith?' I ask. Smith was a British 'security specialist' who was killed six months before when UNITA overran the north-eastern oil-producing town of Soyo. It is a stupid question. 'Philip is a sore subject with us mate, I suggest you don't bring it up. What do you do here, anyway?'

By now the alarm bells are ringing. 'Oh, I'm a journalist,' I say. It is only then I realise these guys have been drinking for quite a while. 'Journalist eh? You fucking journalists have screwed up Philip's wife. You called him a mercenary and now the insurance company won't pay her. If you weren't here with this woman we would kick the shit out of you.' Just when I think it is time to beat a quick retreat, my friend, a woman who works for the World Food Programme, fires back at them that none of the Angolan mothers and wives of those killed in battle have insurance, and besides, 'People like you make fat salaries.'

They start to put their drinks down and I grab my friend by the arm and drag her out of the bar. All the while she is shouting abuse at them, and they at her. The only thing I hear are the repeated references to 'kicking the shit' out of me. The lesson I take away from the Bar Aberto that night is that if you plan to get into an argument with someone at a bar in Luanda these days, it is wise to check first to see if the person is sporting a bulging black waist pouch.

A few days later I run into the same pair at the Espaço 93, but this time they are with a dozen mates, all wearing their bulging waist pouches. A lot of whispering and pointing of fingers is going on, when one of my colleagues comes up and asks me what is happening. 'These guys seem to be pissed off with you. I heard them talking about "the fuckin' journalist".' Feigning a visit to the toilet, I leave quickly for Pandemonium, the large outdoor discotheque. Five minutes later they show up there, completely taking over the bar area. The whispering and pointing continue until I lose myself in, well, the pandemonium of the dance floor. Big beefy mercenaries, it seems, don't dance.

In the new Angola ideology is being replaced by the bottom line, as security and selling expertise in weaponry have become a very profitable business. With its wealth in oil and diamonds, Angola is like a big swollen carcass and the vultures are circling overhead. Savimbi's former allies are switching sides, lured by the aroma of hard currency.

When a colleague working as a television journalist goes to the airport a week after my run-in at the Bar Aberto, he bumps into an acquaintance, a veteran of 32 Battalion's battles on behalf of UNITA, and asks him to carry his film to Johannesburg. The man says he will do so on one condition – that the film contains nothing that would make the MPLA government look bad.

By this time there are several security companies operating in Angola, including the largely British Defence Systems Ltd, an up-market firm known as DSL which recruits ex-Gurkhas and carries out a wide range of tasks, from training soldiers in Mozambique to protecting banks in London. In Luanda its men help to guard the British and American embassies.

Ango-Segu, I later discover, is a far shadier concern. Run by a former colonel in the Israeli security agency, Mossad, it is linked to senior members of the MPLA government, including a former Minister of the Interior. A month after my encounter at the Bar Aberto, the Angolan government announces the expulsion of eighteen Ango-Segu employees, including four Britons, three South Africans, two Israelis, a Kenyan, a Portuguese, an Austrian and a Lebanese. Police raid the company's warehouses and the government says hundreds of illegal weapons are discovered. Several Western military contacts tell me the government suspects that Ango-Segu's foreign employees have been passing sensitive military intelligence to UNITA. Whatever the truth, I feel relieved. At least I can return to Luanda's bars in peace. Unfortunately, by this time the Bar Aberto has closed.

In early January 1994 I pay a visit to the Pretoria offices of another security company operating in Angola, Executive Outcomes, to ask about allegations that the firm is recruiting mercenaries for the government in Luanda. I am sitting on the patio of a suburban house when the company's director, Eeben Barlow, drives up in a sleek red sports car. He walks up, shakes my hand and announces that he believes I am an intelligence agent. 'I don't know who you are working for, but I intend to find out.' Fine, I say, but until you do, would you mind telling me about Executive Outcomes?

For the remainder of the morning Barlow is very civil, offering me endless cups of coffee and explaining that his company does not recruit mercenaries but has a $40 million contract with the Angolan government to help train its army. He shows me a video of his recruits at a training base somewhere in Angola. The day starts at 5 o'clock with several bearded South Africans in military uniforms leading prayers in Afrikaans. The rest of the time is dedicated to normal military training – obstacle courses, unit deployment, weapons inspection and so on. Barlow refuses to tell me the location of the camp, but I later discover that one of the main Executive Outcomes training centres is at Cabo Ledo, about 50 miles south of Luanda.

Barlow admits that he is recruiting former members of the notorious Koevoet (Crowbar) unit which the SADF employed to fight nationalist guerrillas in the Namibian independence war. 'A lot of Angolans were in Koevoet, and they're good because they speak the language and have family back in Angola,' he says. Recruitment is also under way among former members of 32 Battalion, a unit in which Barlow himself served as a long-range reconnaissance scout. In those days he was helping UNITA.

The reason the South Africans, once the regional warriors against communism, are so easily persuaded to fight for the MPLA is obvious. Salaries range between $2,000 and $8,000 a month. Four of South Africa's best helicopter pilots have enlisted.

By mid-1994 the Executive Outcomes operation in Angola had become extremely controversial. The façade that its soldiers are engaged only in training was taking a beating. In July UNITA announced that it was holding several South Africans captured when their plane was shot down near the diamond-producing areas around Cafunfo in Lunda Norte province. UNITA said it planned to execute 'the assassins'. The MPLA army had just captured Cafunfo, the main source of UNITA's financing, with the aid of 100 mercenaries. Barlow confirmed that two of the captured men worked for Executive Outcomes and admitted that at least twelve of his employees have been killed or disappeared. South African deputy president Thabo Mbeki announced that 500 South African mercenaries were fighting alongside government troops in Angola. 'Those people ought not be there,' he declares.

In late June I am standing at the bank in the departure lounge of Jan Smuts airport attempting to purchase some US dollars before departing for Angola. I ask the teller to make sure that he gives me $100 bills with 1990 printing dates, because these are preferred by the *kinguila* street traders in Angola.

'What are you going to do in Angola?' he asks. I am a journalist. 'Are you going to write about Executive Outcomes and the mercenaries?' he asks. Possibly. 'What they're doing there is terrible,' the young man says. 'I was in the parachute regiment here and I was about to go to Angola until my sister's fiancé died there in March. They were lying to us. They said we would be training only, but once the guys get there, they have to fight. They should all come home. I have a cousin there now. If you run into him, tell Bruno that his family wants him to come back home.' I say that I will pass on the message.

13 The New Angola

A crowd of children gathers in the middle of the courtyard at the Cuando Catholic mission, but one boy stands out. It is not that his left leg has been amputated, that he has joined the new species, the *mutilados*, or that he hobbles around on crutches which catches my attention, but rather his alert and determined eyes. It is February 1994 and my BBC colleague Chris Simpson and I have come to the Cuando mission, partly to see what life is like outside Huambo, the UNITA capital about 20 miles to the west, and partly to see the orphanage which the Church is running. The image which will stick with me, though, is that little boy's gaze.

I sit around with the kids on the cement path that surrounds their living quarters, chatting with them to loosen them up and let them get used to us. They have seen visitors before, but not very often. Then I ask if any of them is prepared to talk about how they came to be at the mission. It is a pointless question, because I already know who is going to speak up first. Lourenço Figueiredo propels himself forward on his crutch and announces that he has something to say to the world. 'The people are suffering. I want peace.' Anything else? 'And some shoes too.' Lourenço is a strong, fearless kid. The nuns say he has a dominating personality. He would probably have been a good athlete had the civil war not robbed him of his limb, perhaps even of his childhood. I think that if I had a son, I would want him to be like Lourenço. He is only ten years old, but he seems like an adult, though more focused, more driven than many I know.

When I ask him what happened to his leg, there is no embarrassment, no shyness at speaking with a foreigner, no sense that he is somehow different from other children, and disadvantaged. Lourenço speaks the truth. He is the symbol of everything that is wrong with a civil war fought primarily against innocent civilians, the *povo*, by armies of conscripted youngsters on behalf of power-mad politicians.

Lourenço was a normal kid growing up in a village called Caconda, about 130 miles south of the Cuando mission in the neighbouring province of Huíla. A few days after Savimbi decided he could not accept defeat in the 1992 elections, fled to Huambo crying fraud and ordered his army to drive the government out of the countryside, UNITA launched a mortar attack on Caconda. That was nine days before election outcome was even known and 22 days before the battle of Luanda.

'We heard the explosions and I was hiding under my bed. When I woke up I was like this,' says Lourenço looking down at the stump where his leg should be. 'I have not seen my parents since then.' Red Cross workers found Lourenço and brought him to the Cuando mission orphanage on 8 January 1993, a few days before they themselves had to be evacuated from Huambo because UNITA's 55-day siege was under way.

The 140 children at the Cuando mission represent a tiny fraction of the hundreds of thousands of Angolan kids who have no one to look after them. Most wander aimlessly around the countryside or live by their wits on the streets of Luanda and other major cities, begging for money, washing or even just watching cars. In what should be one of Africa's richest countries, guarding vehicles has become a major form of employment.

As the orphans at Cuando mission line up to sing a couple of songs for us about peace and wanting their parents back, Lourenço moves to the front. His strong voice carries over the rest. His eyes are fixed on me, his face dead-pan until I crack a smile and he breaks into bashful laughter, the only time he seems soft and vulnerable like a normal little boy. When he and his mates finish singing, they break off into small groups chasing each other in games of tag. As we leave Lourenço is running around the courtyard at a remarkable speed, as if he has not yet noticed that he is missing a leg.

The Cuando mission, formed in 1911, has become a magnet for a great variety of victims of the war – the hungry, the homeless, the sick, the blind and those who have simply lost the will to survive on their own. 'It is the work of a mission to be an asylum,' says Father Cornelius Kok, a 55-year-old Dutch priest who runs the mission, in his staccato Portuguese. The mission takes all the orphans brought to it, whether their parents have been killed by UNITA or by government troops. Seventy-seven of the children arrived the previous July from UNITA-controlled areas in the neighbouring province of Bié where Savimbi's men are laying siege to the provincial capital of Kuito.

To the left of the church is a queue of 100 people waiting for blankets, which they can exchange for food in the countryside. They sometimes sit there for several days, hoping a Caritas truck will bring in a new shipment. To the right, behind the orphanage, is an even more distressing scene. Dozens of stick-like people have arrived from the *planalto*, once Angola's breadbasket, in search of food. The hungriest people are immediately sent to a small cement building where the nuns have set up a makeshift kitchen to cook maize and beans in huge metal pots. The food, as well as medicines and clothes, comes from Caritas. I wonder how many Angolans would have starved to death were it not for Caritas, an agency that is consistently able to go to places which the better known, more publicity-conscious UN and international relief agencies cannot reach.

Several dozen people dressed in rags are sitting in the dirt and the tall grass waiting silently for the nuns to prepare the day's lunch. Maria Mamunga has brought her three children to the mission from the nearby village of Nanghenya. She is so thin that her dry skin literally hangs off her bones. 'We would have died if we did not come here,' she says. 'If you want to see real suffering, how the people are dying, please visit Nanghenya.' We promise to do so.

The maize harvest on the *planalto* is still almost two months away and the signs are that it will be a bad one. Rains have been poor. 'We are praying, hoping every day for the rain,' says Father Kok, who came to Angola in 1959 and has been at the Cuando mission for the past fourteen years. 'I have never seen people dying here because they had nothing to eat. A lot of people are going to the city, but there is nothing to eat there. People are selling off everything they have: clothes, shoes, tables.'

Father Kok is disgusted with the whole business of war. He

is tired and, although hardly anything makes sense to him any longer, he is certain of one thing. Neither the government nor Savimbi's UNITA are fighting for the *povo*, freedom or democracy. They are fighting for power. 'If there is ever peace here, everyone has to be pardoned because many things have been carried out by all sides. They were practically equal, and the people felt this,' says Father Kok.

Hundreds of Angolans have passed through the church schools, ordinary people who got on well with each other, until they joined one of the political parties. It is unfathomable to him that the same children and youngsters who attended his classes are waging a war that has ripped the country apart, made a mockery of the dreams of independence and transformed the once proud farmers of the *planalto* into emaciated beggars waiting days for blankets or a plate of maize meal. 'All the people are cynical. Everything we're seeing is impossible to believe. We hear about Somalia and the Hutu-Tutsi conflict and we think that can't happen here. But it is here. We have to remember that many leaders on both sides were students at the missions. This war is incomprehensible because everyone has members of the family on both sides. This is a war within the family, because they are the same people.'

Father Kok says he wants to show us something. He leads us down a path that cuts through a grove of eucalyptus trees at the back of the mission. 'Over there is where the Cubans used to stay when they occupied the mission in the 1980s. They didn't bother me much and in a way they were disciplined. They had three doctors here.' Further along the path Father Kok suddenly veers off the trail and leads us through some thorn bushes. We stand on the edge of a large crater, perhaps eight feet wide and five feet deep. 'That is where one of the bombs fell.' I cannot imagine what the bomb would have done had it hit the church, or the orphanage, which are just 300 yards away.

The bombs were dropped by government jets in late 1993. Why, I ask Father Kok, would the government want to bomb the mission? Perhaps they were trying to hit the dam and the reservoir on the other side of the mission? Perhaps they thought UNITA soldiers were hiding here? 'That's ridiculous. They know we have no soldiers here. What we have are myself, an old priest, the sisters, the orphans and a lot of people looking for food and clothes. The only purpose I can imagine was that the bombs were meant for the dam. If they were intended for the dam, though, they should have been dropped over there. That doesn't seem to me to be a very good interpretation.' My own interpretation is that those who ordered jets to bomb a Catholic mission in the middle of nowhere are truly desperate people. How can such people honestly pretend that they were ruling in the name of the *povo*? But of course, for many, 'These are not people, they are Bailundos.'

As we say our farewells to Father Kok, the old women and men waiting for blankets that might come today, maybe tomorrow, maybe never, continue to sit on a brick ledge in the hot sun. One day these people, or maybe their sons and daughters, will rise up and throw out their self-styled leaders, rulers who have brought them to such a state of utter misery. But perhaps they will not. These people and their ancestors have suffered such atrocities over centuries of the slave trade, internecine wars, Portuguese occupation and now this. Maybe they will bear it and remain silent forever.

Father Kok has given us directions to the village of Nanghenya, where Maria Mamunga described conditions of severe hunger, so we head back down the road to Huambo. Father Kok said we would have to turn off down a dirt road, but dirt roads are common in these parts so we stop to ask a young man walking towards Huambo. He agrees to take us there.

Nanghenya is five miles west of Cuando mission and the road is not really a road at all, more a path through the parched maize fields which, like the people, are waiting for the heavens to open up and provide salvation. The sun is hot, the light bright, but the clear blue skies return the gaze of hundreds of thousands of peasants and their fields with a cold blue stare.

We know we have reached the centre of the village when the path simply stops in a clearing surrounded by huts. Dozens of people suddenly gather, mentally digesting the first vehicle, the first foreigners they have seen for months. Everyone is covered in fine brown dust, their hair, their noses, their legs wrapped in a veil of earthly powder. For a moment they are silent. Many of the children have thin red hair and extended bellies. We ask how things are in Nanghenya, a redundant question if there ever was one. 'There is no food, father. The people are starving,' says an elderly man who identifies himself as a *soba*. Can you show us? 'Follow me.'

We walk through the village centre. There are dried maize stalks and dust everywhere, but no chickens or goats: the normal rhythm of village life has long been stilled. Within minutes my white trousers have a brown tint from the dust. We reach the door of a hut. Some young men enter and there is a commotion inside. They re-emerge with a gaunt man in their arms. He cannot walk. A few withered children, their faces covered in dust, follow the procession out of the dwelling. They do not smile. They do not giggle. They stare.

Nascimento Massambo is a farmer. He knows he is dying. He sits down to explain why he and his children are starving to death. 'When the illness came, it was just slowly, slowly. I cannot cope. Now there is no food in the house and the illness is affecting the children. I have sold off everything and have no way of making ends meet.'

Since his wife and parents died last year, Massambo says, he has been looking after his children. The neighbours are trying to help him, but they have no food either. There is no telling what will happen to the children if he passes away. 'That is all I have to say,' Massambo concludes. I am embarrassed that we have bothered him. Massambo attempts to heave his body from the chair. He cannot. The young men lift him up again and re-enter the house.

We return to the clearing where our car is parked to speak with the senior *soba* of Nanghenya, Mariano Ndelefy, an ancient man wearing a bowler hat and a well-worn sports jacket. There were 675 people in his village, he says, but one-tenth of them have perished in the past three months. 'It began in November and the children were the first to begin dying. We are eating some leaves, but the people don't have the strength to look for food any more.'

By now the sun is setting and we have to begin the fifteen-mile trip back to Huambo. Looking out of the car window I watch the passing fields, the occasional blown-up vehicle, and think of the trip I made in 1991 from Luanda to Huambo. I wonder what Rosa, the woman in Caimbambo who asked if the war would resume, is doing now. If she is alive, she is probably in a refugee camp waiting for food hand-outs. I hope she never remembers that white man who came by one day while she was selling oranges and said that he thought the peace would last because the people were tired of war.

It is sunset when we reach Huambo and we stop off at our hotel, the only one operating in the city. It is a converted clothing factory. The rest of the city's hotels are in ruins, casualties of UNITA's glorious victory in the battle for Huambo, Savimbi's 'liberated' city. The hotel owner, a Portuguese businessman named Alcides Gonçalves da Cruz, asks us if we have had a good day. Oh yes, we say, very interesting.

Chris and I arrived in Huambo a few days earlier courtesy of a UN flight which was bringing a couple of aid officials, including a de-mining expert, from Luanda. The UN aid co-ordination office, known as UCAH, has had to request permission both from UNITA and the government for us to travel to the city. Ours is a somewhat unusual visit for journalists coming from government-controlled territory because we are being allowed to spend the night in Huambo. On landing at the airport I immediately begin to regret the originality of the event.

As we disembark from the plane several UNITA officials conduct us to what used to be the VIP lounge, just to the right of a huge poster of Savimbi welcoming visitors to his capital. They immediately hand us immigration forms, as if we have entered a different country. I am afraid that they are going to stamp our passports with some form of UNITA emblem, which will present us with untold problems back in Luanda, but they merely grab up our papers. One wiry little man sees from the form that I am living in South Africa and begins to question me about the situation in the run-up to the country's first all-race elections. 'Mandela will never win there, will he? Our information is that the South Africans will vote overwhelmingly for President de Klerk. The South Africans won't vote for a communist like Mandela.' It is then that I realise that I am not in another country but that I have just landed on another planet. The mind boggles at how out of touch seemingly intelligent UNITA officials are, how thoroughly UNITA's distinctive form of brainwashing penetrates the minds of its followers. No wonder they were so easily convinced that they were cheated out of the 1992 elections. Savimbi, *O Mais Velho*, says so, so it must be true.

I cannot pass up such an opportunity to shatter the man's world-view. Well, no, I say, Mandela will win at least 60 per cent and de Klerk's National Party will be lucky if it gets 20 per cent of the vote. There is absolutely no doubt that by May Mandela will be president of South Africa. A stunned silence is followed by a smile which is bolstered by the confidence that only extreme ignorance can foster. 'That is not the information we have here in Huambo.' Oh, there is absolutely no doubt about it, I say. The National Party will consider itself very fortunate with 20 per cent. His increasingly uneasy smile signals the end of the conversation and he scurries out to the tarmac with our papers. I see him talking animatedly with several other UNITA officials, probably relaying what I told him about Mandela's imminent victory as proof that I am a communist journalist from Luanda, another victim of MPLA propaganda. When I ask where the toilet is they send someone to accompany me even though it is only five yards away.

After about 30 minutes no transport has arrived to take us into town and I am beginning to wonder whether this visit to Huambo was such a good idea after all. A vehicle is on its way, the UNITA officials assure us. Finally it comes and we begin a slow drive towards Savimbi's capital.

The helicopter shot down in a field near the airport because it flew too close to *O Mais Velho*'s house, the one whose metal blades the kids used to jump up and down on, is still there, but with no children in sight. Savimbi's Casa Branca residence has so many holes blasted in its walls that it looks like a piece of rotting Swiss cheese. Further down a main avenue into the city our UNITA guides take us past the charred remains of a Russian-built tank. There is a human skeleton inside. Its driver had been burnt alive. Despite the destruction, the streets are remarkably clean. Gangs of women move up and down the roads sweeping up leaves and twigs in front of houses that have been blown away by mortars, tank shells or bombs dropped by government jets. I later ask a UN official if the women receive pay for sweeping the streets. 'UNITA makes them an offer they can't refuse,' he says.

The city centre looks almost deserted. The only vehicles are those owned by top UNITA officials, a few businessmen, the Catholic Church and the international aid agencies. The modern buildings look as if a giant has taken huge bites out of them. Most of their roofs appear as if something punched its fist through them and ripped out their insides. At this point the UNITA officials launch into their tirade about how the MPLA is responsible for all the devastation. The diatribe against the government suddenly goes silent when we enter the central plaza in front of the post office, the governor's palace and the MPLA headquarters. The buildings have massive cavities and thousands of bullet holes in them. And who did this? The *guerra*, says one UNITA official, meaning that UNITA did it. On several of the walls graffiti announce 'With UNITA, A New Future' and 'With UNITA, A New Angola'.

The quick tour over, we are driven over to Cruz's hotel in Huambo's old industrial area. The driver drops us off and says he will be back in a few minutes. Cruz is bubbling with excitement at the arrival of more guests. Business is looking up, but he is worried because the conversion of the clothing factory into a hotel is not complete. He barks orders for the staff to start cleaning the rooms, preparing linen and carrying water to the bathrooms. It turns out that water and electricity are major problems in the capital of Savimbi's new Angola.

After an hour our car still has not returned. There is only one option open to us. Start walking. The central hospital is less than a mile away so we will begin there. If UNITA shows up again, we tell Cruz, let them know we have gone to the hospital. Believe it or not, this is a fairly bold step. UNITA, like the MPLA, especially in the old days, does not like journalists walking around unchaperoned in the areas which they control. They become jumpy about the possibility of erroneous conclusions being reached. As we descend towards a small creek, we startle a group of women and children washing their clothes and then emerge from a patch of thick bushes into the Bairro Académico, the wealthy neighbourhood near a huge secondary school on the side of the hill. We pass some buildings peppered with bullet holes, as almost all buildings are in Huambo. Parts of the road are ripped up from the impact of mortar shells.

Some students are lounging around in the sun in front of the school. UNITA, with the help of the international aid agencies, is trying to get children to attend classes again. This is proving to be a difficult task, however, because after UNITA won the battle for Huambo its soldiers and supporters, like their counterparts in Luanda, went on a massive looting spree. Books, desks, chairs – everything has been stolen. UNITA officials later tell us it was the MPLA's fault.

The city's main hospital is also largely empty of fixtures and supplies. The laboratory has far less equipment than the most deprived inner-city high school in the United States, but at least its floors and wards are generally cleaner than the Josina Machel hospital in Luanda. Broken windows and bullet holes abound and part of the roof was ripped off in a government bombardment.

We head for the paediatric ward to see the condition of the children. About 90 youngsters are being treated for severe malnutrition. One little two-year-old looks like a living skeleton. Others have red hair and extended bellies. The chief of the ward is Fandila Chilonga Lopes, a cheery nurse who has been in charge for the past five years. I ask her why there is apparently so much hunger in Huambo, a city surrounded by fertile farm land. 'All the children you see here are from the city. They're from families which were accustomed to a certain type of life. They worked for companies or for the government and they had salaries at the end of each month. Later with the war they became unemployed, without any way of surviving and now they're in this situation. This child needs to be fed in a hyper-protein, hyper-calorie way. She also needs medicines, antibiotics and anti-malaria drugs, because the malnourished are hit by infections. They get scabies and urinary infections. The hospital doesn't have the necessary medicine. We have received medicines from international organisations but in insignificant quantities that aren't enough for all the kids in the hospital.'

Nurse Lopes's explanation about the destitution of the city folk, the people who formerly had paid jobs, is obvious. All over town there are maize stalks on unused land, in stream-beds and in people's back gardens. It gives Huambo an eerie feel, as if, in line with UNITA's early Maoist ideology, the city is being returned to the countryside.

That night at the hotel Cruz sends a young man out to buy some beers for us. He is trying to make us feel welcome. When the beers arrive we notice that they are Windhoek lagers, the first hint that Huambo has contacts with the outside world. Cruz, now one of Huambo's leading businessmen, explains that once in while a convoy of trucks winds its way down to the Namibian border to trade wood and ivory for food and beer. If it is lucky the convoy takes fourteen days to reach the frontier, a few days to carry out the trading and another two weeks for the return trip. Business people in Huambo can make small fortunes from such trade. Convoys also haul goats and cattle in lorries up to the meat-starved diamond-producing areas of north-eastern Angola around Cafunfo. A head of cattle worth $100 in Huambo can fetch more than $1,000 in Cafunfo, he says. I begin to understand why Cruz and a handful of other Portuguese did not join the evacuation of 400 foreigners carried out by the Red Cross after UNITA captured the city.

Cruz says he lives by the adage 'The more difficulties there are, the better the opportunities.' He was born in Aveiro in central Portugal 49 years ago and came to Huambo in 1968 after serving for three years as an infantry soldier with the Portuguese army on the eastern front. In Cruz's version of local history, those were Huambo's golden days. In the last years before independence Portugal attempted to make up for centuries of neglect and exploitation by funding schools, hospitals and factories. 'The world doesn't appreciate what the Portuguese did for Angola,' he says. He becomes irritated when reminded of the slave trade or how in terms of literacy and economic development in Africa, Portugal came last among the colonial powers.

He is typical of Portuguese colonials who have sided with a particular ethnic group in Angola. Africans aligned with the MPLA are lazy blacks who 'wreck everything', but Savimbi's Umbundu people 'are very hard working', which means that they are paid very little money and their bosses earn handsome profits. I am sure the Portuguese plantation owners who sent the Ovimbundu to work the coffee and cotton fields in the north said much the same thing.

Soon after he came to Huambo Cruz began to work as a painter and then began to produce briefcases and luggage, examples of which still adorn his hotel. Despite the turmoil of Portugal's withdrawal from Angola, Cruz decided to stay on. 'Independence has brought nothing but trouble, but I knew there were many opportunities for someone who was willing to work.' By the 1980s Cruz established a consortium involved in the manufacture of light fittings, clothes and food products. In Huambo his company struggled as the civil war worsened, but he was earning valuable hard currency by renting out property in Luanda to foreign oil companies.

During the battle for Huambo Cruz drove around the city loading the wounded and the dead onto his truck and taking them to the UNITA clinic outside the city. He sent his wife and three children out with the Red Cross evacuation but decided to remain behind, explaining that, 'I have a lot of wealth here. I built this factory. I didn't want to run the risk of being evacuated and losing everything.'

Cruz's decision to remain behind ingratiated him with Huambo's new rulers. His first move was to take advantage of the destruction of the city's hotels by converting two floors of his clothing factory into a small inn, which UNITA recommends to journalists, aid workers, foreign advisers and occasionally even to visiting generals. A room and three meals a day cost $20. The kitchen and laundry are in the back warehouse alongside 150 idle sewing machines.

We settle in for the evening and Cruz cranks up his generator for electricity. General Beja, UNITA's commander in Huambo, passes by for a drink in Cruz's office. I enter to introduce myself and ask for his help in arranging an interview with Savimbi. He says that he will see what he can do, but Savimbi is not in town at the moment. I have bad memories of my endless waiting for an interview with Savimbi in November 1992 and tell myself not to count on anything. As we sit around chatting, Beja discusses the peace negotiations in Lusaka which have entered their fourth month.

No matter what happens at the talks, Beja says, 'UNITA will never give up Huambo. The MPLA wants to force us to return to the bush, but we lived in the bush for long enough and we will never go back. We are here and we will stay in our beloved city of Huambo.' There is evidence to confirm his thinking. UNITA has set up the skeleton of an alternative government in Huambo, complete with ministries of education, health, humanitarian affairs and housing. A UNITA police force drives around the streets in a Land Rover.

Cruz tries to strike a lighter note and asks if we would like to watch a video. His selection is extensive and after some debate we settle on *Body Heat* with William Hurt and Kathleen Turner. I cannot fight off sleep, however, and head off to bed before the film ends.

The next morning we set off early to one of the Save the Children feeding centres in the shanty-towns on the east of the city. We arrive at the Bom Pastor centre at about 9 o'clock to find over 600 children standing with their mothers in a queue waiting to receive a dish of maize meal. The children are thin but look in relatively good shape. Most have been coming to the kitchen for the past three weeks. I sit down next to a tall, strong woman named Elizabeth Casilva to ask her what she is doing there. She has brought her four-year-old son, Erickson, who seems a normal child except for his slightly blond hair. Three weeks ago, she says, his hair was red and his legs were severely emaciated. Many of her neighbours' children starved before the food kitchens started to open in January. Elizabeth speaks excellent Portuguese and is obviously from the city. So why has she and her family fallen to such a state?

Her husband António is a mechanic who had a job until the siege shut down the town's businesses. Since then he has been out of work. The family had some money saved, but that quickly went on food for the five children. The eldest child, António José, worked for the government and disappeared during the fighting. Like most people who once had jobs in the city, Elizabeth's family was starving by November. They began to sell off everything in the house, including their clothes and furniture, at the central market.

I ask how Elizabeth spends her average day. 'Each morning I make a bit of maize meal and stir it in the water to give it to the children. Then I gather whatever I can find in the house, a chair or a shirt, and go to the market to see if I can sell it for some maize. I can usually get one kilo of maize for a shirt. Some days no one is buying. If I don't sell anything I return home and make some more maize soup. We don't have any salt or oil. We have to feed the children first or they would die. Then what is left over is for my husband and myself. António has anaemia. In November his legs became so inflamed that he had to stay in bed all the time. Since then the family has been starving. If it wasn't for this kitchen, Erickson would have died.'

As we speak I feel sure that this woman has become comfortable enough with me to say what she thinks about the war, about politics, about which party she supports. I am disappointed. She is like most civilians in Huambo. No one except strong UNITA supporters and UNITA officials wants to discuss politics, while UNITA militants talk of nothing else. So when I ask Elizabeth what she thinks, her response is firm. 'It's better for us not to discuss such things. All I can say is that it would be a great pleasure if this war would stop. No one understands why the fighting continues.'

One of the kitchen workers approaches me to ask if I will taste the children's gruel. The children watch in amazement. I put a little in my mouth and the thick porridge of potato, maize and sugar tastes surprisingly good. I turn to the assembled children, smile and rub my stomach in satisfaction. They roar with laughter and dig into their food.

We decide to return to the town centre to photograph the ruined buildings. At the corner of First of May Avenue and the city's central park there is a particularly badly hit building, so we go around the back to have a look. We walk through the ground floor of a building and reach a small patio. Maria Sasfates is preparing lunch for her sixteen-strong extended family there. Her patio is surrounded by huge piles of rubble, the remains of two buildings destroyed by bombs dropped by government jets six months before.

Miraculously, Maria's apartment block and luncheonette survived more or less intact. One of the bombs hit the very spot where her parents had been sitting 30 minutes before the attack. Luckily, they had gone inside to play cards. 'We think it was a miracle that nothing happened to them,' she says. Sasfates was serving soup to customers when the warplanes roared overhead. 'We were used to it so when we heard the sound of the MiG we ran and hid.' None of her family was hurt, but one pedestrian and an elderly shoemaker named Fernando were killed in the street outside.

I have to ask what she is still doing in the centre of the city when she knows that the jets can return at any moment. 'This is my home. My husband ran away to Luanda and hasn't come back, but we'll stay here for ever. I hope the war will end, but I don't know if it really will. War destroys everything, hungry children ...' she says as she breaks down sobbing.

When we return to the hotel that afternoon, Cruz is giddy with excitement about a new opportunity that has come his way. He is holding a letter in his hand and says, 'This is from Dr Savimbi.' The letter from *O Mais Velho* says that Cruz can choose any of the derelict hotels in town to rehabilitate and manage, so he sits down to make the calculations about what it will cost to rebuild the Hotel Roma or the Hotel Almirante, both of which have suffered extensive damage. It does not matter – Cruz knows he will receive full support from UNITA and I watch him doing the sums in his head. For some, at least, the future is bright in Savimbi's 'new Angola'.

That evening I hear a familiar voice in Cruz's room. It is that of Brigadier Armindo Urbano, Chasanya, the pony-tailed white commander. Chasanya has risen to become UNITA's operations chief and he is as arrogant as ever. When I enter the room he is obviously uncomfortable until he recognises me from our meeting in November 1992, a few months before UNITA launched its final siege of Huambo. Chasanya is very curious about life in Luanda. He has heard that it is difficult. 'They say that Luanda is about to explode, that it's total chaos,' he says gleefully. The implication is that life in Huambo is infinitely better, that Huambo is proof of UNITA's superior capacity to govern. But Huambo is in ruins, thousands of its people are starving, there is no water and electricity. I do not see how life is any better for the average resident than in Luanda. Chasanya does not feel the pain. He drives around in a landcruiser with his own bodyguard. Like their government counterparts in Luanda, UNITA officials do not suffer from the war. They want for nothing.

'The good thing about what's happened in Huambo is that the problems have forced these people to work for the first time. The city people are lazy, and finally they are being made to work,' he says. I wonder how Elizabeth Casilva, whose family is on the brink of starvation, would feel about such a statement. She could not possibly work any harder, and yet only a feeding centre kept her son Erickson from dying. Huambo might be UNITA's urban paradise, but it is a false one.

Chasanya echoes General Beja's view that no matter what happens at the Lusaka peace talks, UNITA will never give up Huambo. There are strong hints that, whatever the outcome of the negotiations, UNITA plans to keep on fighting, that a peace deal would simply be to provide some breathing space to prepare for the final march towards Luanda. The May 1991 peace accords signed in Bicesse have helped carry UNITA from its headquarters in the remote south-eastern village of Jamba to Huambo in the heart of the country. Despite the collapse of the electoral process in 1992, UNITA has made vast strategic gains. Chasanya's parting words are haunting: 'We haven't been able to reach the Atlantic coast yet, but one day we will.'

After five days in Huambo there is still no word about when an interview with Savimbi might be possible. Some UNITA officials say that he is in town, others that he is not. They are working on it. By now UNITA has tired of our presence in Huambo. The only official who tries to help is Tony Chivukuvuku, the younger brother of UNITA's former foreign affairs spokesman who was captured during the battle for Luanda and is now staying at the plush Hotel Tivoli in Luanda under a loose detention order. Tony is a bright, honest young man who never minds walking around the city, is always as helpful as possible, and does not spew forth the routine UNITA propaganda favoured by his colleagues. He supports UNITA but does not have the brainwashed world-view of most of the movement's supporters.

I reckon this will be my last day so I decide to visit the old UNAVEM camp by the post office where I had met Lieutenant-Colonel Mortlock, the New Zealand commander of UNAVEM, on various occasions both before and after the elections. During the 30-minute walk to the camp I tell Tony how things had been on my previous visits, including the time I met UNITA's General Wiyo and Colonel Jorge of the MPLA in November 1992 when they were desperately trying to halt the final battle for Huambo. I tell him that

General Wiyo in particular was anxious that the peace should hold, how he said that he did not want to waste any more of his life on a senseless war. Tony tells me that Wiyo is still fighting today over on the western front. Colonel Jorge is in the MPLA army and Lieutenant-Colonel Mortlock, I say, was evacuated from Huambo in the early days of the battle in January 1993, an emotionally drained man.

When we turn into the camp everything is silent, a far cry from the buzz of activity when idealistic young soldiers and UN personnel from around the world were rushing to and fro, and helicopters were lifting off and landing in an effort to transform one of Africa's worst disasters, Angola's civil war, into an international success story.

All that is left now are spent mortar shells and cartridge cases littering the ground. Where the smart tents and prefab houses once stood, complete with a canteen and a satellite phone installation, there are only overgrown trenches where Lieutenant-Colonel Mortlock and his group of unarmed UN soldiers and police officers huddled for several days awaiting their evacuation. I wonder what they must have felt then, spending the night in those shallow trenches with missiles, shells and bullets racing overhead. The former hospital building which served as the UNAVEM headquarters is now abandoned, pockmarked by bullets. I can still see General Wiyo standing next to his supposed enemy, Colonel Jorge, saying, 'I lost my whole youth to sixteen years of war, and the last thing I want is to see it start again.' That day the two men were not enemies but comrades in a battle to stop Angola from destroying itself. It was a battle which they lost.

We walk over to inspect the last piece of UN hardware left at the compound. It is a Russian-built MI-8 helicopter that was used to ferry UN soldiers out to inspect demobilisation camps and to carry food, ballot forms and election equipment to remote polling stations to ensure that all Angolans had a chance to vote. Now it is a wreck. Everything that can be removed has been taken. A strong stench emanates from the aircraft's belly. The helicopter has become a public toilet, a perfect symbol of how Angola's political leadership, particularly the UNITA 'freedom fighters' led by *O Mais Velho*, literally shat on the commitment of the international community and the Angolan people to seek an honourable way out of the madness.

Tony too is moved by the scene, so I ask him the question. Savimbi lost the election by a mere 9 percentage points and he had a chance to contest a run-off vote and to lead a strong opposition against a government which was likely to collapse soon under the sheer weight of its own corruption. Is all this suffering, this incredible waste, worth 9 percentage points? Tony shakes his head and thinks for a moment. 'The problem is that you have two forces fighting for power, and each one believes that if it lays down its arms, the other will subjugate it,' he says. 'The logic is to keep on fighting.' Maybe it is that simple, one side fighting the other until one dies. They just cannot stop. Fight or perish.

Hopes for so-called 'national reconciliation' are naïve, the idea of compromise a mirage, no matter how many people die and suffer, step on landmines or fall victim to kwashiorkor. All in the name of a cause, not of the *povo*, but of power. Ideologies come and go, negotiations are a matter of tactics, the cause of absolute power ever enduring. The old adage that power corrupts people is misplaced. It is people who corrupt power.

While Tony and I are stomping around the desolate remains of the UNAVEM camp, my colleague Chris Simpson is on the other side of town running into trouble with the authorities. When I return to the hotel Chris is distraught. While he was interviewing some residents of a derelict building some women asked him to take a few letters to Luanda to tell their families that they are all right. They had not been able to communicate with their relatives and Chris told them that he was willing to help them out. A young boy had followed him and saw him take the letters. As he finished the interviews and walked out of the building, the little boy asked him to deliver a letter to Benguela for him. Chris said he could not because he was travelling to Luanda, but the boy is actually a UNITA spy and a couple of young toughs in fatigue trousers and Savimbi T-shirts immediately stopped Chris and identified themselves as 'immigration police'. They said he had 'broken the laws of the country'. They confiscated the letters as well as the cassette with his interviews. I find him back at the hotel.

I assure him that everything will be all right, that General Beja and the other UNITA officials will be able to straighten out the problem. When they arrive the next morning, they are accompanied by two security men. They insist that Chris is guilty of an infraction and suggest his action was deliberate. The officials say there is nothing they can do, that this is a security matter, yet they are keen for us to stay, promising that we can attend a church service with *O Mais Velho* and perhaps have an interview in the next few days. We tell them that if they return Chris's cassette we will consider staying for a few more days, but if not we are leaving today. Returning the cassette and the letters is impossible, however, so we depart on a UN flight that very morning. It seems that in Savimbi's 'new Angola' sending a letter other than through the usual channels is a crime.

14 Kuito Madness

Olegário Cardoso walks down the gloomy hall of his Casa Ford general store and points towards the cement floor in between rows of empty metal shelves. 'Thirty people sleep there, twelve over there, and another four families next to them,' he says. 'We have more than 300 people in all living in Casa Ford.' For 34 years Cardoso's store stocked building materials, car parts and, until recently, school books for the children of Kuito. Now dozens of the city's youngsters sleep here along with their mothers and fathers, if they are among the lucky ones whose parents are still alive. People even live under the marble stairs to the second floor. 'The kids from the street break everything, but there's nothing we can do. They have nowhere else to go.' Casa Ford has become a refugee camp.

At the end of the corridor a door opens to another world, Cardoso's house, which is attached to the general store. Here the wooden furniture and mirrors are freshly polished and everything is in order. We pass through the kitchen where Cardoso's cook is preparing a lunch of maize, beans and salad. Cardoso may be the most prominent businessman in Kuito, but he too lives on a refugee's diet. It is a sign of the times. When he apologises that he cannot offer me coffee, his cook looks on with sympathetic eyes, as if saying to himself, 'Imagine, the *patrão* cannot serve his guests properly.' Cardoso says he has not been able to find coffee for months.

As we ascend a wooden staircase at the side of the house, we are covered in a veil of bright white light from the winter sun of Angola's central plateau. 'The best view of Kuito is from the roof,' Cardoso says.

Below stands the ruined heart of Kuito. A dozen three-

and four-storey buildings in the city centre are blackened shells, ripped apart by thousands of bullets and scores of mortar shells. Kuito was once a beautiful colonial town, Cardoso says. By May 1994 it has become a scene of utter devastation, the bell-wether of Angola's civil war, the site of its fiercest battles and the international aid effort to save civilians caught in the crossfire. Attacks by government forces on rebel positions in other parts of the country inevitably bring UNITA retaliation against Kuito or a suspension of aid supplies.

Looking across the street, Cardoso points out the municipal court which has been reduced to a concrete skeleton filled with piles of rubble. To the right and left are the Hotel Kuito and blocks of flats and shops which, like Cardoso's Casa Ford shop, are refugee centres, home to thousands of people, mainly women and children, who endure conditions of sheer squalor. They are permanently covered in a thick grey smoke from cooking fires that burns the eyes and fuels a non-stop chorus of coughing children.

The war has sliced the city in half. Looking down to the left, Cardoso points to a main avenue which serves as the frontline which divides the MPLA troops from the UNITA soldiers who have laid siege to the city for the past eighteen months, ever since Savimbi rejected his election defeat and Angola returned to war. The opposing soldiers are so close that they can, and frequently do, throw stones at each other. Many people who have taken refuge in Cardoso's Casa Ford shop and nearby buildings can look across the square and see their old houses now occupied by UNITA.

The war for what Savimbi says is the dignity of his UNITA movement and what President dos Santos describes as the defence of democracy has come down to this. The city's 30,000 residents are confined to an area of about one square mile, scrounging for survival in the debris of buildings blasted away by mortars and machine-gun fire, looking for water and food, maize and beans when the international aid flights can get in, rats and roots when they cannot. Some of my more excitable colleagues have written that the people of Kuito resorted to cannibalism, but that story remains just that, a story, as if the tragedy of Kuito needs to be exaggerated.

Nearly every family has buried one of its members killed in

battle, by the mortar shells that rain down on the city, or by cholera, malaria and the other illnesses that race through the city like waves of plague. Even disabled men tote AK-47 assault rifles. The city is one big armed camp. When a crowd of people were chasing a thief the day before my arrival, the outlaw turned around and threw a grenade at them. His pursuers were not deterred, however, and the police had to save him from being lynched.

Savimbi's struggle for the survival of his Umbundu people has become perverse. The overwhelming majority of residents in Kuito and the entire province of Bié are Ovimbundu, and in September 1992 nearly 80 per cent voted for Savimbi. Today UNITA is shelling the people of Kuito in order to save them, just as the government is sending its jets to liberate the people of Huambo by bombing them.

'UNITA has bombarded the city indiscriminately and killed parents and families, which has created a certain revulsion among the people,' says Cardoso. 'The majority of the people in Kuito voted for Savimbi and now they're being sacrificed. That is what they don't understand.'

By some estimates 500,000 people have died since Angola's civil war resumed in late 1992, perhaps one in ten of them in Kuito, about one-third of the city's original population. The United Nations was unable to begin a massive food airlift to Kuito until October 1993, nine months after UNITA launched the siege. By then thousands of people in the encircled government-held sector had starved to death. When bands of 150 people crossed the battle lines to forage for food, sometimes only half of them returned alive. 'Dante's *Inferno*' was the way one of the first outsiders to visit the town, Manuel Aranda da Silva, head of the UN Department of Humanitarian Affairs office in Luanda, described the scene at the time.

The first relief work by the UN and foreign aid agencies began in Kuito after UNITA, bowing to international pressure, temporarily halted its siege on 21 September 1993. A familiar pattern then developed. The fighting resumes, the aid flights are suspended and the foreign aid workers hide in their residences or cower in their bunkers as shells fall all around until UN officials in Luanda can negotiate a brief ceasefire to evacuate them. A few weeks later relative calm returns, the bodies are cleaned off the street, the aid effort starts afresh and the aid workers re-appear.

Battles often start when government soldiers try to sneak across the lines into UNITA-held territory to retrieve supplies of foodstuffs, cigarettes and ammunition from high-altitude parachute drops by Russian-built Ilushyn cargo planes. Even when the parachute drops hit their target they provoke clashes among government soldiers and police. During my visit casualties from those fights comprise the majority of the twenty young men who are receiving treatment for gunshot wounds at the main hospital, which Médecins sans Frontières has built in the offices used by the International Committee of the Red Cross before it fled from a previous round of fighting.

Before the food airlifts began most of the patients were women who had stepped on landmines while searching for food in the nearby fields. When the airlifts are forced to halt the number of anti-personnel victims will rise again. It is the same story I had heard in Malange the year before.

Minor spats can erupt into intense shelling at a moment's notice. An argument over the branch of a tree caused a particularly heavy week-long round of UNITA shelling and government bombing of rebel positions in February 1994. Cardoso remembers it well. 'It started at the blue building over there,' he says, pointing to a large house which served as the Chamber of Commerce during colonial times and soon after independence was converted into the local headquarters of the MPLA.

Several government soldiers attempted to drag a fallen branch back to their side for firewood. UNITA soldiers objected. Shots were fired into the air at first, but later the soldiers took aim, prompting mortar gunners some disance outside the town to unleash a barrage of shells. Cardoso recalls that UNITA snipers in the city centre made it impossible to recover the wounded. He helped one injured woman by throwing a rope from his shop into the street and dragging her inside. 'Living in Kuito is like being an imprisoned animal,' he says. 'There is just no way out.'

The civilians huddled in the buildings and in the handful of mud-hut neighbourhoods held by the government are a mixture of people from all over Bié province and beyond. Many were in Kuito on business or to visit relatives when the siege began. They remain trapped here. They have had no news of their families for the past eighteen months. One eight-year-old boy I meet, Júlio Evangelista, came to Kuito with his father hoping to receive a prosthesis to replace his left leg, which a landmine ripped away while he was playing in a field. His chance of a new limb was dashed after mortar shells destroyed the hospital and the siege has kept him from returning to his village five miles away.

A typical case is Eduardo Sauro, a man I find one day while travelling around the city with Hans Peter Vikoler, the Italian World Food Programme base manager. Sauro looks embarrassed as he struggles to keep the three shiny tin plates he has just received from rattling in his trembling hands, which leprosy has left as deformed stumps. Nor can he control the smile which explodes onto his face as soon as several relief workers jump out of Hans's UN landcruiser and begin handing out kitchen utensils to a group of war refugees living in tents.

'Now I can eat properly,' Sauro announces proudly. Maize porridge is cooking in a battered pot on a small wood fire, but I cannot work out how with just his two stumps he is going to pour it into his new plate, much less eat it. The answer comes moments later when two tiny barefoot girls, daughters of a neighbour who has gone to town to look for food, enthusiastically offer to serve him the meal. For the first time in ages they too are about to eat from plates.

Sauro is staying next to a community of refugees who have put up tents under a patch of mango trees. Unlike most of his neighbours, Sauro lives completely alone. He thinks his wife and four children are just a few miles away. For the past year they have been trapped behind UNITA lines. He has not seen them since he walked to the market a few hours before UNITA began another series of bombardments. The chances are that they were evacuated to the countryside along with the rest of the civilians in the rebel-held part of town, but I do not have the heart to tell him this as he takes comfort in believing that they are close by.

Now Sauro is a refugee in the government-held half of town. Like millions of Angolans, he has no control over his own life. Survival depends on the willingness of the rebels and the government army to halt the fighting for long enough to allow relief agencies, such as the World Food

Programme, the International Committee of the Red Cross and Médecins sans Frontières, to deliver food and medicines. Still, the day is a happy one for Sauro. He has shiny new tin plates so he can eat properly.

Across the way, an old man shouts, 'We are completely surrounded and we can't do anything.' The voice is that of António Quisapa, a 74-year-old *soba.* He still wears his light brown *soba* uniform and hat issued decades ago by the Portuguese colonial authorities. When I meet him he is standing outside his tent in a tiny camp for refugee *sobas.* 'You see those ruins on the hill over there,' he says, pointing to a few shattered mud huts about 500 yards away. 'No one can go beyond there because of the mines. It is as if we civilians are trapped in a cooking pot.'

Quisapa miraculously reached Kuito with his wife in May 1993 after fleeing the village he once ruled over just days before UNITA occupied the area. Previously a figure of ultimate authority for thousands of people, Quisapa is now struggling to maintain the fading shreds of his dignity, living in a tent, cooking in the dirt, surviving on hand-outs from foreigners. He says he had to flee the UNITA advance because as the *soba* he had co-operated with the MPLA government. He had no choice. Quisapa is particularly distressed because he has received news that the UNITA rulers of his village have installed their own *soba.* The government has their *sobas* and UNITA has another set. 'No one respects traditional power any more, they just use us for their own ends,' he says, staring at the ground. 'If I go back now, they'll kill me.'

As the conversation with *soba* Quisapa reminds me, I have little stomach for the depression that I knew Kuito would provoke. Kuito brings back too many memories. When I visited the city in September 1992 as dos Santos and Savimbi brought their electoral campaigns to the city, Angola was celebrating its first elections. During those two days Kuito was the focus of the carnival fever gripping the nation. I can still hear President dos Santos promising his supporters *O futuro certo.* And there was Savimbi in his baseball cap and T-shirt, threatening, cajoling, warning that, 'If they provoke me, this is going to get ugly.' The young man at the microphone screaming '*O nosso gallo*?' and the massive crowd responding '*Voa*'. How many of those people are dead now, sacrificed for a cause no one understands anymore?

I decided to make the trip to Kuito after the United Nations in Luanda arranged for Nicholas Shaxson of Reuters, Alex Vines of Human Rights Watch/Africa and myself to spend the night there, a rare opportunity for foreign journalists.

As we circle above the city in a UN plane, Kuito looks much as it did when I visited during the election campaign, but once we touch the ground the scale of the devastation comes into focus. The chants of the crowds wearing hats and party T-shirts in September 1992 echo only in my ears. Everywhere I turn I hope to wake up from the nightmare, to see the children clutching flowers and dancing to merengue music, holding their parents' hands and trying to catch a glimpse of the visiting politicians.

The airport is largely in ruins, occupied by a small garrison of government soldiers who are hanging around in the arrival hall. Their commanders are easy to spot. They are riding around on bicycles, prized possessions in a city with few cars and no petrol. Occasionally shooting erupts in the distance and an officer lends a soldier his bicycle to go and tell the men to stop fooling around.

Two dozen stevedores employed by the World Food Programme lounge around on the tarmac waiting to unload cargo planes bringing food, clothes and medicines flown in from the coast. As soon as an aircraft touches down, two lorries race over, one to deliver half of the loot to the government-held part of Kuito, the other to the UNITA side. The equal division is a UNITA condition for its permission for the aid to cross enemy lines into the city. Some would call it blackmail.

At this point the WFP is flying in 90 tonnes of food each week, sometimes more, which is enough to provide 100,000 people, or 50,000 on each side, with a minimum diet. Since there are no more than 30,000 people living on the government side, there is some cushion for the inhabitants when the flights are halted by another outbreak of fighting. UNITA profits even more by the arrangement as there are no civilians at all on its side of the city – Savimbi's men have forced them out into the countryside. A warehouse a few miles from a major UNITA logistics base is the destination for its portion, which can feed most of Savimbi's army.

Leaving the airport the trucks pass through the first checkpoint, a 'barrier' of string manned by a couple of government soldiers who lazily wave them on. As the food lorries head towards town, they immediately run into a remarkable sight: small groups of UNITA and government soldiers, supposedly arch enemies, are mingling in the middle of the road, effectively the no man's land. It is further confirmation that the young soldiers are not fighting for a cause. This is not their war. They just do what they are told: fight or perish. They break off their conversations for long enough to allow the vehicles through before continuing to chat to one another. At sunset they return to their trenches on either side of the road in case their commanders issue the orders to resume the *guerra*.

Fraternisation with the enemy, it turns out, is not unusual. At the various military checkpoints government and UNITA soldiers engage in cheerful banter. Sometimes they play cards, gambling for salt, which government planes drop by parachute, and firewood, scarce in the city but plentiful in the rebel-controlled countryside. Residents say the rival soldiers have even been known to organise bicycle races. Trade across the frontline has become so regular that UNITA troops have set up makeshift breweries to produce *cachipembe*, the potent maize-based drink, for sale to the government side. Sometimes the drink is exchanged for salt and clothes, as is the precious firewood and fruit and vegetables brought in from the countryside. Small markets in the city regularly sell produce from UNITA-controlled areas.

Given the ferocity of the fighting and the scale of destruction, such trade seems ludicrous. When I ask Cardoso about it he just laughs. 'Once in a while the government decrees a ban on trade with UNITA, or UNITA issues orders to stop selling to the city, and the business stops, but it soon starts again because we need the firewood and they need salt and clothes. There are cousins, sometimes even brothers, fighting each other across that line,' he says.

Gazing from Cardoso's rooftop, I see what looks like a column of ants appear in the distance, on the outskirts of Cunje, a town about four miles north of Kuito. It is a human caravan bringing wood from the countryside to the UNITA troops in Kuito who trade or sell it to the government side. 'This is a war of crazy people. One minute they do business together and the next they kill each other,' Cardoso says.

Nowhere is the taste of Kuito's madness stronger than at the UNITA checkpoint guarding the entrance to the city about one mile from the airport. It is run by a certain Captain Pepe whose task it is to ensure that the rebels receive their fair share of the goods sent by the outside world. When the lorries come from the airport, they stop at Captain Pepe's checkpoint where a UNITA driver mounts one of the trucks to steer it towards the rebel warehouse close to the UNITA army logistics base. The other lorry is cleared to drive on to the WFP warehouse in the city.

The checkpoint consists of two small red 'stop' signs facing opposite directions, two pieces of string across the road and a crudely painted sign which announces in English that 'Savimbi is our man' and 'Savimbi is the king of peace'. Perhaps UNITA has a sense of humour after all. Captain Pepe does not seem to have one. When we approach him, he sports that arrogant half-smile that is typical of Africa's roadblock dictators who have the power to decide whether unfortunate passers-by escape with their money, clothes and even their lives. From his swagger, he would be at home in Liberia, Nigeria, Mozambique or a dozen other countries where the line between police work and banditry is very fine indeed. Since the WFP is handing over generous food supplies, which UNITA is free to distribute to whomsoever it likes, the good captain is pleasant enough.

Hans, the WFP base manager, makes the required small talk, but within minutes the game begins. Captain Pepe's smile tightens slightly as he announces that he has a small worry: headquarters in Huambo has not informed him of a visit by journalists and Brigadier Karinala Samy, the commanding officer who can authorise our visit to UNITA-controlled areas, is out of town. Captain Pepe is lying. Several hours later we learn that Brigadier Samy was meeting with the International Committee of the Red Cross in Kuito at the very moment when Captain Pepe was insisting that he was elsewhere. We see him several times that day and inquiries about a meeting with Brigadier Samy, standard fare on the journalists' tour, are met with the same response: there is still no word when he will return.

After a while, it seems that he knows that we know he is being less than truthful, but the half-smile never leaves his face. Our suspicion is that a visit by journalists at that moment is, as they like to say in Angola, *inconveniente* for UNITA. The government radio is broadcasting hourly reports that UNITA is massing troops around Kuito for a major assault.

Another mile down the road brings us to a second army checkpoint at the gateway to the government-held sector. There Kuito's insane sense of humour is again on display. MPLA campaign posters, slightly sullied now, picture President dos Santos's soothing smile with the inevitable slogan, *O futuro certo*. A few hundred yards to the left is the field where two years ago President dos Santos made the promise of *O futuro certo* to a crowd of 25,000 people.

We ride into a scene of collapsed buildings and houses riddled by machine-gun fire and gaping holes blasted by mortar shells. Whole floors of multi-storey buildings have simply been blown away. There is a pot-hole in the middle of one road around which someone has drawn a red circle to alert drivers to the presence of an unexploded shell. As we cruise through the destruction towards the WFP warehouse, Hans turns up the volume on the landcruiser's stereo playing his favourite opera, *Il Trovatore*. It seems he too has a sense of humour, his own way of coping with Kuito's madness.

The WFP warehouse is situated in the city centre, next to Cardoso's Casa Ford shop and 50 yards or so from the frontline. The craziest part of it all is that, apart from the bombed-out buildings, daily life seems remarkably normal. There is a strange energy in Kuito, the energy of resistance. Young boys are making neat piles of stones they have gathered from the rubble of the municipal court to sell to residents taking advantage of a lull in fighting to rebuild their homes. Some of their friends are playing football while others are chasing each other in a game of tag. On many corners women are sitting by tiny street markets, hawking soap and tins of maize meal brought in by the aid agencies.

Barely standing supermarkets, hardware stores and office buildings are bustling with thousands of refugees. Behind their walls is an entire world, almost universally shrouded in the irritating smoke from the cooking fires. There are kitchens, cemeteries, pharmacies and, at the Hotel Kuito, even a shoe repairman.

When I stumble upon António de Castro, he is working in

complete darkness under the hotel's stairwell, carving new heels from strips of rubber he has salvaged from the tyres of burnt-out vehicles that litter the streets. Castro says he had left his home village of Caconda, about 250 miles south-west of Kuito, 33 years ago to make his fortune. He has been a shoe repairman for the past 30 years. 'There is always work for a shoe repairman, especially now,' he says with a broad smile. 'When I have the materials, I can fix seven or eight pairs a day. Since there is no way of finding new shoes in Kuito, I just keep fixing up the old ones.'

Kuito might have been bombed almost back to the stone age, but the spirit of getting on with life is infectious. Near the main hospital, rebuilt and run by Médecins sans Frontières, students attend driving classes even though there are virtually no private vehicles or petrol. Daily cleaning rosters are posted in several buildings whose walls have disintegrated in the mortar fire.

Kuito's residents simply refuse to give up. 'If we thought about the situation we are in, we would become very frustrated,' says Fernando Augusto, a history teacher given to extreme under-statement. 'I am working out of good faith. We have to have faith, because if we didn't we would be lost. There are other teachers who would like to work but they can't because they do not even have clothes or shoes.' Fernando is one of 500 teachers instructing 6,000 primary and secondary students in twenty schools that have been opened with help from the Irish aid agency, Concern. When I meet him, his students have just begun sitting for their exams.

His teaching career began seven years before when, after graduating from the local *liceu*, he became a *brigadista*, one of the young activists whose task it was to bring literacy to the rural poor. Now, like everyone else, Augusto is living as a refugee. His home has been destroyed and the only food he receives comes from the World Food Programme. He and his colleagues work for no pay. 'We would like to be paid, of course, but if that happened then the nurses and all the government workers would be demanding their pay. There would be big *confusão*,' says Fernando Pequinino, a mathematics teacher and head of the Bié provincial education department. 'Most of these teachers are working because they love it. Since I was a young boy I always wanted to be a teacher.'

The story is much the same over at the open-air

orphanage, where 137 children live in a dozen white canvas tents set up on some abandoned land. The head of the camp is Evangelista Chamale, a stout woman who has been caring for Kuito's orphans for the past fifteen years, although for most of that time in far better circumstances. She and the children live from day to day, never knowing when the fighting will start again, when a mortar shell will fall on their cluster of tents, when the food will run out.

They are preparing for the worst. In a clearing at the back, workmen are digging a bunker about fifteen feet long and six feet deep. Although it is a start, it will clearly not be big enough to shelter all the children if Savimbi's troops restart their mortar bombardments in another attempt to save the people of Kuito. As it is, ten to fifteen children sleep in each tent, which contains one reed mat the size of a double bed resting on a platform of bricks. Chamale and her staff of five, all volunteers, cannot possibly cope with the number of orphans so they ask the older children to look after the little ones, in her words 'to give them comfort, especially now that it is so cold'.

Provided there is no fighting, Chamale's day begins at sunrise. She rouses the children from the tents and organises breakfast, one of four daily meals consisting mainly of rice, beans and maize which she is able to serve thanks to donations from the international aid groups. They provide blankets and medicines too. Her big problem is finding shoes for the kids.

Chamale knows that she and her colleagues are almost out of their depth. Many of the children are suffering from physical and mental illnesses which she and her staff are not equipped to treat. 'We found these children wandering around the streets crying out for their mamas,' she says. 'Some had malaria, some were suffering from diarrhoea, but the worst thing was the trauma of the war. The shelling gives children mental problems, especially when they have no parents to hold them.'

As we drive off to another refugee camp, I wonder how Hans can do this day in and day out. People are always coming up to him, asking him to help bring more food, or soap, or blankets, to help to open another feeding centre. He is a celebrity, and since no one can pronounce his name properly, Hans is known simply as 'Anstee', after the the former Special UN Representative. Some families have even named their children after him. When I ask him why he does this, his explanation is simple: 'If we don't feed these people, they will certainly die.'

While we are driving, Hans takes a break from *Il Trovatore* and tunes in to the news broadcast of UNITA's Vorgan radio station. It is carrying an item on the UN-brokered peace negotiations that began in Lusaka on 15 November 1993, a process to which Savimbi and the UNITA leadership have repeatedly committed themselves. The Vorgan commentator does not give much cheer to those of his listeners hoping that the talks, now in their seventh month, will bring about a new peace agreement. He likens the Lusaka peace effort to 'talking to prostitutes'. Vorgan likes to talk about 'prostitutes'. When Margaret Anstee was scrambling to save the peace process in 1993, Vorgan suggested that she too was a *puta*.

Vorgan's dismissal of the peace talks, coupled with Captain Pepe's refusal to let us visit UNITA-controlled areas, suggests that mortar shells will soon be falling on Kuito once again.

The next morning is our last. I want to have one more chat with Cardoso over at the Casa Ford shop. What will he do if UNITA captures the town, will he try to slip out with the retreating government troops? 'I have a wife, seven children and a 90-year-old father. I don't think my father could survive an evacuation and I can't leave him here alone. My problem is that UNITA doesn't like the colour of my skin,' he says, brushing his arm with his hand. 'They don't like *mestiços*. They believe the *mestiços* are responsible for this war. Their hatred of us continues. It's a hatred which goes back a long time.' Could it be the memories of the Bailundo war? 'Yes, it could be, but I think it's just UNITA leaders stirring up anger against the *mestiços* as a way of mobilising their people, using hatred for their own political purposes.'

Hans pulls up in his landcruiser to announce that the plane is arriving. Our time in Kuito is up. We are angered that the UN officials in Luanda will not allow us to stay another night. We get on the radio to our contact at UN headquarters, Sarah Longford, to demand that they relent and permit us one more day. Longford is adamant. She does not want to be responsible for a group of reporters stuck in Kuito should the fighting break out again. As it is, there is barely enough bunker space for the foreign aid workers, let alone three more journalists. We must leave. We start plotting with Hans, who jokingly suggests that we could fake a delay at a checkpoint and miss the plane, but that would irritate our UN benefactors and jeopardise future trips by journalists. Reluctantly, we climb aboard the next UN plane leaving Kuito.

Back in Luanda the next day our childish irritation with Longford turns into sheepish gratitude. The fighting starts again in Kuito that night, apparently after drunk UNITA soldiers throw first rocks then hand grenades at a house in which the government military commander is holding a meeting.

It all goes according to script. Hundreds more civilians are killed and wounded. The airlifts are suspended and the last foodstocks run out a week later. Hans and eleven foreign aid workers from Médecins sans Frontières, the Red Cross and Oxfam huddle in underground bunkers for nine days before a brief ceasefire is arranged and a special plane flies in from Luanda to evacuate them. Two Red Cross workers stay on, but they too are flown out several weeks later. The new bunker at the orphanage does Chamale's children no good. During the fighting, rampaging government soldiers, supposedly their defenders, sack the camp in search of food.

The fighting lasts for about a month and when it ends in late June the MPLA forces and their armed civilian supporters have driven UNITA ten miles from the city centre. This last battle for Kuito proves to be one of the most humiliating defeats ever inflicted on UNITA, delivered largely by people who had voted for Savimbi in September 1992. It is the latest in a series of sharp military reversals for UNITA, following the fall of the provincial capital of N'Dalatando in April and in July of the diamond mines around the north-eastern town of Cafunfo which had helped to finance Savimbi's army.

UNITA's struggle for the honour of the Ovimbundu people is literally running out of steam. The government begins landing planes at the Kuito airport by early September 1994, ferrying in arms and supplies, and the army starts preparations for a final assault on UNITA's headquarters at Huambo.

15 Promises and Lies

> Luanda. Angolan government forces have penetrated the outskirts of the rebel UNITA stronghold of Huambo, an aid worker said, in fighting that could decide the fate of an accord aimed at ending 20 years of civil war.
>
> 'The government controls the eastern edges, the western edge and possibly the airport,' the foreign worker said on Wednesday.
>
> Reuter
> 9 November 1994

A light drizzle is falling from grey afternoon skies on a city that rises up from a green plateau. A 30-year-old Russian plane descends through a bank of thick fog and touches down on the tarmac amid a scene of near anarchy. Above the din of the propellers rises the clamour of several thousand people's voices – ashen-faced old men, women with infants strapped to their backs and dozens of little boys pushing and shoving in giant queues in the hope of boarding the aircraft to escape from the city. Several hundred soldiers, some of them so small they cannot yet have reached puberty, armed with AK-47 assault rifles, rocket-propelled grenades and long whips threaten and cajole the crowds in a vain attempt to keep order while army stevedores unload a cargo of 50-gallon drums of diesel fuel. Fights break out in the rolling sea of humanity. As soon as one fight is quelled another erupts somewhere else. A barefoot man in torn trousers screaming, 'I didn't do it, I didn't do it,' runs in circles fleeing an elderly soldier with a wooden switch. The hunter does not seem to realise that if he simply stopped his quarry would land right in his arms. The chase provides a fleeting moment of levity and the throng roars with laughter. At the front of the airport building thousands more people push against helmeted soldiers and form ill-disciplined queues 500 yards down the road. Occasionally the guards fire shots into the air, but as soon as the echoes fade into the thin mountain air chaos erupts anew. Huambo is back in government hands.

It has been two weeks since the FAA army entered Huambo and put an end to UNITA's eighteen-month reign in Angola's second city and Jonas Savimbi's dream of building the capital of his 'new Angola'. The UNITA troops fled the army's advance on 9 November 1994, abandoning without a fight the city they vowed never to leave alive. Angola's civil war has, at least temporarily, been put on hold. Eleven days later after Huambo fell, UNITA and MPLA government negotiators signed the Lusaka Protocol in the second attempt in three years to bring an end to Africa's longest war.

Staring blankly into the distance at the airport entrance is Maria Isabel Wasovava holding her nine-month-old daughter. Not much chance of leaving today, is there? My question seems to wake her from a dream. '*Confusão*, just a lot of *confusão*,' she says. So why do you want to go to Luanda so badly? 'There's nothing left for me in Huambo,' she says. 'My husband Horácio Tito was taken away with three friends by UNITA and we've had no word from him. I'm sure he's dead.'

Maria's friend Julietta looks as if she is about to cry as she listens to the tale and nods her head in agreement. A group of UNITA soldiers came for Horácio at 4 o'clock in the morning and dragged him away, Maria says. He and a few friends were planning an escape by walking to the coastal city of Benguela. They were among hundreds of Huambo's residents killed by UNITA in the days and weeks before the government forces entered the city. Some were shot or stabbed at the police headquarters, others were clubbed over the head or strangled with barbed wire and thrown down wells.

Maria, who is from Luanda, and Horácio, a native of Huambo, married two years ago around the time of the elections, a matrimonial symbol of the hope that the people of the coast and those of the interior could live in peace. Horácio's disappearance left Maria completely alone, with no family in the city. She and Julietta moved into the servants' quarters of a house and eked out a living by baking muffins to sell on the street. It was a tough business since during UNITA's rule, when Huambo was cut off from the outside world, few people had money.

The roar of another plane touching down provokes wave-like surges in the masses as their hopes of joining the exodus flare afresh. The stevedores run back and forth into the recesses of the huge craft and emerge with stacks of the two commodities found in abundance in Angola: bags of donated maize and boxes of rifle ammunition. When it takes off 30 minutes later, the plane carries only twenty people with it. It is the last plane of the day and everyone trudges home hoping for better luck tomorrow.

The light is fading now and Nicholas Shaxson of Reuters and I decide it is time to find some shelter for the night. Brigadier Suco, the local army public relations officer, marshals the only vehicle he can find to give us a lift into town. Our destination is a house once rented by Concern, the Irish aid agency, before its personnel were evacuated two weeks ago. It is one of the few buildings not looted during UNITA's retreat from the city.

A dozen international aid groups, including the International Committee of the Red Cross, Save the Children and UN agencies, lost everything, even the clothes off their workers' backs. Food, cars, generators, air conditioners, cutlery and plates were removed by the UNITA commanders and their followers as they fled north to their refuge in Bailundo, seat of the traditional Umbundu kingdom where the rebellion against the Portuguese had begun almost a century ago. UNITA's glorious rule in Huambo ended in one tremendous explosion of larceny. Whatever was left behind was gobbled up a few days later when the government soldiers entered the city like a pack of rabid dogs. Before we leave the airport, a barefoot soldier approaches me with an offer: 'I have a television, a big Sanyo – do you want to trade it for some clothes? I can't carry the television very far and my family needs clothes.

I have driven down the road lined by flame trees from the airport to central Huambo on half a dozen occasions over the past three years and each time the destruction appears worse, as if its resistance to the virus of humanity has simply worn out. There are hundreds of houses and buildings blasted into piles of rubble, burnt-out vehicles and tanks littering the streets, even some unexploded bombs dropped by government planes in the army's campaign to 'liberate' the people of Huambo. By dusk there are few civilians on the streets other than those returning from their unsuccessful wait at the airport.

As our army lorry revs its engine and tumbles around the muddy streets of the Baïrro Académico neighbourhood, I notice that the civilians standing in front of their homes recoil in fear at the sight of the soldiers. We ask several people for directions to the Concern house and finally a young boy agrees to climb aboard and direct us.

I open the gate at the side of the house, and immediately *Dona* Isabel, a tiny Portuguese-born woman of about 60, runs out and gives us a big hug as if we were her long lost sons. In fact, we have never set eyes on her before. But the sight of Nick and I, foreigners, visiting her house has obviously given *Dona* Isabel new hope that the nightmare is ending. We pass on greetings from the Concern staff in Luanda and *Dona* Isabel insists we stay with her for as long as we remain in Huambo.

How *Dona* Isabel has survived the various battles and looting raids is impossible to imagine. About five feet tall, she is not an imposing figure, but her rapid-fire Portuguese suggests her tongue could be a lethal weapon. Perhaps her apparent fragility actually saved her, maybe the fighters on both sides just could not bring themselves to attack so meek a creature. *Dona* Isabel lives alone, never having married, which is why she still insists that her neighbours call her *menina*, girl. She has come through everything – the 55-day siege by UNITA in 1993, the government's aerial bombardments over the ensuing months and the FAA's final conquest of the town earlier this month – physically unscathed. The only apparent damage to her house is a crack in the wall caused by a 500 pound bomb which landed nearby. A number of UNITA bigwigs had been living in Bairro Académico, so it was a special target for the government's MiG and Sukhoi jets.

Dona Isabel rushes to the kitchen to prepare us a dinner of boiled potatoes. She brings in a huge chunk of Dutch cheese left behind by the Concern workers which we nibble on with fresh bread while we await the main course. It is dark outside by now and a lone candle lights the dining room. Huambo has not had electricity for nearly two years. Nick is staring intently at his plate. I ask what he is looking at. 'I don't want to tell you,' he says. I insist. 'Just look closely at your plate,' he replies. Initially I see nothing special in the bread, the cheese and the white cheese crumbs spread out in front of me. Then I hold my breath. The crumbs are wiggling. Luckily I have brought a bottle of whiskey from Luanda and we both guzzle down a glassful.

It has been raining for the past quarter of an hour and in the distance there is what at first sounds like thunder, but it soon becomes clear that the noise is the crackling of dozens of rifles. Huambo has erupted into a wild shooting spree, sometimes far away, sometimes just down the road. Occasionally the thump of mortar explosions makes the heart skip a beat.

Dona Isabel hardly seems to notice. We ask if this is a battle between UNITA and the FAA. 'Looting,' she responds calmly. 'They're *mal educados* [ignorant ruffians]. It's been like this every night since the government troops came. They have nothing to do, so they get drunk and then they start robbing or shooting at each other.' This is why so few people were on the street this afternoon and why those who were out appeared frightened of the soldiers. Fear is so rife that wealthier residents who have generators and vehicles refuse to use them because they are worried that they will attract the soldiers by day, armed robbers by night.

When I ask her if the people of Huambo are not pleased that UNITA's occupation is over, her response is hardly a ringing endorsement of the government. It is a question of survival, she says. 'There was great happiness when the government troops arrived because the people knew they were free from the MiGs. With the government back in Huambo they knew there would be no more bombs.' The racket unleashed by the soldiers-cum-armed robbers continues for another hour or so until the rains intensify and drive everyone inside for the night.

The next morning we contact the Lopes brothers to see if they can arrange a vehicle to take us to Caala, a town about thirteen miles west of Huambo. The brothers, it emerges, are fix-it men. During UNITA's occupation they helped to organise the convoys of lorries which travelled up to the diamond-producing areas around Cafunfo and down to the

Namibian border to bring supplies of food, diesel and beer for the city. The convoys were Huambo's only contact with the outside world until UNITA was able to organise flights from Kinshasa and, some said, remote airstrips in South Africa, thereby making a mockery of the UN Security Council sanctions against Savimbi.

Both men are strongly pro-MPLA, however, and explain their co-operation with UNITA by saying that they simply did what was necessary to survive. The older brother, Mário, used to provide rations for the government army before UNITA captured the city in 1993, and the younger one, Rafael, is an electrician. Now that the MPLA has returned the Lopes brothers are temporarily back in business. Rafael, though, wants to leave. 'If the peace agreement sticks and UNITA decides to send its members to parliament and joins the government, then perhaps I'll stay,' he says. 'Otherwise I'll join my family in Luanda. Enough is enough. People here just want to get out of Huambo as soon as possible. Huambo was like a cage and now they're desperate to experience a new reality.'

A pick-up truck driven by a man named Miguel and his son João arrives at *Dona* Isabel's house. For $100 the truck is ours for the day, but first we must return to the airport to buy some fuel and to find a soldier to accompany us to Caala. Before we depart *Dona* Isabel scribbles a note and asks us to deliver it to her old friends Dr Manuel Joaquim da Silva, a psychiatrist, and his wife Maria França.

On the way to the airport Miguel explains that before the elections and the resumption of the civil war he ran a small general store and João was at school. Once UNITA gained control of the city there was virtually nothing to sell, so he lived off the only thing of value he owned, the pick-up. For much of the time he kept João hidden, first in the countryside with some friends and later in the deeper recesses of his house. As a young man, João was a target, liable to be drafted into the UNITA army, or if he was deemed to be insufficiently dedicated to Savimbi's cause, to be 'disappeared'. His fear that João would be kidnapped heightened during the last days of UNITA's rule because with the FAA approaching the UNITA troops were desperate to round up as many young boys and men as possible. 'All the families I know were in the same situation.

That's why you never saw men in the streets of Huambo. They were all in hiding.' This, surely, is what had happened to Horácio Tito, the husband of Maria whom I had spoken to at the airport.

As we bounce down the airport road we see that the massive crowds have gathered again, poised to make a mad dash for the next airplane to leave Huambo. *Confusão* reigns. On the left military police are back to their threatening ways, whips raised high, occasional shots fired to keep order. On the right about 30 young men, mostly barefoot, all of them in ragged clothes, are marching towards the army barracks under the direction of a couple of soldiers. 'They are joining the army to fight UNITA,' Miguel says. 'Volunteers.' Of course.

Miguel's pick-up is familiar to the airport guards so he drives straight onto the tarmac towards the fuel depot. As he bargains with the soldiers for diesel, Nick and I join Brigadier Suco for an inspection of the military hardware captured by the government forces when they entered town. There is an impressive display of vehicles and weapons, most of it made in the United States or Russia. Amazingly, there are two of the squat jeep-like vehicles known as Humvees, which the US forces used in the war against Iraq and which later became the favourite means of transport for the Americans as they plied the streets of Mogadishu in their failed campaign to impose the new world order on Somalia. Over at the warehouse there are thousands of American claymore mines, stacks of Russian or Chinese AK-47s and an American anti-tank weapon still in its original packing. Sometimes the world's generosity towards democracy knows no limits.

An hour later we are bouncing along towards Caala with a soldier named Tears standing in the back of the pick-up truck, staring down a dirt road that leads to a home he has not seen in two years. Suddenly he is banging his fist on the roof of the cab, signalling the driver to stop. The truck skids, throwing up a cloud of dust as Tears leaps over the side and sprints towards a woman who is bent double and holding a hand to her mouth in disbelief. For the next few minutes they alternate between embracing and standing back to gaze into each other's eyes, between shaking their heads and breaking out into peels of laughter. A final hug and Tears skips like a little boy back to the pick-up.

'My cousin,' he says climbing aboard the vehicle. 'She thought I was dead. Everyone in my family did. They have had no news of me for two years.'

It was this prolonged absence, Tears says, that spawned his nom de guerre, *Lágrimas*, which he has scribbled above the pocket of his camouflage jacket. 'I cried for them and they cried for me: Tears.'

The pick-up resumes the journey down the red dust road and as the cool, crisp air of the central highlands rushes into Captain Elías Chivuka's eyes, tears are welling up in them. Perhaps the touch of wind is the real source of the nickname given to Tears by his army friends as they ride around in military trucks. Or maybe the anticipation of what he will find back at home is getting to him.

We have covered about half the journey when we reach the River Cunhongama and a depressingly familiar sight. A ten-yard-long cement bridge over the fast-flowing river has collapsed, blown apart by saboteurs to take its place as another signpost on Angola's road to destruction.

As we approach to take a look at the bridge, women and children emerge from several wattle and daub huts on a bluff above the river. Tears warns that there could be mines about and suggests that we avoid the mud and walk only on the patches of tarmac, mere scraps of what once was a paved road. Tears' talk of mines calls up images of hundreds of amputees, the *mutilados* I have seen in villages, hospitals and hobbling along the streets of the capital. There are between 9 and 20 million mines in Angola and they have made working the fields, or even the simple pleasures of rural life, strolling by a stream or running in an open field, a game of Russian roulette.

Following Tears' instructions is like crossing a stream by hopping from rock to rock except that in this case a stray foot would not get wet, it could be blown away. I step gingerly.

There is no doubt that the demolition of the bridge was UNITA's handiwork. A rebel unit detonated the charges two weeks before in a vain effort to block the government army's advance from Caala to Huambo. In the end, of course, it did not matter. The government army simply found a narrow point a few hundred yards upstream, built a makeshift bridge out of strips of wood and chunks of cement and proceeded down the road to chase the rebels out of Huambo. A few days later, on 20 November 1994, the entire war was supposed to have stopped when negotiators for the two sides signed the Lusaka Protocol peace agreement mediated by the United Nations.

Tears is not too confident about the new peace, but he has decided to take advantage of a chance to escort us to Caala to have a look at his home. We spend most of the morning in the town itself, interviewing civilians on its wide Portuguese-style streets, now strewn with rubble and rubbish, and inspecting the looting carried out by the UNITA fighters hours before they fled the government advance.

Caala shows few signs of its erstwhile glory as a vital gateway in the trade between the farmers of the *planalto* and the more pastoral people of the south. The hospital and all the houses have been ransacked. Government troops are now in control and they are up to their old tricks. Last night, several residents whisper, a group of them raped six peasant women and forced their husbands to watch.

All in all, Caala is a fairly typical town in the Angolan interior, better than places such as Kuito, 110 miles to the east, which is as badly ravaged as Beirut and Mogadishu. Most of Caala's one-storey buildings and strangely middle-class suburban houses remain standing, but their faded pastel walls have been chewed by hundreds of rounds fired by AK-47s. They are without life. There is no electricity, no piped water and damn little hope.

Before completing Tears' pilgrimage we must deliver the message which *Dona* Isabel gave us for Dr Joaquim da Silva, the Portuguese psychiatrist who has been living in Angola for the past 27 years. It takes only a few minutes to locate his house. Caala has a small-town mentality and everyone knows where everyone else lives, so it is just a matter of asking directions from the first person we meet.

Dr da Silva's house on the central avenue is abandoned, but some passers-by lead us to a place on a back street where he and his wife are staying with friends. The moment Tears sees Dr da Silva, he remembers him. 'I'll never forget that big dog you had,' he says. Dr da Silva smiles, doubtless imagining Tears as one of the little boys whom the dog had chased around years ago.

We wander over to his home and as we stroll through it the locust-like efficiency of the looters is a marvel to behold. They have taken everything from the kitchen sink to carpets and wooden tiles on the floor, even the toilet, the thoroughness of their work revealing a maniacal desperation. Anything associated with modern civilisation has been removed in the frenzy. Behind the house is a pile of burned papers and documents. 'That is ten years' work,' Dr da Silva says. 'Those papers were the draft of my book for the university. Why did they have to burn them? They could have just left them to one side.' Not satisfied with its untold death and destruction, the civil war has turned predator of the mind.

The looting began just before the government troops arrived on 5 November. As UNITA soldiers were preparing their retreat, they demanded that all civilians leave with them, no doubt to show the depth of their support among the *povo*. 'We're going house to house,' they said, 'and we'll kill anyone we find,' Dr da Silva's wife tells us. The civilian caravan was marched to an outcrop of rocks about six miles south of town and told to remain there with no food, no blankets and in many cases no shoes. A week after the UNITA soldiers disappeared, the civilians trudged back into Caala.

The people who flocked to the UNITA looting gangs were mainly the poor, refugees from the countryside, and in order to survive they immediately started to sell most of the stolen goods in the open-air market. This has led to comical scenes. A few days ago an elderly woman selling shoes came by the house where the da Silvas were staying. 'She had a pair of my high heels, and when I said they were mine, she replied, "If you recognise your own shoes, you don't have to pay,"' Mrs da Silva says laughing. 'Someone also tried to sell me my own parasol.'

The hospital grounds across the street are deserted except for Zacarias Kalepa, who has worked as the security guard there for the past fifteen years. He is barefoot, dressed in rags, hungry and drunk. All he wants to know is when the Concern aid workers will return from Luanda to restart the food kitchen they ran at the hospital before their escape from the recent fighting. 'If you see *Senhora* Sheila, please tell her that all the children are starving,' Kalepa shouts.

This was not the first time the hospital has been in such a state, and it is hard to believe it will be the last. In recent years it has functioned properly only when foreign doctors like Dr da Silva and volunteers from agencies such as Médecins sans Frontières were around and when international aid groups flew in medicines. Angolan doctors have long since pulled out, or they have perished, leaving the hospital in the hands of courageous local paramedics and nurses who work for months with no pay.

I have often wondered how long the war in Angola and similar conflicts elsewhere would have continued if the United Nations and the assorted international aid agencies had not been so ready to fly in thousands of tonnes of food, medicine and clothes to help keep the remnants of society functioning, if they had not been there to sweep up the human rubble strewn around in the wake of battles waged in the name of the *povo*, if they had not provided just enough food to keep the country alive, to let the authorities avoid responsibility for their own citizens, to fatten up the young boys living in refugee camps so that they could be dragooned by one of the warring armies. The answer is probably that international aid or not, the fighting would have continued.

'When's Sheila coming? When's Sheila coming?' Kalepa keeps asking us with an irritating tone of dependency in his voice.

Caala's hospital consists of several empty cement rooms. There are no beds, no doors, no medicines, not even an aspirin. In an area where malaria is endemic, Caala, once a town of 10,000 people, does not have a single chloroquine tablet. This we discover when a young man runs up to Dr da Silva begging for some treatment for his sister, a former hospital nurse, who is dying of cerebral malaria. There is no treatment in town, Dr da Silva explains, but he suggests that we could take the woman back to Huambo, where some chloroquine, preferably something stronger, might be found.

After we pick up the young woman at her home in the slums behind the railway tracks, we travel across a green field to some huts in a neighbourhood called Firewood because it once was a forest of eucalyptus trees used by the railway company. Tears yells at the driver to halt at an abandoned lot. For a moment he says nothing, seemingly in a state of shock, until I ask him where the house is. 'This is it,' he says, pointing to a concrete slab overgrown with weeds. Tears looks heart-broken. Three of the walls are missing and the fourth is well on the way to dissolving back into the earth. 'After I ran away two years ago, UNITA set fire to the thatched roof and allowed the rains to finish it off,' he says.

Tears ran away from Firewood in November 1992 after UNITA had rejected its electoral defeat and occupied municipalities like Caala. Like Deofina's sons Alberto and Inácio, he joined one of the massive human columns which marched to the coastal towns of Benguela and Lobito. They were reminiscent of the nineteenth-century legions of traders and porters sent by the independent Umbundu kingdoms to sell rubber, wax and slaves to Portuguese merchants. This modern day exodus, however, was concerned not with profits but with survival.

In Benguela the FAA's chief of staff, General João de Matos, re-organised and re-armed the routed troops like Tears and enlisted refugee men and boys into a new force to recapture the central highlands. It took them two years.

His jaw set tight, Tears walks through a maze of mud-hut compounds, curtly greeting some of his old neighbours, before striding off again. After 50 yards, he stops at one, opens a piece of rusty sheet metal that serves as the entrance gate and catches his daughter Carolina as she leaps into his arms. Tears, for a fleeting moment the returning hero, breaks out into a broad smile, but the joy quickly fades as he turns to face his ten-year-old boy, Domingos. Tears' first son, with stick-like limbs and a distended belly, is starving.

There is no hiding Tears' anger now, nor his embarrassment at the state of his son, his home, his country and his own life. Tears just wants to get away from the place. After exchanging pleasantries with his sister-in-law, he begins to walk back to the pick-up. 'When are you coming to stay?' a neighbour asks. 'There are still too many UNITA soldiers around,' Tears replies. Tears is lying. It is not UNITA he fears, but the shame of his family's condition.

As Tears climbs back into the truck, his son Domingos gazes up at his father, admiring him like a giant warrior in the green army fatigues. But his eyes show that he senses his father's disappointment. Young boys, first sons especially, are supposed to be out with their friends hunting game, looking after the cattle and getting into mischief. 'I'll be back tomorrow, son,' Tears shouts. As we speed off, he pulls out some banknotes and throws them into the dust. Domingos scrambles for them. 'It's a disgrace,' Tears says more to himself than the rest of us. 'A big man like me. My son looks like a refugee.'

On the way back to Huambo Tears keeps to himself, speaking only when spoken to, and as he stares into the wind tears fill his eyes again. At the River Cunhongama another lorry has broken down on the far end of the temporary bridge. A boy is working alone unloading massive bundles so the vehicle can be pushed aside, while the rest of the 25 passengers, among them several soldiers, sit on the ground waiting for something to happen. At this rate it will take days to move the truck out of the way. Tears starts an argument with one of the soldiers by asking him why he and his colleagues are doing nothing to help the boy to empty the lorry. The discussion ends with one of the soldiers yelling, 'It isn't our problem, it's the driver's fault.' It is not his problem and he seems to be willing to sit around all day waiting for a miracle.

Tears is irritated, impatient to reach Huambo, to leave behind the memory of his home, so he begins to direct our driver to squeeze the pick-up through a slender gap past the disabled vehicle. As soon as we pile back in, the soldiers make their move and before Tears can ward them off, three of them are stashing their bags and settling in for the ride to Huambo. Just ten minutes ago, we seemed to be certain of spending the day at the River Cunhongama and now we are on the road again. Travelling in Angola is best practised as an act of faith.

As we reach the giant open air market at São Pedro on the eastern outskirts of Huambo, João points out the groups of young men milling around at the street corners. Many of them, like himself, were in hiding before, but others are UNITA soldiers who have hidden their weapons, donned civilian clothes and mixed in with the population. 'A lot of the UNITA troops I saw around town are still here,' says Miguel, 'but we don't know if they are spying for UNITA or whether they too are simply tired of war. This war always goes back and forth and nobody here thinks it's over.'

We deliver the young woman from Caala who is suffering

from cerebral malaria to the central hospital's emergency ward and I decide to stay to have a look around. Unfortunately, the hospital's interim director and most of the staff have left for the day. I meet a grey-haired orderly who chats for a while, shows me a few rooms filled with the ill, the hungry and the wounded, and the courtyard where dozens of people are cooking pots of maize meal on tiny fires for their sick relatives.

Suddenly a smart landcruiser pulls up and two soldiers run in demanding to see a doctor. The orderly informs them that no one is around at the moment. 'Who's in charge?' an officer screams, 'We have a wounded man who needs attention now!' The orderly says there is nothing he can do, but if they will bring in the man, the first doctor to arrive will have a look at him. The young soldier has a nasty leg wound. The orderly clicks his tongue. 'The soldiers are always shooting each other,' he says. 'When the government forces came to Huambo they brought in eight wounded and now there are 42 of them. They get drunk at night and shoot each other.'

I want to find out what has become of Alcides Gonçalves da Cruz, the Portuguese businessman who maintained such a cosy relationship with UNITA and had a dream of rebuilding one of Huambo's hotels to serve Savimbi's new Angola. After asking around, I discover that he is virtually in hiding at an old warehouse about 500 yards from the hotel he was running during UNITA's occupation.

Cruz is suffering from malaria and is extremely depressed. As soon as UNITA fled Huambo, the city's residents took their revenge on someone many viewed as a profiteer. They invaded his factory and hotel in a looting frenzy and made off with anything they could carry – beds, generators, sewing machines, his television, video machine, even the videos. FAA soldiers, he says, robbed him of $5,000 in cash. He has reached the end of his patience and as soon as he can he wants to travel to Luanda, collect the hard currency he has been earning by renting office space to oil companies and join his family in Portugal. The International Committee of the Red Cross has promised to put him on one of its planes. 'There is nothing for me here any more. These people are savages,' he says. It is hard to feel much pity for him. He benefited handsomely from UNITA's capture of Huambo and now he is paying the price. Other businessmen had an easier time of it, getting on just as well with the new government rulers as they did with UNITA.

Cruz has been staying for the past two weeks with Virgílio Farinha, a Portuguese businessman who was once the technical director of Huambo's Coca Cola factory. When the war restarted in 1992, he passed up the chance to join most of the other Portuguese nationals who were evacuated by the Red Cross. He had been working at the plant since 1972 and did not want to see it all go to waste. Farinha survived by renting out factory and warehouse space to foreign aid agencies, such as the Red Cross and the World Food Programme, when they needed a place to store their food before distributing it to the city's residents. 'Without the WFP and the Red Cross, there would have been nothing here,' says Farinha. Other shops and businesses throughout Huambo were wrecked, and the industrial area, which used to produce furniture, textiles, beer and soft drinks, is abandoned and gutted.

Miraculously, the Coca Cola factory remains largely intact. Looters broke into the administrative offices the day before UNITA fled and removed all the doors, threw the factory's records all over the floor and generally wrecked the place. The main warehouse is empty now except for stacks and stacks of empty bottles. In its heyday the factory was one of the most efficient in Angola, producing 4,000 bottles of 'the real thing' every day. The hope was to supply drinks to shops and bars all along the road from Huambo to Benguela, but the civil war made that an unfulfilled dream, with too many lorries waylaid by bandits and UNITA soldiers or destroyed by landmines sent from South Africa and America. In some places, even the allure of Coca Cola is not enough.

Farinha is not discouraged by the mess. 'All this will pass, God willing,' he says. 'I plan to be here a few more years, to help to put the factory back in shape, then I want to get on with my life.' His hope, like that of many business people on the central highlands, all over Africa for that matter, is that foreign investors are poised to rush in to help resurrect the region from the ashes of war. Their optimism is a pipedream.

As we walk out of the factory and board Miguel's pick-up, we see two Russian-built tanks abandoned by government troops in March 1993 when UNITA occupied the area. Their guns face the factory. In front of them one of Farinha's guards is sitting by a small fire ranting and raving to himself. 'He's a lunatic,' says Farinha. In the circumstances, he seems rather sane.

The next morning we are standing in front of the Red Cross compound at Bomba Alta waiting for a lift to the airport to catch our return flight to Luanda. Suddenly the window panes are rattling and the earth is trembling. Three young government soldiers guarding the complex say in unison, 'A bomb.' There are not supposed to be any more bombing raids or any more fighting at all following the signing of the Lusaka Protocol. For another twenty minutes the faint reports of artillery shells rumble in the distance to the north-east, the direction in which UNITA fled two weeks ago. 'Those are the areas where there are still problems,' says one of the soldiers. His nom de guerre, scribbled on his uniform, is *O povo sabe*, The People Know.

16 Postscript

Ricardo de Mello walked into the building in which he lived in central Luanda just after 1 a.m. on 18 January 1995 and began climbing the stairs to his tenth-floor flat where his wife and four-year-old son were sleeping. He never reached home. In the darkness of the second-floor landing de Mello was cut down by an assassin's bullet. No one heard the shot. The gunman, a professional, used a silencer. A neighbour saw the body at about 1.30 but assumed de Mello was a drunk who had wandered in from the street to sleep it off. His corpse was found the next morning.

De Mello had been the director of *Imparcial Fax*, a muck-raking daily which drew inspiration from the independent press that emerged in eastern Europe in the late 1980s. The idea was to use a fax machine to undermine the government's tight grip on the media. De Mello and two colleagues started publishing in February 1994 and *Imparcial Fax* soon became required reading for diplomats and senior government officials because of its investigations into corruption in President dos Santos's administration and the FAA and into faction fighting within the MPLA.

In March 1994 he started receiving death threats. Upper echelons in the military were outraged when de Mello published a secret army document in October which revealed plans to launch a campaign of psychological warfare against UNITA. *Imparcial Fax* also described André Petroff, the Minister of the Interior whose control over the secret police made him one of Angola's most feared men, as 'one of the most worn-out faces of the government'. Contacts in the Ministry of the Interior told de Mello that his life was in danger.

Two days before his death de Mello wrote a story entitled 'MPLA: Two Steps from Crisis' detailing the deepening divisions in the government. The next day General António dos Santos França, 'Ndalu', the former chief of staff who had tried to negotiate a ceasefire with UNITA during the battle for Luanda in 1992, asked him to lunch. Ndalu urged him to hire a bodyguard. De Mello was investigating rumours of an imminent military coup d'état.

President dos Santos duly issued a condemnation of the killing and said he did not think that it was politically motivated. No one took his statement seriously. 'This was a conspiracy organised at the highest level,' said Arminda Mateus, de Mello's widow. Ironically, the murder was reminiscent of the assassination in 1992 of Dr David Bernardino, director of the *O Jango* newspaper in Huambo, allegedly by UNITA gunmen. UNITA and the MPLA were soul mates in their hatred of independent reporting.

Arminda, her son and colleagues at *Imparcial Fax* were living in a state of terror, despite round-the-clock police protection. 'Almost every day vehicles with armed men drive past our house to intimidate us,' said Mariano Costa, one of two *Imparcial Fax* reporters who were assaulted just hours before de Mello was killed. Costa was attacked at the airport while awaiting the arrival of the UN Special Representative to Angola, Alioune Blondin Beye. The assailants mentioned that *Imparcial Fax* had published a story linking President dos Santos's wife, Ana Paula, to diamond trafficking.

Costa had been in trouble with the law before. He was jailed for a week in September 1994 and accused of spying for UNITA. Ten days after de Mello's assassination two carloads of men assaulted Costa again and said they were taking him to police headquarters. He managed to escape.

De Mello was once a stringer for the BBC and the Voice of America. He fell in love with Arminda, then a fourth-year law student in Portugal, and convinced her to join him back in Angola. 'He was filled with optimism,' she said. 'He and a friend from Mozambique decided to return from Portugal to their home countries and begin practising free journalism.'

A young man is sitting listlessly in the dust in front of a walled compound with his left leg chained to the rusty rim of a car wheel. He is working as a security guard to deter anyone with evil intent from entering. He has no need for guns or nightsticks. One look at him and any potential trespasser will think twice about breaking in. If they do this to the guards, one can hardly imagine what goes on inside.

The compound's metal gate opens to reveal the Papa Kitoko Traditional Medical Centre, a place for Luanda's ill, its destitute and above all its insane. The centre is located in the Cazenga *musseque* on the northern outskirts of Luanda and is run by a young traditional healer named Kitoko Maiavangua. Everyone calls him Papa Kitoko.

The guard at the gate, like many of the patients inside, was once a soldier in the government army. No image is more symbolic of Angola's *situação* than ex-soldiers, several of them *mutilados*, chained to engine blocks and wheel rims, as if some barbaric feudal dungeon has found a place in the African sun. Some of the patients rattle their metal bonds in anger. Others sit staring at a brick wall, their minds no longer linked to the outside world. They and the dozens of women and children with them are the spiritual waste of a society that is bordering on insanity.

For all the killing and suffering of the civil war, perhaps its most tragic impact has been on the psyche of an entire generation of Angolans for whom violence, hunger and the rule of the gun have become a way of life.

Chaining people up has become good business. 'The years of civil war have driven the Angolan people crazy,' says Papa Kitoko. 'As long as the war continues, many crazy people will turn up looking for help from Papa Kitoko.'

Several thousand patients have passed through his centre in the past eighteen months and some have responded well to Papa Kitoko's treatment of applying secret plants and herbs, sometimes modern drugs like valium, occasionally even mud, while strengthening the medicine with prayers and chants. 'We have our own spiritual law and rhythm,' he says.

The president of the Kitoko Foundation, Maria de Fátima, is herself a former patient, as are most of the other workers at the centre. 'I had mental problems because of conflicts with my family, but I was cured here,' she says. 'I decided to stay and work to thank him for what he did.'

Papa Kitoko learned his treatments from his mother, Muta Maria, who set up the first centre in 1975 in the town of Maquela de Zombo near the border with Zaire. 'My mother taught me the secrets and sent me to Zaire to gather the necessary plants,' he says.

In the 1980s he opened his own clinic in Negage, near Uíge, the scene of fierce battles between UNITA and the MPLA after Savimbi claimed that the government had cheated him out of victory in the 1992 election.

Papa Kitoko makes no apologies for his methods. 'The patients are chained up so they can't run away,' he says as if it were the most obvious thing in the world. 'If we don't take these measures, the crazy ones will run outside, smoke marijuana and become even more crazy.' It would be hard to blame them.

He is not considered a quack, especially among the poor and forgotten in Cazenga, where he started to practise in April 1993. Police bring around tramps whom they find living in rubbish dumps, and the state newspaper, *Jornal de Angola*, regularly reports on his activities. Papa Kitoko often hires a car to scour the streets of Luanda for mentally ill vagrants. 'When I approach them, they're calm,' he says. 'They may be sick but at least they understand that finally there's someone who wants to care for them.'

His beard is flecked with grey now, but even at 57 he still has a cherubic face that breaks easily into a broad, youthful smile. Only his eyes betray immense pain. Dignity is the word that comes to mind when one meets him.

He used to be a businessman in Huambo, a driving instructor, and the owner of a lorry. He used to have a happy marriage, five children and respect in the community. Even during the worst of the war years, he used to live a relatively comfortable existence.

A month after the Bicesse peace accords were signed in Portugal, the government asked the city's lorry owners to pick up a delegation of UNITA fighters stationed in the town of Alta Hama, just to the north of Huambo, and bring them to the city. Since it was a government request, he agreed and helped to bring in UNITA's Huambo commander, Brigadier David Wenda, and his aides so that they could set up the UNITA office at the Hotel Roma. After all, peace was dawning.

As an Umbundu, he sympathised with UNITA's call for 'equality' between the less educated people of the central highlands and the more cosmopolitan Bacongo, Mbundu and *mestiços* of the north and the coast. Yet in the 1992 elections he crossed ethnic lines and voted for the MPLA, believing the party to be better equipped to lead the nation.

After Savimbi denounced the polls in October 1992 and resumed the war, UNITA caught one of his sons, who was 21 at the time, wrongly accused him of being an MPLA soldier and slit his throat.

When UNITA launched its siege of Huambo in January 1993 it was his turn to be picked up by gunmen, this time by the pro-MPLA *ninja* police. They called him a UNITA sympathiser because he had helped to transport Brigadier Wenda's rebel delegation to town in June 1991, conveniently forgetting that the government had asked him to do so.

They threw him in the back of a lorry with 32 other men and women, drove them to an abandoned migrant workers' hostel in the São Pedro neighbourhood and stuffed them down a sewer. Huddled in the darkness they could hear the battle raging as UNITA poured up to 1,000 mortar shells a day into MPLA-controlled areas and government MiGs bombed rebel positions.

'We stayed down there for five days,' he says as he peers in disbelief down the tunnel. Then the killing began. Every few hours the *ninjas* would drag four or five unfortunate souls out of the sewer, march them 50 yards over to a cluster of trees and execute them.

Six prisoners were left and he knew his turn was about to come when an army commander arrived and stopped the *ninjas* from finishing off the rest. The officer said they could not just kill people like that, but the *ninjas* did not understand his objection. He learned later that one of his sons, a government soldier, had begged the commander to free his father.

His wife was injured when a mortar hit his house near the end of the siege in March 1993. As his eighteen-year-old son was helping her to the hospital, a group of UNITA soldiers stopped them on the way. They tied the boy up and dragged him off. He has not seen him since.

Today, two years later, there is a small maize field growing under the trees where he watched the *ninjas* carry out their executions. 'At least something good is coming out of this place.' He can still remember where the bodies are. Five men over to the left and two women are buried beside a mound. 'One of them was mentally ill, poor woman.'

He wanted to show me something in front of the abandoned military hospital in the centre of Huambo. A human skull and some other bones were lying in the grass next to the shreds of a soldier's uniform. Angola, he said, has sacrificed its youth on the altar of power. 'Children of thirteen or fourteen are taken by force, by UNITA or the government, it doesn't matter. They remain illiterate, *mal educados*, and all they know is how to rob and kill. They lose an arm or a leg and then go home to stay in their parents' house, illiterate and *mutilados*. This is the state of Angola's children today.'

When the FAA drove UNITA out of Huambo in November 1994, government secret police came around to his house three times looking for him. Obviously he was still listed as a UNITA supporter in someone's file. Luckily, he was never in, and after a few weeks the police seemed to lose interest. Today he is doing what he knows best, driving. He still lives with his wife, who is healthy but whose right arm has been permanently deformed by the mortar wound. He asked me not to write down his name in case the secret police or UNITA decided to come back.

Bibliography

Andresen Guimarães, Fernando, *The Origins of the Angolan Civil War: Foreign Intervention and Domestic Political Conflict,* New York 2001

Anstee, Margaret, *Orphan of the Cold War: The Inside Story of the Collapse of the Angolan Peace Process, 1992–93,* Basingstoke 1996

Bender, Gerald, *Angola Under the Portuguese: The Myth and the Reality,* Trenton, New Jersey, 2004

Birmingham, David, *Empire in Africa: Angola and its Neighbors,* Athens, Ohio, 2006

Bridgland, Fred, *Jonas Savimbi: A Key to Africa*, Edinburgh 1986
The War for Africa, Johannesburg 1990

Crocker, Chester, *High Noon in Southern Africa: Making Peace in a Rough Neighborhood*, New York 1992

Heitman, Helmoed-Römer, *War in Angola: The Final South African Phase*, Johannesburg 1990

Heywood, Linda, 'UNITA and Ethnic Nationalism in Angola', *Journal of Modern African Studies*, 1989, Vol.27, No. 1

Hodges, Tony, *Angola: Anatomy of an Oil State*, Bloomington, Indiana, 2004

Human Rights Watch Africa (formerly Africa Watch), *Angola: The Violations of the Laws of War by Both Sides*, New York 1989
Angola: Civilians Devastated by Fifteen-Year War, New York 1991
Land Mines in Angola, New York 1993

Angola: Arms Trade and Violations of the Laws of War Since the 1992 Elections, New York 1994

Jamba, Sousa, *Patriots*, London 1990

Kapuscinski, Ryszard, *Another Day of Life*, London 1987

Marcum, John, *The Angolan Revolution, Vol. I, The Anatomy of an Explosion, 1950–1962*, Cambridge, Mass., 1969

The Angolan Revolution, Vol. II, Exile Politics and Guerrilla Warfare, 1962–1976, Cambridge, Mass., 1978

Mendes, Pedro Rosa, *Bay of Tigers: A Journey Through War-torn Angola*, trans. Clifford Landers, London 2004

Minter, William, *Operation Timber: Pages from the Savimbi Dossier*, Trenton, New Jersey, 1988

Apartheid's Contras, London 1994

Moorhouse, Karin and Cheng, Wei, *No One Can Stop the Rain: A Chronicle of Two Foreign Aid Workers During the Angolan Civil War*, Toronto 2005

Neto, Agostinho, *Sacred Hope*, Luanda 1974

Pepetela, *As Aventuras de Ngunga*, Lisbon 1978

Mayombe, Lisbon 1980; trans. Michael Wolfers, London 1983

O Cão e os Calús, Lisbon 1985

Yaka, Lisbon 1985

Lueji (O nascimento dum Império), Luanda, 1989

A Geração da Utopia, Lisbon 1992

O Desejo de Kianda, Lisbon 1995; trans. Luís R. Mitras as *The Return of the Water Spirit*, Oxford 2002

Roque, Fátima, *Angola: Em Nome da Esperança*, Lisbon 1994

Stockwell, John, *In Search of Enemies: A CIA Story*, New York 1978

Van der Waals, Willem, *Portugal's War in Angola, 1961–1974*, Johannesburg 1993

Vieira, José Luandino, *The Real Life of Domingos Xavier*, Luanda 1976

Vines, Alex, *One Hand Tied: Angola and the UN*, London 1993

Wolfers, Michael and Bergerol, Jane, *Angola in the Front Line*, London 1983

Index